KEN BRADSHAW
& MARK FOO

ANDY MARTIN

BLOOMSBURY

First published in Great Britain 2007
This paperback edition published 2008

Bloomsbury Publishing Plc,
36 Soho Square,
London W1D 3QY

Bloomsbury Publishing, London, New York, Berlin

A CIP catalogue record for this book is available from the British Library

ISBN 9780747592853

Typeset by Hewer Text UK Ltd, Edinburgh
Printed in Great Britain by Clays Ltd, St Ives plc

10 9 8 7 6 5 4 3 2 1

All papers used by Bloomsbury Publishing are natural, recyclable
products made from wood grown in well-managed
forests. The manufacturing processes conform to the
environmental regulations of the country of origin.

www.bloomsbury.com/andymartin

ACKNOWLEDGMENTS

This book could not have been written without Ken Bradshaw, SharLyn Foo, Mark Foo, Matt Warshaw, Steve Barilotti, John Callahan, Randy Rarick, Dennis Pang, Heather Martin, Alec Cooke, Roger Erickson, Michael Willis, Milton Willis, Peter Cole, Brock Little, Spud, Mark Dambrowski, Bodo van der Leeden, Ted Deerhurst, Clyde Aikau and family, David Godwin, John Gomes, Jack, Mike Parsons, Titus Kinimaka, Al Hunt, Layne Beachley, Darrick Doerner, Laird Hamilton, Jay Moriarity, Dan Moore, Mike Jones, *Surfer* magazine, the *Independent* (Matt Tench), the *Independent on Sunday* (Mark MacKenzie), Expedia.co.uk, Rip Curl, O'Neill, Billabong. Or the universities of Cambridge, Columbia, and Rutgers. Or a few others who remain mysterious but not forgotten.

BY THE SAME AUTHOR

Walking on Water
Waiting for Bardot

For Spencer and Jack

Sharing the wave

'Everything is water'

Thales, 6th century BC

CONTENTS

Idols

When I was about fourteen or fifteen I had to write an essay at school entitled something like 'My Hero (or Heroes)' and explaining why I found X or Y to be so heroic. I found this one of the most challenging essays I'd ever had to write. And not just because it was in French. It was more because I didn't really have any heroes. I ended up writing something about the Apollo moon missions (what was 'rocket' in French anyway?) and the joys of flying to the moon and leaping over giant craters. But in truth I was faking it, to some extent anyway. Astronauts, soldiers, athletes, writers and intellectuals – they were all interesting and some of them were doing or had done a fine job, but were they really *heroic*? Did I want to be like any of them?

It was another decade or so before I discovered who my true heroes were. You could call them anti-heroes, but it amounts to the same thing. Most of them were surfers. Now some of them are dead. This is a story about two of them. There are a lot of waves in this book, but it's not really about surfing. It's about love and death, rivalry and friendship, and two very different men who came from opposite ends of the earth – Texas and Singapore, East and West – and ended up meeting in the middle, in Hawaii.

It is a mistake to think of Hawaii as a land of pleasure and happiness, a mid-ocean centre for R&R. The spirit of *aloha* is a myth invented by shipping lines to suck in gullible tourists. Hawaii is an arena of gladiatorial conflict and always has been. The island is a natural coliseum with a history of violence. As in ancient Rome or Troy, so in Hawaii: the exploits of its heroes arouse pity and terror in the heart of the observer. In mine anyway.

Hawaii comprises the most isolated chain of islands on the planet: a bunch of volcanoes that poke up out of the middle of the Pacific like periscopes. This land is cooled magma that boiled up out of a geological 'hot spot' beneath the earth's crust. Even now, a few aeons later, colonised by plants, insects, animals, birds and one and a quarter million human beings, it remains prone to eruption. All islands are harsh, unforgiving environments in which there is a permanent struggle for extremely finite resources. There is no Garden of Eden here, no 'paradise' beloved of the tourist brochures, only a strenuous Darwinian struggle for survival.

The Hawaiian legend of the *menehune* refers back to a race of 'little people' who preceded the Polynesians and first peopled the islands more than a millennium ago. The *menehune* were kindly, easygoing, peace-loving, benevolent folk, innocent souls, full of the milk of human kindness. Recent archaeology suggests that this was no legend – the *menehune* were real, a species of smaller humans, scared to death of the larger, lumbering monsters who were destined to take over. It seems probable that the Hawaiians (as we know them now) slaughtered the lot of them. The *menehune* were completely wiped out in a merciless inter-species holocaust. All that remains of them is buried skeletons, a distant stirring of the collective memory and a few surf contests for kids under the banner '*menehune*'.

To understand Hawaii we have to forget palm trees and sultry breezes. Hawaii is a metropolis made out of water, a brutal exercise in the reality principle. Like New York, with its limited space, it has had to build up. Hawaii is to big waves what New York is to tall buildings, and the North Shore – extending from Turtle Bay to Kaena Point, 'the biggest impact zone in the world' as the captain of lifeguards described it to me, twelve miles of highly corrugated water – is its Manhattan.

Waimea Bay is its Empire State.

The beach is a jungle. When, in 1778, the Hawaiians did to Captain Cook exactly what his name seemed to be inviting them to do – when he was clubbed, stabbed, battered and drowned for good measure at Kealakekua Bay on the Big Island and finally sacrificed to the gods – it established a precedent and a *modus operandi* for future Hawaiians. Most of the action in this book takes place at another bay, Waimea Bay, on the main island of Oahu. Waimea means 'reddish water' – the colour may have something to do with the iron-rich earth washed down from the mountains, or it may be a reference to all the blood perpetually being spilt to incarnadine the multitudinous seas. A smooth crescent moon of flawless white sand and tranquil turquoise water in the summer, come the winter it turns into a tempestuous, explosive seascape out of which monstrous waves burst forth like new volcanoes, framed by jagged pinnacles of cooled lava at both ends.

In 1792 Captain George Vancouver, who had served under Cook and was in command of another vessel named *Discovery*, anchored at Waimea with a notion of encouraging the islanders to desist from their deadly inter-island warfare. He sent a party ashore to collect fresh water. What is known in military parlance as a 'skirmish' ensued in which several men were killed, including two English sailors. It is believed that their bodies were burnt, partly eaten, and offered up to the gods at the *heiau* – a temple and sacred site – which still sits in ruined splendour on the black crumbling cliffs that tower up above the Bay. Human sacrifices used to be made here in association with prayers for big surf. Since ancient times, Waimea has been a place of myth, miracle, madness and murder. In the last quarter of the twentieth century, two more men, Ken Bradshaw and Mark Foo, would be making their own sacrifices at Waimea Bay as they clashed in the hunt for extremely large waves. This book is the history of their skirmishes.

I first met Bradshaw in the late 1980s. I was supposed to be writing for *The Times* about 'Pottz', Martin Potter, the Brit who was threatening to become the UK's first surfing world champion. Just as *The Times* had sent a reporter to Everest to cover Edmund Hillary's ascent in 1952, so they had sent me to Hawaii to bear witness to our conquest of the waves. The main difference was I had to talk them into it. Born in east London, far from any beach, but umbilically connected via the Thames with the open sea, I used to dream as a child of giant waves sweeping upriver and flooding the capital and flushing away school, friends and family while I surfed to safety atop a passing tree or door. It was never very likely, and it looked even more improbable in Cambridge, where I wound up teaching French, and you needed a punt and a pole, gondolier-style, to glide along the face of the tranquil River Cam. I visited assorted rugged outposts in Europe, Australia and California, but I knew I would have to make the pilgrimage to Hawaii if I was ever to live out my dream and face up to the ultimate, brutal, punishing, purifying, trans-cendent, all-redeeming wave. Pottz was my ticket and I should have been faithfully reporting on the ASP (Association of Surfing Professionals) Triple Crown contests in which he was performing. But inevitably I got distracted, mainly by the big-wave matadors, the high priests of Waimea Bay.

In Hawaii I learned that a big wave is not big in the way a building is big or the way a mountain is big: it is always bigger. It eclipses everything else in your life. Especially when it is coming straight at you. Like everyone else on the North Shore, I stuck the talismanic 'Eddie Would Go' sticker in my car window in tribute to the exploits of native Hawaiian Eddie Aikau: there was no such thing as a 'Pottz Would Go' sticker. The 20-foot-plus guys were somehow deeper, more obsessive, warped, twisted, sublime, courageous, insane, and radically dysfunctional than the pros on the ASP tour, who finessed anything up to 15 feet. The truth is, I had fallen in love, I can see that now. They were my heroes. These were the men I wanted to be like. I resolved that I too would ride a 20-footer – or die.

Bradshaw 'has muscles the way a fish has scales', I jotted down in my notebook as I watched him sculpting a new board in that big wooden house of his off the Kam Highway that looks out over Sunset Beach. He had a beard and even his chest and back had beards too. He was to waves what Tarzan was to trees. I felt obliged to ask him about his eccentric habit of biting chunks out of people's boards.

'It's not as hard as it looks,' he said, grinning and revealing powerful, gleaming incisors. 'It's just a question of getting your mouth at the right angle.' He treated it as a purely technical issue, as if I too might like to try it, like a circus Hercules showing me how to tear up telephone directories or to pull a truck with his teeth – as if my question had been *how* rather than *why*. The idea that I could be expressing any moral qualms about the whole exercise was alien to Bradshaw. He seemed to feel that putting boards together – which is what he did, as a shaper – gave him the right to take them apart again. We talked of this and that and then I said to him: 'Ken, I've heard rumours, is it right that you're at war with Mark Foo?'

He gave the question serious consideration. 'Andy,' he finally replied, in his most meditative, professorial style, 'I can't be at war with Mark Foo. If I wanted to go to war with somebody, they would cease to exist. I would win.'

I used to follow Foo around. I was first introduced to him at Sunset Beach Elementary School, where he was teaching an after-school class on the ABC of big waves. He was dazzling, bewitching, mysterious, enchanting. He glowed like radium. Even his scars were good-looking scars. He was a good writer too – he had even won 'Sports Story of the Year' in Australia for his article, 'The Unridden Realm' – and he used to think he could learn something from me (even though the only award I had won was for 'French Poetry Reading' at school). Meanwhile, I was hoping to learn something from him. I paddled out behind him at Laniakea one time on a medium-to-heavy kind of day. Our paths intersected briefly: we were going in opposite directions, like trains in a relativity experiment, not just travelling at different speeds but occupying radically distinct frames of existence.

He was skimming towards shore as I was toiling out to the line-up and facing up to an extremely large wave – he was poised on top of it – that was about to unload on my head. Seeing me trying to windmill my way out of trouble, he smiled down at me, with compassion and benevolence, as he went flying by. 'You're going to die out here,' he said.

1

The Longest Ride

Festooned with *leis*, the surfboards stood planted in the sand like tombstones. They described a serrated circle around the orange lifeguard tower that looked out over the Bay from the top of the dune. Not mere 'thrusters' but *guns*: long, thin and stiletto-nosed, dedicated to the pursuit of big waves, lances for tilting at dragons. In the early-morning sun at the end of March 1978 they cast elongated shadows over the sand.

The thousand or so people on the beach watched a whale breach and spout a half-mile out. 'The open sea is to the Hawaiian people,' the preacher intoned, 'as the desert was to Moses and the Israelites. It is where they go to meet God.' Outrigger canoes ferried family and close friends out into the middle of the Bay. A hundred or more surfers paddled out behind them and held hands, forming an immense circle, the circle of life, like a gigantic wreath floating on the surface of the tranquil waters. A sacred volcanic rock was placed in a secret location on the bottom. A helicopter unloaded a thousand blossoms on the Bay and everyone else threw hibiscus flowers and rose petals across the face of the water.

They had to. There were no ashes to scatter. But Eddie was dead all the same.

Ken Bradshaw turned to the man next to him. 'Eddie was the best there's ever been,' he said. 'He was fearless.' Bradshaw, with a heavy beard and built like a grizzly bear, was sitting on his board out in the Bay. He was just one of the congregation on the water, but he was holding the hand of one of Eddie's family. He was almost an honorary member of the clan. Like table settings at a wedding, a rough kind of hierarchy was implicit in this funeral formation. Mr K. Bradshaw was sitting at the high table, as if he was being acknowledged as the heir apparent to the crown, the next in line. He had staked his claim, bulldozed his way right into the genealogy.

Somewhere in that circle, far out from the core, like a powerful but remote star, on the outermost periphery of the circumference, amid the masses, sat Mark Foo. Almost nobody knew who he was. Nobody invited him. He had just paddled out there spontaneously, of his own accord. He thought he ought to be there, to register his respects, but also to leave a calling card. Barely twenty, with short hair and slightly built, he looked like a beardless boy. But he would be back. He had an obscure sense, even then, that he belonged here, that he too deserved a place at the high table.

Just then a set came through, out of nowhere, on a calm day, and everybody scattered. Only Clyde, Eddie's brother, caught the wave. He had been sitting where Eddie had once sat. But perhaps everyone let him take the wave, deferring to him, as a sign of respect.

Eddie Aikau had been the universally acknowledged master of Waimea Bay. Even while he was still alive he was already a legend. He was the effortless numero uno on the biggest waves in the world; his name was synonymous with grace under pressure. Technically, he worked as a lifeguard at Waimea, and saved many lives, but he was more than a lifeguard: he was the Bay's presiding spirit, its resident genie, at once its ruler and icon. The man and the place had become inseparable. The *Honolulu Advertiser* called him 'Mr Waimea'.

Eddie Aikau was a native Hawaiian from a family that could trace its ancestry back beyond the days of Captain Cook. His father was a stevedore and sometime gravedigger in a Chinese cemetery. Eddie was brought up on Maui, then moved to Honolulu, and made his debut in giant surf at Waimea one day in late 1967, aged twenty-one. He was a revelation. It was the biggest swell for a decade (and had swept away and killed a couple of unsuspecting Marines the day before). Some say it has never been bigger. When Eddie finally left the water six hours later on that Sunday afternoon in November he had already established himself as one of the finest big-wave riders of his generation. Over the next ten years he steadily built on his reputation at the Bay. However deep you sat, Eddie would always somehow be on your inside, deeper still, closer to the exploding core of the wave, right on top of the curl. Sometimes he paddled out alone on his 11-foot, fire-engine-red Hobie board, when no one else dared to. But he liked to have companionship in the water. He didn't have any competition. On his home ground, no one even tried to compete with him.

Just as his ancestor Hewahewa had once ruled over the entire valley as chief *kahuna* (or priest) and witnessed the twilight of the old idols in the post-contact era, so now Eddie rose to become the natural ruler of the Bay, with a lifeguard tower for a throne, poised on the crest of a renaissance in Hawaiian culture. If, over the last century, America had annexed and purloined most of the Hawaiians' land, at least the beach and the ocean were still theirs by right. Edward Ryan Aikau was modest and shy, a high school dropout who didn't say too much, but he was King of Waimea.

When he won the Duke Classic (named after Duke Kahanamoku, the most influential Hawaiian surfer of the twentieth century and an inspiration to the young Eddie) in 8–12-foot Sunset in December 1977 he was thirty-one and at his peak. He would disappear into the biggest, hollowest tube – the spinning vortex formed by the breaking wave, its briefly throbbing heart, that is the quintessence of surfing – and then re-emerge, miraculously, as if reborn, back into the light at the end of the tunnel, like Jonah being spat out of the whale. He didn't know he had only a few months left to live, but the news would not have altogether surprised him. In accepting his winner's statuette at the Duke banquet, Eddie gave a speech which everyone remembers. 'What is important in life is not competing against each other,' he said. 'It's your family and loving each other.' And he finished with the words, 'None of us know how long we are going to be on this earth. We have to love each other and take care of each other 'cause you never know when your time is going to come.'

Eddie adorned surf movies like: *Golden Breed* (1968), *Waves of Change* (1970) and *Fluid Drive* (1974). Pictures of him appeared in *Life* magazine and on billboards advertising the Bank of America. One photograph preserves Eddie forever tracing a clean high line across the face of a Waimea wave roughly five times his height, just under its curling lip. The sun picks out the trapezoid and deltoid muscles in his back. He is wearing long white shorts with a black waistband, he appears perfectly poised on his long spear of a board, slightly crouched, legs akimbo, arms spread like wings, a single rail carving out a trail of white water, while the other rail hangs out in space, seemingly unsupported, like a cornice of snow sticking out over a crevasse. He is not a big man, perhaps 5 foot 8 or so, but he is symmetrical and sinuous, the incarnation of balance, like a tightrope walker strolling nonchalantly along a high wire over Niagara Falls.

There is an earlier photograph of him aged eight and a half, smartly dressed and wearing a huge smile. Eddie is receiving *The Boys' Book of Knowledge* in an awards ceremony at St Anthony's Catholic School in Maui, with his proud parents and brothers looking on. As it happened he didn't go down the academic road. He was a waterman. But he had the Book of Knowledge, where Waimea Bay was concerned, seared into his soul: he knew it all off by heart, word for word, he could read it upside down, back to front, and inside out. 'Maybe he wasn't educated,' said Kimo Hollinger, a North Shore fireman and mentor to Eddie, 'but when it came to surfing big waves, that guy was a genius.'

To Eddie, Waimea was not an arena of combat, it was more a playground and a temple. Surfing was not a struggle against the elements but an exercise in communion and homage to the god of the ocean. He was an instinctive surfer, who couldn't even remember when he began surfing, he had always surfed. It was in his blood. It was as natural to him as breathing. He surfed without anxiety, almost without thought. He would ride the most savage seas with a broad easy smile on his face, sometimes hooting with sheer joy. He wiped out once on a big day and split his head open. He swam in, wrapped his head up in a towel and paddled right back out again. He liked to see others catching waves alongside him and would actively encourage them: 'Come on, brother! You and I! I'll be on your inside.'

He called just about everybody *brother*. He was a benign force at the Bay, a symbol of solidarity among surfers. Ken Bradshaw – whom he called 'Brother Brad', having understood his name as Brad Shaw – said, 'I never once saw him get upset or angry.' At the height of the Vietnam era and beyond, he believed in love not war. Once, when some brash loud-mouthed Australians had ruffled local feathers with their cocky attitude (exemplified by Wayne 'Rabbit' Bartholomew's bragging, rabble-rousing 1976 article for *Surfer* magazine, headlined 'Bustin' Down the Door' – asserting inevitable Australian dominance), and a group of native Hawaiians were on the warpath, Eddie brought the two sides together and persuaded them to settle peacefully. 'You've got to learn to live together,' he would say. 'The ocean is for everybody.'

Another time it was Bradshaw who was looking for blood. James Jones, a serious Waimea contender, had 'burned' Bradshaw, so he thought, getting in his way and stealing 'his' wave. Eddie gave Brother Brad a lift in his lifeguard truck and spent an hour explaining the meaning of *aloha* to him and calmed the raging bull down. 'He taught us to be more loving and understanding of each other,' Bradshaw remembers. There was no sense in argument or dispute. Surfing in a big-wave environment was tough enough already even without any extra aggro in the water. Eddie was the godfather of Waimea, but a fairy godfather who healed rifts and headed off quarrels and conjured up an aura of harmony. He could be found wearing a multicoloured bandanna and singing and strumming his slack-key guitar on the beach: 'I'm leaving on a jet plane, don't know when I'll be back again . . .' But any time anyone got into trouble at Waimea, Eddie would be there to fish them out and save them, almost miraculously manifesting himself amid the deepest darkest boiling chaos, perched on a cloud of foam. He had brought drowned men back from the dead. No one was allowed to die while he was around. Once he was supposed to be competing in a contest and he stopped to save one of his adversaries.

Eddie was a Hawaiian Hegel who believed that the final synthesis had already been attained. The real was ideal. There was no more conflict between thesis and antithesis. In some sense, history was already at an end. History began with Hawaiians being the supreme surfers on the planet and now history had come full circle. Eddie was therefore a natural for the crew of the *Hokule'a*.

The *Hokule'a* had more or less blown the *Kon-Tiki* out of the water. The Norwegian anthropologist Thor Heyerdahl conjectured that Hawaii had been colonised by roaming South Americans. In the 1950s he managed to sail his hypothetical boat west from Peru but the arguments for an alternative migratory course always looked like winning. The name 'Polynesia' – meaning 'many islands' – didn't take hold until the eighteenth century, but the people who would ultimately become known as Polynesians began their travels, a few millennia ago, along the east coast of Asia, shoving off from China in the north down to Indonesia in the south, and gradually making their way across the Pacific, from Fiji to the Marquesas, and at their most easterly extending as far as Easter Island. Sometime in the last quarter of the first millennium they sailed northwards, perhaps from Tahiti (as legend has it) or, more likely, from the Marquesas, steering by the stars and tracking land by seabirds and ocean currents. But whatever their origin, their final destination, some two and a half thousand miles to the north – and the most northerly point of the vast Polynesian triangle – was Hawaii.

The history of the *menehune* suggests that the Hawaiians as we now know them may not have been the first people to step ashore on Hawaii. But the newcomers made Hawaii their own and invested it with their mythology and history. And they brought surfing with them. Legend tells of a Tahitian chief, Moikeha, who sailed to Hawaii and, largely thanks to his prowess on a surfboard, succeeded in marrying not just one princess but two and thereby becoming King of Kauai. When his sons returned to Tahiti and were asked the fate of their father, they said:

> He is dwelling in ease in Kauai,
> Where the surf of the Makaiwa curves and bends,
> Where the kukui blossoms of Puna change,
> Where the waters of Wailua stretch out,
> He will live and die on Kauai.

The classic long-distance Polynesian vessel in which Moikeha and his sons made such massive voyages was almost certainly a double-hulled canoe. The brainchild of anthropologist Ben Finney from the University of Hawaii and the Polynesian Voyaging Society, and with two hulls 60 feet long, V-shaped sails and a big steering paddle at the back, the *Hokule'a* was an attempt to reproduce the original ancient craft. The idea was to mirror the primordial expedition and sail the canoe all the way back from Hawaii to Tahiti and beyond. There was no motor on board, no radio, no satellite navigational equipment, no way of communicating with the rest of the world beyond what the ancient Hawaiians had themselves had. They would be using the same centuries-old techniques of astral navigation and water knowledge. *Hokule'a* represents Hawaii's zenith star, Arcturus, and means 'star of gladness', so called because it once guided Hawaiian sea-goers home from their nomadic journeys.

On 16 March 1978, the *Hokule'a* set out from the harbour in Honolulu on its epic journey south. Eddie was one of the sixteen-man crew who were all as trained, honed and rigorously prepared as astronauts. Or astronomers: they had spent weeks in the Bishop Museum Planetarium studying the constellations and committing to memory the way they rose and set on the horizon. Eddie was not the captain, nor (at thirty-two) the oldest on board, nor the navigator, but he was the canoe's good-luck charm, spiritual father and guardian angel of the *Hokule'a*. They sure needed one.

It was not the *Hokule'a*'s maiden voyage. The first time round, in 1976, this great spiritual journey had ended in a mass onboard brawl. The tight living quarters were like a pressure-cooker in which the racial tension between ('stupid, lazy, fat') Hawaiians and ('who do you fucking think *you* are telling *us* what to do?') *haoles* (of Anglo-Saxon origin) had nowhere left to go. It became known as 'the hell-on-high-seas incident'. It was more like a mutiny. Buffalo Keaulana, the strapping, short-fused Hawaiian lifeguard from Makaha, flattened the captain and gave Ben Finney a black eye. The quest for a noble past, for truth and beauty, had led only to violence and mayhem. Eddie was recruited as a mascot of mutual tolerance and mellowness and brotherhood. He in turn looked on the vessel as a symbol of Hawaiian history and, more than that, as a miniature Noah's Ark, a vehicle of salvation, an immense olive branch to the world. He thought of the crew as his 'second family'. On this voyage, unlike the previous one, there would be no support vessel to escort them. With Eddie along, they didn't really need one. That was the thinking anyway. Before they departed, on the harbourside in

Honolulu Eddie pulled out his guitar and sang the assembled crew a song he had composed about the *Hokule'a* and everything it meant to him. He sang of sun and moon and stars, of wind and sail, of pride and freedom, and the ship that would carry a man to Tahiti and swing him back again to Hawaii. It was a prayer to the old Hawaiian gods of water and sky. And it was a love song. It was no secret that Eddie's marriage was breaking up and it was as if he had fallen for the *Hokule'a*. She was his mistress, his sweetheart, his beloved. A picture was taken of Eddie – the last – wearing his trademark bandanna and paddling his surfboard away from the canoe. It was an image that, later, would seem to foreshadow his fate.

In the minds of more than ten thousand people, including the governor of Hawaii and the Mayor of Honolulu, who had gathered at Magic Island to join in the celebrations and the send-off, the winds and currents were set fair on that sunny Sunday afternoon in March. Captain David Lyman, a veteran of the first, violent voyage, reflected wryly that the original Hawaiians had not had to put up with all this hoopla. To the cheers and applause of the crowds lining the harbour walls, and the mournful crooning of massed conch shells, the *Hokule'a* moved smoothly away, out past Diamond Head, leaving the flotilla of accompanying yachts and small craft behind them, heading south from Oahu, to the west of Molokai, cutting through the whitecaps and steering swiftly towards the Big Island at the southernmost tip of the Hawaiian chain, and beyond to Tahiti. The twin hulls of the *Hokule'a* were loaded with dried and canned food and three hundred one-gallon containers of water. They had 2,400 miles to go. If everything went according to plan, the voyage had been estimated to take around a month.

They were hardly out of sight of land before they ran into gusty winds and heavy seas. Some of the crew were starting to have second thoughts about taking off in these conditions, and debating fears and premonitions. One man had already bowed out on account of bad omens. Maybe he was right. Now it turned out that neither the captain nor the navigator, Nainoa Thompson, mindful of gale warnings, had really wanted to set sail, they had just been putting a brave face on it. And, more crucially, the nagging question of the open-water effectiveness of the seals in the theoretically 'watertight' compartments hadn't been resolved either. When he woke up that morning, David Lyman told his wife straight out, 'I don't want to leave today.' He had had bad dreams. But the Polynesian Voyaging Society had set the date for departure, and politicians and photographers had turned up to send them off, so they had to go. All those qualms were dismissed as nothing more than sailors' superstitions. Retrospectively, the Coast Guard would refer to 'questionable conditions'. But, at first, the great voyaging canoe made good time as it sailed into the night.

The sun had set on that first day when an ugly squall blew up in the channel known as Kealaikahiki, or 'the Path to Tahiti'. The *Hokule'a* was due west of the island of Lanai. Soon the craft was flying over the top of 20-foot waves in the darkness and taking on water. They kept on pumping it out again, but soon the canoe was listing heavily. David Lyman cursed those damn seals: he had known all along they were never going to be robust enough for mid-ocean conditions. He was intent on keeping the boat at 90 degrees to the oncoming waves, tackling them head-on, and carving a line straight through them. But the multiple currents swirling around and between the islands were treacherous and the big swell was amplifying the general turbulence. Around midnight a rogue 25-footer came at them at an angle out of the darkness and, before the crew could spin the boat around to absorb the blow, the wave hit, the *Hokule'a* went careering up the face at 45 degrees and capsized as it shot off the peak. It was like a Polynesian *Poseidon*.

The crew swam out from under the canoe and attached themselves to the upturned port hull. Nobody was hurt. Everyone was safe. For now anyway. But it was impossible to right the craft. Hours passed. No one panicked, but they became colder and more dispirited. Some were sick and there was a fear of sharks. The emergency radio beacon had been lost. They had travelled less than a hundred miles on a journey of more than two thousand and here they were – already upside down and disabled.

The sun had not yet risen when Eddie said he was going for help. He didn't want to just rescue everyone: he wanted to redeem them and turn disaster into a good-news story. 'At a deeper level,' said Nainoa Thompson, years later, 'Eddie tried to rescue not only the crew of the *Hokule'a* but the symbolism and dignity of the canoe because he knew it carried the pride of his people.'

'Are you crazy?' yelled Lyman, above the howling wind. 'It has to be all of twenty miles to land.' It was a cardinal rule of the ocean to stay with your boat, so long as it was still afloat. But, as usual, Eddie was fearless. All his training and his instinct called on him to act rather than keep treading water. And they could see the lights of the airport tower on Lanai winking invitingly in the distance.

'It's OK,' he replied. 'I'll take my board. It'll be the longest ride ever.' Eddie had brought his 12-foot big-wave surfboard along. He had been planning to use it in Tahiti (legend has it, the birthplace of surfing). It was on this board that he had saved so many lives at Waimea. Now it would save a few more. Eddie had no difficulty paddling for miles at a stretch. And the big waves were meat and drink to him. Eddie dived under the canoe and unlashed his board.

'Don't worry,' he reassured Lyman. 'I can do it. I'll get to land and send a message.' Lyman didn't like it, but it was finally agreed: Eddie would go. Nainoa Thompson held his hands and looked into his eyes, saying nothing. Maybe it would have been better if he had said something. 'If you were to ask me if I could make it, I would say no,' Thompson admitted later. 'But Eddie was godlike, he was like a miracle-man – he could do anything.'

'I'll be OK,' says Eddie, ever the optimist. 'Don't worry, everything will be OK.' He pushed off calmly from the *Hokule'a* and paddled away into the maelstrom with quick firm strokes, cresting the waves, discarding his lifejacket as he went, and vanished in the half-light. The lifejacket just got in the way. Soon he was stroking into that great immensity in which there is no more land, where there is nothing but waves and more waves, an infinity, an eternity, of waves.

The crew were picked up later that same day by Coast Guard helicopters. The promised miracle had duly occurred. – Eddie got through, then, they said. We knew he would. But nobody knew anything about Eddie. There had been no word from Lanai. The helicopter trawled back and forth across the channel in a frantic search for the man who was now the only missing member of the crew.

They finally spotted the big white board with the word 'RESCUE' inscribed on the deck in red letters; but of Eddie there was no sign. The board was just being blown across the surface, rolling in the wind like tumbleweed in the desert. The desperate search continued for several days. Everyone knew by then that it was hopeless but they went on anyway, guided by hope and the intervention of Californian psychics. The body of Eddie Aikau was never recovered. There was no corpse, no body to commit to the deep. It was as if he had been spirited away to heaven. At the memorial service an urn of Waimea sand, representing the ashes of the dead man, was voided upon the waters. In a way the whole of Eddie's brilliant, flaming career had been built on sand – and it was vulnerable to a turn in the tide.

While Eddie was alive it was like an endless Christmas – peace, love and goodwill to all men. It was an age of innocence, of faith, hope and charity. It was a prolonged season of *Makahiki*, the period of recreation when Captain Cook first arrived in Hawaii and was briefly, bizarrely, mistaken for Lono, god of light, god of sport, god of surfing. Cook was dead but Eddie took his place in some ways. He was Lono: a god, but a peacenik god, devoid of wrath and vengefulness, who preached and embodied love-thy-neighbour. And now god was dead, aged thirty-two. 'Don't worry' had been Eddie's last words; 'everthing's going to be OK.' But everything was not OK. In years to come the *Hokule'a* would sail triumphantly back and forth across the Pacific, attaining the extremities of the scattered Polynesian civilisation. But that achievement would never erase the experience of going down and losing Eddie Aikau to the sea.

In retrospect it seems as if the era during which Eddie ruled at Waimea was no more than a truce, a brief cessation of conflict, almost an illusion. The age of harmony was over. War had not yet been officially declared in the islands, but it was imminent.

I was on my first date with the Bay. It was summer. Eddie Aikau had been dead for the best part of ten years. I stumbled across the commemorative bronze plaque, scrupulously maintained, framed by flowers and stones, near the water fountain. It reads: 'Greater love hath no man than this, that a man lay down his life for his friends' (John 15: 13). The memorial is the closest Eddie came to a tombstone. His status as Hawaiian hero had been immortalised. But the death of Eddie meant that there was a little less *aloha* in the world and especially on the North Shore. It was the armed-to-the-teeth eighties: Reagan and Thatcher were carving up the map, Stallone and Schwarzenegger were blowing away the box office, and Foo and Bradshaw were about to embark on a duel that would span the decade and beyond. Life was due to become more brutal and, in some cases, shorter. On that day in March 1978, the day of his funeral, Eddie's orange tower on the beach at Waimea Bay was empty, but the message board was clear: 'NO LIFEGUARD ON DUTY'.

2

The Perfect Day

It was a 10–12-foot day at Sunset. Early morning, still clean and glassy, before the trade winds kick in, one day in winter. It was a predominantly western swell, with a little bit of north in there too. The peak was jumping about the way it always did at Sunset, but the strong offshore breeze was pinning the waves back, holding them off, and keeping the walls well formed and steep. Cloudless skies too, bathing the faces of the surfers in a quasi-transcendental radiance, like haloes around the heads of saints.

And – perhaps because it was still early – only a handful of guys were out, no more than a dozen, maximum. The muster included Ken Bradshaw and Mark Foo and a handful of ASP pros in training for the next contest. The couple of surfing-magazine photographers who had already installed themselves on the beach and screwed on their long-range lenses, the size of bazookas, were calling it *perfect*: 'the perfect day'. But they exaggerated for a living. For true perfection you would have to double the size and reduce the numbers to one and even then you could still dream of better. But all in all this was about as good as it gets. There were plenty of high-class waves to go around and not too many takers. Far away, low-pressure systems prowled the ocean looking for trouble, but here in Hawaii, if there were such a thing as a surfing barometer, it would surely have to be set to 'fair' or even 'sunny'.

I used to rent a room in Banzai Betty's yellow house at Backyards (Betty had been nicknamed after 'Banzai Pipeline' and was at the time the ballsiest big-wave woman surfer on the whole North Shore). There was a huge picture window that looked right out on Sunset Point a couple of hundred yards away. I marvelled, as I prepared breakfast, at how pristine, how enticing it looked, framed by the fronds of palm trees and hazy Kaena Point ten miles distant. I used to think: this is as close as I'll ever come to heaven. Sunset aroused in me an obscure but powerful sense of grace descending on the world. Hawaii seemed to me like an oasis of purity and truth in an otherwise corrupt and screwed-up world. But that morning, sometime in the mid-eighties, paradise was about to be lost, yet again, the way it always is.

Every so often a bigger set would come thundering through. That was one of the things you had to be ready for at this unpredictable break. Having slotted into a few of those fickle, voluptuous curves, I knew that you couldn't afford to take your eye off the ball, otherwise the ball would come right up and smash you in the face. Around the time most people would be kissing their partners goodbye and getting in the car to go to work, the pack sat up on their boards and stared hard at the horizon. Sensing as much as seeing an abnormally large troupe of waves approaching, they flattened themselves into the paddling posture and started moving into position, at first tentatively then, as the waves got closer, and the lead wave was looming up and feathering at the crest, with increasing urgency. Soon most of this small group were digging in and scrambling for the horizon. They were aiming quite deliberately to get out of the way of this set. Wave selection is one of the crucial components of the art of surfing. This one virtually de-selected itself. Starting to rear up and stagger so far out, it looked too big to handle, a risky proposition for this hour of the morning. Why bust your board and blow the entire day (and – who knows? – sustain injury) for the sake of one outsize wave? This was not a percentage wave. Too much of a gamble. Better to play safe.

One man, however, paddled confidently, almost complacently, in the opposite direction, away from the pack. They were heading out so he was heading more in, or at least sideways, manoeuvring and correcting and checking on the wave and then correcting again, to place himself in the optimal spot for take-off. For every wave, he knew, there is really only one window. And he wanted to be on it when it opened up. As far as he was concerned, the bigger the better. There was no such thing as too big, not at Sunset anyway. The idea of playing safe never occurred to him.

Gambling didn't enter into it, this was not chancy, not a long shot, no, this was all down to knowledge, experience, skill and timing. He laughed to himself at all the guys – ASP guys! – going the wrong way. But this was how it was meant to be. He had put in the time and almost superhuman effort into conquering and mastering and dominating this break. He had bought a house only a few hundred yards away. He had an intimate understanding of all its moods and vagaries.

He had it all mapped out in his mind, so clearly that he could see the way things would happen long before they happened. He knew for a fact that he would make this wave and make it his and ride it powerfully and indestructibly until he had sucked out all its juice, drained it of life, and killed it, and it collapsed exhausted, useless and impotent, and slunk back into the sea whence it came. He had bested countless others. With all the clarity of his prophetic gaze he foresaw the moment in which he would leap to his feet and get a stranglehold around this massive foaming beast and wrestle it into submission. The *thing* stood no chance, none; it only *looked* like it could mow down and obliterate anyone who dared to stand in its path. For, the man knew, everything in his vast experience told him, that he would prevail. Nothing – no *thing* – could touch him out here. This was his domain, his manor. Here he was invulnerable, omniscient, infallible.

No wonder then, that bright December morning, with no cloud on the horizon, that he paddled so commandingly, so authoritatively, so serenely, with an air of calm conviction, with no shred of doubt in his mind, no fibre of weakness in his body. The masses humbly eclipsed themselves before him. Muscular, with long brown hair and big but strictly barbered beard, Ken Bradshaw could pass for Moses (or Charlton Heston playing Moses). From the perspective of the photographers on the beach, from my window at Backyards, he looked as if he could part the waters, never mind ride them. At Sunset, he ruled.

Bradshaw had the wave. There was no question about that. He was on it. He was lined up. He was in position. He had paid his dues, he had earned this wave, he deserved it. He was locked on target, he was implacable, there was no calling him back. And then another man came racing out of the pack. He appeared massively junior to Bradshaw. He was not just younger, he was smaller, slighter, lighter, slimmer, a bantamweight to Bradshaw's heavyweight slugger. And he was Asiatic, no hint of the biblical, more Tao, beardless, almost hairless apart from the mop of unruly black hair on his head. More of a Bruce Lee in shorts: sinewy, tight, hard, with a surprisingly, disproportionately, penetrating punch. Maybe, in retrospect, Bradshaw had been just a little too commanding, a little too authoritative, a little too slow. In motion he was as majestic as a large battleship, an aircraft-carrier, but he was bulky too and slightly lumbering. He couldn't be outgunned but it was possible to sneak under his radar. Mark Foo did just that: whipped past him, streaked by – 'snaked' by, Bradshaw would later say – stealing up on his inside, the last place Bradshaw could have expected to find anyone, and took up pole position. It was with a kind of astonishment that Ken Bradshaw briefly contemplated the sight of someone in front of him, jumping the queue, muscling in, usurping the throne. The water plumped up voluptuously under both men and hoisted them up towards the sky like an open-air elevator.

The wave generally has a short but intense existence. The mother swell, conjured up out of a frothing cauldron of wind, sun, moon and rotational energy, may well have travelled thousands of miles from the Aleutian Islands up near Alaska or north of Japan. But the manifest wave is only born out of it when the jutting, perpendicular reef that is Hawaii thrusts up into all this amorphous energy and pumps up a great slab of water that rises up precipitously before attaining its full ferocious height, only to expire, shortly thereafter, and collapse in a tumbling, exploding fury of white water, thus finally releasing the original storm out of which it was composed. But in its buoyant youth it is hungry and unforgiving. It yearns to consume anything and anyone in its way. And so it was that the great maw that was the inside of the wave opened up in front of and directly under Foo and Bradshaw. Foo, slightly ahead of Bradshaw, dived down into the great void, leaping to his feet.

Bradshaw, on the very brink of doing precisely that, had already visualised it fully, saw Foo ahead of him and pulled up in shock and amazement, letting the wave slide past underneath him, like a bad dream in which you have a gun in your hand and it turns into a bar of soap, no bullets, nothing but bubbles – but not before he had caught a glimpse of Foo already up and cutting a jagged scar across the face of the once flawless wave. *You're dropping in on me?* he said to himself, outraged and perplexed. It was typical of surfing that one of the cardinal sins should be not – as it was in landlocked society at large – dropping *out*, but dropping *in*, which anywhere else would be considered a harmless, even positively sociable, thing to do. In serious hardcore surfing, everyone had already dropped out, become socially dysfunctional beings, outsiders, beyond good and evil; in these circumstances, the worst thing you could do was to drop back in again.

YOU dare to drop in on ME?

In Bradshaw's view of the world, Foo had just stolen *his* wave; it was flat-out broad-daylight robbery, as plain as if Foo had reached into Bradshaw's pocket and prised it directly from his billfold. The wave, already his, had been taken away from him. The day, which had been so close to perfection, had been shattered. More than this, the natural order of things had been disturbed, subverted, turned on its head.

But Bradshaw would recover from this glancing blow to his pride. Foo had barely drawn blood. It was a mere pinprick, no more than scratch. Foo was an annoying insect who could be flattened at any time with a single swipe. But an injustice had taken place nonetheless and that would need to be corrected.

Foo was a felon who would have to be brought to book, be shown the error of his ways and rehabilitated as a decent citizen. And this was not the first time, either. He was a serial offender.

What Sunset really needed was an effective police force and impartial judicial system for meting out swift justice. In their absence, Bradshaw was Sheriff. He had been taken by surprise. But he wasn't furious with Foo, he wasn't angry or hotheaded about it, he just had a cold, impersonal, abiding sense of duty. Someone had to see the Law enforced. And it was incumbent on him, as the great Enforcer, to draw the line in the sand.

Bradshaw waited. Finally the outlaw – the Sinner! – paddled back out to the break, as Bradshaw knew he would, returning to the scene of the crime. He had ridden his ill-gotten wave for several hundred yards and now he was coming back for more. More illicit waves. Bradshaw would have to do something about it. It was all in the interests of the community, the republic of wave-riders. It was nothing personal. Bradshaw bore Foo almost no ill will. Foo scarcely registered on his barometer. This was not Tom and Jerry. This was not a grudge, not a touchy, infected, boiling abscess of resentment and jealousy that Foo had enflamed yet one more time. No, this was the awesome machinery of justice being fired up and brought to bear.

Bradshaw would waste no words of reprimand. The delinquent wouldn't understand anyway. Firm action was what was needed. Foo was sitting up on his board, scanning the horizon for his next misdemeanour, when Bradshaw came up behind him, soundlessly. The long arm of the Law came up out of the water, reached up and grabbed the Fugitive by the throat in an armlock, dumped him in the water and shoved him down. The board was vacant, floating free. Taking no further notice of Foo, Bradshaw flipped the board over and inspected the bottom. Just what he had anticipated: a three-fin pin-tail thruster. Foo's usual flashy purple and yellow design. Beyond rage, coolly, methodically, implacably, one by one he whacked off each fin with the base of his hand. Foo came spluttering up. He looked at Bradshaw open-mouthed, incredulous, as if he were contemplating a lunatic who had recently escaped from confinement. He backed off discreetly, still umbilically connected to the mangled board by a 15-foot leash strapped round his ankle. 'Somebody had to teach you a lesson,' the madman was muttering.

There are conflicting accounts, all distorted by the passing of time, of what took place next, and even whether anything took place at all. But it seems possible that Bradshaw somehow understood that the true majesty and weight of the Law had not yet been fully brought to bear. Now he examined the board carefully. No, it was not too thick. He brought it up to his great jaws. Then savagely, suddenly (according to Foo), he chomped down on it, bit a great chunk out of the rail section. Had Foo's board been the *Titanic*, it would have gone down then and there. But instead it just floated uselessly, ruined, beyond repair, bobbing on the now-calm turquoise waters, looking as if a particularly indiscriminate shark had taken a lunge at it. Foo, having unleashed himself, was treading water a few yards away, looking on with awe at this spectacle of justice being rigorously applied. Well, it had been a long time coming, but maybe he would learn something at last, if it was not too late, perhaps he would behave himself in future, conduct himself properly and show due deference and respect to the master.

This close encounter was not the beginning of the rivalry between Bradshaw and Foo, the Old Guard and the Young

Gun. And it was not the end either. This day, this morning, this moment, this incident torn out of the annals of the mid-eighties, was rather an exemplary episode within that larger, more epic and enduring narrative. Some say that it would never have happened that way had it not been for all the ASP guys out there and the photographers on the beach: Bradshaw felt he was under public scrutiny and could not let a slight such as Foo inflicted on him pass unpunished.

Foo and Bradshaw: the North Shore was just not big enough for both of them.

3

The Boy of Steel

Sergeant Ken Bradshaw Snr, Special Forces operative, kitted out in full Nazi uniform and knee-high leather boots, and driving a Volkswagen staff car (with swastikas) behind enemy lines, was sizing up German towns for the next advance. He didn't take any notes, in case he was arrested. He couldn't speak any German, so he masqueraded as a deaf-mute. Every now and then he would signal to people who were speaking to him that he didn't have a clue what they were saying (he found that tapping his head on the side as if it was hollow worked quite well). He carried a fake ID with a message on it explaining that, as far as communication went, he was *hors de combat*. Fortunately he was accompanying a lieutenant who spoke the language fluently and explained to anyone who was interested that his driver was incapable of speech. He was born that way, he would say. Sad, *ja*?

It wasn't a great cover story. Not everyone was going to fall for it. Maybe it was not so surprising, therefore, that Ken Bradshaw's father had a grand total of seven bullet holes in him. Enough, in fact, to kill seven men. His body – back, stomach, face – looked as drilled as a wallful of incompetent DIY fixings. The entire German Army had failed to nail him and finish him off. He was starting to frighten the Nazis. During the Second World War he was twice sent home from the front after being shot and twice he returned to duty as soon as he could walk again.

A couple of the wounds were inflicted in later years by would-be assassins in the course of his duty as an officer in the Houston police department. *Eat lead, pig!* Over and over again. But he never seemed to get the message; he ate it, and just got on with the job, slightly better ventilated than before, as if the role of a punch-holed deaf-mute suited him down to the ground. It may have been a fake ID to begin with, but it was a role he adopted and grew into.

In the course of time, Ken Bradshaw Snr became Sheriff Bradshaw (technically, a captain in the sheriff's department) and finally 'Mayor Bradshaw' of Spring Branch, a small town near Houston. Fellow Texans appreciated the fact that, even if he didn't listen too much, he didn't say too much either. When he was not being shot to pieces, running for Mayor, overthrowing tyranny or chasing felons through the mean streets, he was running a successful pipe-fitting business that kept Texan oil flowing. In his off-duty hours he turned into a Commander of the Sea Scouts. Not to mention President of the Rotary Club and Chairman of the Board at assorted local trade or philanthropic organisations. How he ever found time to get married and bring up a family remains a mystery.

It was not for want of imagination that Ken Jnr was named after his father. His parents wanted young Ken to follow in his father's remarkable footsteps. After all, it still left him with plenty of options: Special Forces, Captain, Sheriff, Mayor, CEO, Commander. Or football player. Kenny slotted into the mould of football player as if he had been born to it. He didn't really need all that armour and body reinforcement; he already looked that way with his kit off. He was big and he was aggressive, like one of those wild animals you daren't shoot for fear of making it angry. You just back away quietly into the undergrowth. While still at junior high school he made the All-City team, as an ass-kicking linebacker. He wasn't expected to do anything too subtle, like pass the ball, just block, tackle and bring down the opposition as hard as possible. It was something he enjoyed doing. He was a natural. He was hard and he knew no fear. Even as a little kid he was never afraid of the dark.

All in all, he was the perfect son, the apple of Ken and Allyne Bradshaw's eye. Maybe he would even be President one day. After all, there was already a Texan in the White House, Lyndon B. Johnson, the Vice-President who had stepped in following Kennedy's assassination and had set about stoking up the Vietnam War. A Texan ruled the world – why not Kenny? This lesson from the political arena would have been driven into the ten-year-old boy's head: you acquired power over the dead and bloody body of your predecessor or rival. There was room for only one at the top. *Vice*-President was never going to be enough, that was for sure.

When not out bushwhacking unwary adversaries on the football field, Kenny dressed neatly and spoke intelligently to his parents' friends and business contacts. He was a model of politeness and good manners. He had good regular features, he didn't spill food down himself, he could be taken out anywhere, he wore a buttoned-up shirt and a tie: a son to be proud of. He was half bloodthirsty warrior, half suave social sophisticate who still went to church on Sundays.

It's hard to say where it all went wrong, where the model,

all-American boy, the son who was a perfect replica of his dad, the presidential candidate-in-waiting, started to come apart at the seams. Perhaps it was partly because, if he wanted to speak to his father, he had to attend a mayoral meeting, pay a visit to the police station or burrow down a pipeline. As Kenny grew up, he found that his father was pulling the old deaf-mute trick again. Or it may have been because he had to make his own bed every day and tuck in the sheets so tightly that you could bounce a penny off them (not a metaphor but an old army ploy). And shine his shoes so that he could shave in them (he was the bristling kind of youth who started shaving young). It could have been because a kid can only take so much military-style discipline and regimentation and over-bearing, domineering ordering around before he cracks and chaos starts to seep into his soul. Yet another factor could have been the potent dose of revolution and revolt and Molotov-cocktail-Kent-State-Bob-Dylan-and-Rolling-Stones anarchy that was being injected simultaneously into the veins of teenagers all over America in the mid- to late 1960s. On the other hand, it might have been that Ken Bradshaw was born backwards and started off as a good citizen in a suit and tie and then regressed into shorts and nakedness and all-round barbarism.

But it's a fair bet that surfing had something to do with it, too.

You could say it was all his older sister's fault. *Janice* – she loved to drive the seventy-five miles to Surfside, south of Galveston, Texas. Her parents didn't have her entire destiny mapped out the way they had with little Kenny, but all the same she was glad of the air. It could get a little claustrophobic at home. And then there was that nice-looking surfer boy called Ted, with the long fair hair and broad muscular shoulders and tight little butt. All those restrictions on how late she could stay out, the rules about laundry, cooking, homework, going to bed, dreaming, breathing. It was like living in an army barracks. Love your parents, of course, but every now and then you still want to go AWOL. Love them, but you have to live. And if I have to take my goofy little brother along too, I'll do it. Anything to get out of this house. Or I'm going to *freak out*.

The young Bradshaw already knew how to swim and sail. His father had had him messing around on boats early on, in a variety of inland lakes, splicing his mainbrace with salty Sea Scout commands. It wasn't until he was nearly in his teens that Ken Bradshaw discovered the alternate universe of the beach, in 1965, at Surfside. He was shocked by it at first, dismayed, almost disgusted. Where were all the neatly marked-out grid lines, where was the end zone, where were the goalposts? Where was the grass anyway? What kind of game could you possibly win on this field? And how the hell could you win? And, finally, who (or 'whom' he would have said in his neat, precise way) could you flatten and pulverise? It was a mystery, mind-boggling madness, random quantum logic at work. This was no place for a live-wire, ballsy, carnivorous kid.

And yet – he kept being drawn back to it. It made everything else seem too easy: the classes, the fraternising, the conquering of other teams, the submission to the long arm of the law and the deaf-mute rod of the father. Here at last was something seriously challenging, beyond mere human power, and requiring a transcendent will. Bradshaw's Law. He had imbibed all the iron discipline and the inexhaustible puritan work ethic that any self-respecting adolescent could ever need and more. Now, at last, he had found something gigantic that all of that could be applied to in a spirit of pure scientific empirical enquiry: the ocean. It was nothing to beat the stuffing out of other kids on some football field. But to get on top of the mighty ocean wave, to dominate the Gulf, to drill that maddeningly wayward geometry into some kind of order – now there was a goal to aim for. Before, it had seemed to him that the sea was just an infinite compendium of details, pure chaos, inscrutable, but as soon as he started graffitiing lines across the surf, it was, almost magically, as if this sprawling great mass had acquired a unity and continuity that were not there before, as if the waves sprang into life as an army, an armada, that he alone, Kenny Bradshaw, had to overcome and command.

His parents didn't approve. In fact they flat out disapproved. Surfing was not on their A-list of duties and aspirations. It wasn't even on their B- or C-list. But the boy persisted, and when Boy Bradshaw persisted you knew about it. The more enthusiastic he was, the less enthusiastic they were (and vice versa). But they let him have his way, most of the time, for the sake of a quiet life. And then they realised it gave them the power of sanction: 'You'd better do this, Kenny, or we're not going to let you go surfing this weekend.' That soon brought him into line. Surfing was bad, all right, but the silver lining was that it was another stick to beat him with. They could always lock his board in the cupboard. That would teach him.

By 1967, by his own reckoning, Bradshaw had been thoroughly taught. He was fifteen, in his freshman year at high school, and all he could think about was surfing. Surfing infiltrated and occupied his mind until all his waking thoughts were wave-shaped. He dreamed of surfing: at night a giant wave sprang up and flooded the whole of Spring Branch, engulfing and obliterating at a stroke parents, sisters, teachers, school, while a lone fifteen-year-old boy surfed away to freedom and glory on a passing tree-trunk. Bradshaw and I were around the same age; with only minor differences, we shared the same dream. It wasn't a death wish; it was an immortality wish. But we both knew, unconsciously, that someone would have to die for that wish to come true.

Janice probably affected – or infected – the way he thought about the ocean. *Thank God!* she would exclaim when they hit the beach road again and the spicy tang of the sea kissed their lips. *It feels like a million miles away from Spring Branch.* To Bradshaw the ocean was always something feminine: different, moody, fickle, perfumed, opaque, shifty, slightly incomprehensible, just crying out for the application of some rigorously masculine discipline. She was a big sister who could nevertheless be shaped and swung around according to your needs and desires. Whenever the outer rim of a hurricane rolled through Spring Branch, his parents would go into overdrive: 'Everybody inside! Out of the wind! Lower sails! Save yourselves from the elements!' Meanwhile Boy Bradshaw was secretly smiling to himself. He knew there would be some good waves down at Surfside and all he had to do was charm his sister into driving him over there. (Hey, Janice, you're looking a bit pale today. Do you think so? Yes, you really ought to be getting some sea air. Ted must be missing you. Wait, if you're going anyway, I'll just get my board.) Compared to his parents, she was a pushover, a piece of cake.

In those days the Texan waves were not insignificant; they were a perfect learning platform for a growing boy. Big, long, easygoing, soft-centred, uncrowded peaks, they gave you paddling experience and the beginnings of wave knowledge without ever punishing your mistakes too severely. When he was at school he hated the thought that there were waves out there that were getting away without his attention. All free, all his, and all going to waste. Suddenly, football didn't seem so important any more. He had bigger fish to fry: he had waves to block and tackle and bring down. When he got out there he was intent on making up for lost time and no sooner had he ridden one wave than he was turning around to paddle back out again and catch another, a glutton coming back for yet another helping, until he was stuffed and exhausted. Except that he never was, not entirely.

He read the surfing magazines cover to cover; he watched ABC's *Wide World of Sports* to see, unforgettably, his first glimpse of the Duke Kahanamoku contest being held at the legendary Sunset Beach, Hawaii, several thousand miles west of Texas and a whole world away. He couldn't believe how heavy the waves were. Then, at the local movie theatre, he watched, wide-eyed, *Ride the Wild Surf*, a movie which featured epic footage of big Waimea. *Real* Waimea. Twenty-foot-plus. Waves as big as houses, as big as office blocks, as big as . . . No, there wasn't really anything else as big as this. Nothing else as powerful and relentless and unforgiving. At last he had discovered something even more formidable than his old man – that might scare even *him*. He went back to see it again and again (his parents thought he would be safe at the movie theatre, not realising that he was, in fact, watching yet more waves.) It was like his personal pornography, in which size was everything. Big, in Bradshaw's opinion, was beautiful (small? That was just pathetic – what was the *point* of small?). Soon he knew the sound-track off by heart and he would go around singing the title song to himself:

The heavies at the Pipeline are OK
But they can't match the savage surf at Waimea Bay.
It takes a lot of skill and courage unknown
To catch the last wave and ride it in alone.

It was around then that he vamoosed and ran away from home for the first time, still singing, and took the Greyhound to California. He had outgrown Surfside. No more challenges there. He had pretty much wrapped up the East Coast; it was time to have a shot at the West. His parents tracked him down and brought him right back home again and this time, instead of the board, they took him and locked him in the cupboard. He ran off all over again. Sheriff Bradshaw called out the cops (all he had to do was whistle) and had him arrested. He was ordered not to go outside the house. They kept a squad car waiting outside to pick him up. Finally the Mayor persuaded – required – his miscreant, unfathomable son to undergo a psychological evaluation, a test designed to see if he was insane or not. Well, they already knew he was crazy, going off surfing all the time like that; but how bad was it exactly and was there any way to make him better again, to get him back to how he was before, when he was just a little boy in a collar and tie? Could it, in some perverse way, be *their fault* that he had turned out this way?

The boy of steel took the test. He told the psychologist exactly what his intentions were and the doctor handed him a questionnaire with about five hundred questions on. What do you want to do with your life? What do you like? What do you dislike? What do you think about girls? What is your favourite colour? How often do you think about murdering your father and having sex with your mother? It didn't matter what the questions were, the answer was always surfing,

surfing, surfing. That was all he really wanted. A couple of days later he went back for the results. 'Look,' said the doc, 'your parents are on their way over. I want you to wait until they arrive.' The boy of steel hung his head in despair. He sat around the waiting-room, feeling that he'd failed. He expected the psychologist to tell him he was an idiot, that he had to go back to school, be a good boy, behave himself, be a good citizen and settle down and get a job – conform. It was the answer he dreaded. His parents arrived and sat sternly, awaiting confirmation of their worst fears.

What none of them realised was that this psychologist was groovy, he had read R. D. Laing's *The Divided Self*, he was an existentialist in leaning and he didn't see it as his job to fit round pegs into square holes. He was a liberated, progressive psychologist. Maybe a strict Freudian who believed in the joy of sublimation and how the whole of civilisation was built on the repression of desires would have kept Ken on the football field. As it was, this schizophrenia-friendly authority figure addressed Ken Jnr rather than Ken Snr and gave it to him straight. 'I'm going to support your decision,' he said, looking him square in the eye. 'You don't have the normal wants of an adolescent male. But nobody is normal anyway. Normality is just a mathematical average. At least you know what you want to do with your life. I'm going to tell your parents that if you want to go, they have to let you go. It's not going to make you happy to lock you up.' The boy of steel was back and he walked out of the office on air – he was home free. Or rather not home. In his mind he was already gone.

His mother took it on the chin. She could adapt. The doctor must know what he was talking about. Big Ken regretted ever bringing a damned bookworm with a college degree into this, he didn't have an ounce of common sense.

Mayor Bradshaw went into his old deaf-mute routine and kept up the *omertà* for the next couple of years.

But Kenny scarcely noticed. He spent just two more weeks at home, time enough to say his farewells, to his mother, to his big sister, to his undercover dad, and iron his shorts (he was always fanatically tidy), and then he took the Greyhound bus one more time for the West Coast and never looked back.

4

Once Upon a Time at Waimea Bay

Once upon a time, Waimea was murder. Too big to ride, simply unsurvivable. There was no one out there. Then, in the middle of the Second World War, two men put it to the test.

Woody Brown installed his lookout point directly above the Waikiki Tavern in Honolulu. Pearl Harbor was still fresh in the memory, and maybe he should have been keeping an eye open for another sneak Japanese attack, waves of Japanese fighter planes screaming across the island and swooping down. But those weren't the kind of waves he was really interested in. Woody had the surf under close surveillance. He was a New Yorker, high-school dropout and conscientious objector. But although technically a pacifist, he was actually praying for bombs – of the big, blue, watery kind. He thought that if only Hitler had surfed, there never would have been a Second World War. On 22 December 1943 he scanned the horizon hopefully with his powerful binoculars, looking for surf. There wasn't any. Not a ripple, not a glimmer. Sunny, tranquil, contemplative, beautiful, terrible. Strictly 2-D. So he and Dickie Cross drove out of Waikiki and took the road north across the island. The South was the side to go surfing. The South was the land of Duke Kahanamoku and the Beach Boys. The South was fun. The North, unless you counted sugar cane and pineapples, was virtually uncharted territory. But Woody had surfed the North Shore a few times before. He thought he was one of the first ever to go out at Sunset Beach. So that was where he took Dickie, who at seventeen was a regular at Waikiki but had never surfed the North Shore before. He still had to be blooded. Dickie might have found it safer to go round to the local recruiting office and sign up for duty in the front line at Iwo Jima. Maybe he could have dealt with wave after wave of fanatical enemy soldiers, armed to the teeth, coming right at him.

By the time they got to Sunset it was late afternoon. It was big but there was no one else out and the channel out was clear, so they didn't think it would be dangerous. Looking back, it's easy to see that Woody's and Dickie's good ideas weren't so good after all. In fact they had no idea what was waiting for them out there. They caught a few minor waves, but it kept on getting bigger, so they had to paddle out further to stay outside the impact zone. They paddled out; the swell kept on getting bigger; they kept on paddling. Finally a major set, bigger than anything they'd ever seen, appeared on the horizon. Woody thought it looked over 100 feet high, but whatever it was it was a monster. The wave seemed to stretch right across the horizon, from Sunset all the way down to Waimea Bay, in a solid wall. It broke and dissipated long before it reached them, but it put the fear into Woody and Dickie. Here they were, sitting outside a 15-foot break, or it could have been twenty on this exceptional day (on which the waves would travel right over the far side of the Kam

Highway and the Haleiwa restaurant would be flooded), and still there were waves bigger yet breaking way outside. They decided to opt for discretion rather than valour and hightail it out of there.

They didn't fancy their chances with the waves and thought they would lose their boards in the raging white water, so they tried to make it back in through the channel and struggled against the outgoing current. It was another of their not-so-good ideas. After twenty minutes or so, Dickie sat up on his board and took a breather. 'Hey, Woody,' he said thoughtfully, 'you know where we are, don't you?' Woody did know: they were exactly where they had been twenty minutes earlier. They hadn't progressed one inch towards the shore. And it was starting to get dark. And bigger and still bigger sets were rolling through all the time. If they couldn't get in they'd have to go out.

Woody doesn't remember which of them had the idea of paddling several miles to Waimea. It seemed like a good idea at the time. When they had driven past the great U-shaped bay on their way to Sunset, it looked as if it was only breaking on the point and the rest of the Bay was clear. They thought they could probably make it through the beachbreak in the middle. So they started paddling. All the way along the North Shore it looked huge, the biggest surf they'd ever seen in their lives. Dickie kept trying to get close to shore, but Woody stayed 100 yards outside of him, fearful of getting caught inside. Dickie joined him after only just making it, flying up into the air, over the top of a set they estimated at 60 feet.

In the end they made it all the way to Waimea. In these conditions, that was an epic achievement in itself. Dickie tried to cut in too soon, to Woody's way of thinking, too close to the point, before they made it into the middle of the Bay, and promptly lost his board to the flood. Woody yelled at him to come out further so they could regroup and plan how to get in. Dickie called back: 'I can't, Woody, I'm too tired.' So Woody paddled towards him while Dickie tried to swim out to meet him. Then, over his shoulder, Woody saw a 40-foot wave bearing down on them and he spun his board around and sprinted for the horizon again. He could see he wasn't going to make it over: the giant wave was already feathering and cresting, on the brink of folding. So he flung his board away and dived for the bottom, praying that Dickie would do the same. He dived down a full 30 feet and still there was turbulence all around him, thrusting him deeper still. When he finally came up again, he looked around desperately for Dickie. There was no sign of him. Maybe he's been washed in, Woody said to himself.

Woody no longer had a board but he knew he had to get in. It was now almost completely dark. He ripped off his shorts, fearing they might drag him down, and swam naked for shore. Breaking waves pounded him and held him under until his lungs were screaming for air and then let him up only to bounce him back down again and again. But each time he was pushed a little closer to the beach. Eventually, in the darkness, he landed up on the sand, whether through skill, prayer, or blind luck, he didn't really know.

An army sergeant on shore said he had seen Dickie get 'wrapped up in that last big wave'. Woody thought that maybe he was trying to bodysurf the wave in rather than dive under it. Either way, Dickie was never seen again, dead or alive. 'We never found any part of him,' Woody said. He felt remorseful for ever taking a kid out there. 'Sure I went back to the North Shore,' Woody said in an interview many years later, 'but never with the same old fire.' Maybe Woody and

Dickie had made some significant errors of judgement. But that didn't mean that anyone else would have done much better. Waimea was unsurfable and that was that. Going out there was pure suicide. Waimea was the Pearl Harbor of surfing. Go out there and you were sunk. It was just one damn sneak attack after another. The place was *kapu* (as the ancient Hawaiians had it), sacred and sacrificial, off limits to mere mortals.

And so it remained until the end of the 1950s, when Greg Noll and a few others finally broke the taboo. The cloud over Waimea, the bad voodoo, lasted a full decade and a half. It was possible nobody had surfed the place in a couple of hundred years, not since the days of ritual sacrifices up in the *heiau* on the cliffs. In a sense no one had ever surfed it before, not Real Waimea. 'Real Waimea' (defined as holding waves in the 20-foot-plus category) was, in fact, an accidental construct. Without human intervention it would have been, say, comparable with Sunset. But some time in the 1920s and 1930s, when Duke Kahanamoku still ruled surfing on the south side of the island, at the time of the construction of the Kamehameha Highway and the massive expansion of Honolulu, Waimea Bay served as a convenient quarry: its bottom was hoovered clean of sand, which was then mixed into the road and other buildings. The whole contour, the configuration, of the Bay was changed, and its full potential as the biggest of big-wave spots along the whole of the North Shore was unlocked. Waimea became Waimea for the first time. Which is when Woody and Dickie encountered it – and when Dickie came to his untimely end. Nobody had even seen anything like it before. No human being could deal with it.

Precisely because surfing is so bizarre and eccentric and incomprehensible, right out on the edge of the map of culture, it tends to get picked up and reabsorbed back into the mainstream (advertising, for example, or fashion) as a token of outsiderdom and marginality. What is more surprising is that it should reflect and reiterate, with all its own 'insane', 'radical', 'awesome' inflexions and connotations, the whole bundle of non-surfing landlocked society. Surfing, in short, is a microcosm. In particular, Waimea Bay has a habit of reproducing the whole twisted blood-soaked history of Hawaii and the outside world. Not long after the gods died, Waimea and the community around it, and Eddie Aikau's ancestors, went into the twilight zone, abandoned, ignored, virtually forgotten about. So Woody and Dickie were discovering it, in a way, for the first time. Dickie, like Cook, two centuries before, had to be given up in exchange. He was taken and sacrificed to the gods of the ocean. And so we lived in fear and awe of Waimea Bay. You'd have to be an idiot to go out there.

As it turned out, there was no shortage of idiots, fools, wild men, maniacs, out-of-work would-be kamikaze pilots, crackbrained geniuses, inspired lunatics, all queuing up along the Kam Highway. Greg Noll was at the head of that queue and he was big enough to block out the rest of the crowd. Noll, a Californian exile, became known as 'Da Bull' for good reason. Somebody called him 'bull-headed' for just stubbornly staying on his board at Pipeline even when the wave was about to crack him on the head and anyone else would have dived off to save themselves. But he had something of the demeanour and muscle of a bull, too. He was a tall man, 6 foot 2 or so, but he didn't strike you as tall so much as broad. He weighed some 225 pounds and looked about as wide as a Mack truck. Da Bull was always more chunky than hunky. He was solid, immovable, unyielding, a man-mountain. When he stood impassive on the sand with his board gazing out at a monstrous sea, he looked like Obelix, menhir in hand, contemplating the Roman army. He had the reputation of having surfed one of the biggest waves ever (a 'death-wish wave' Fred Hemmings called it), somewhat in excess of 30 feet, at Makaha, on the west side of the island, where he and a group of friends lived in shacks and survived by fishing. He pioneered Pipeline, when it was 10–15 feet, vertical and tubing. He explored Outside Pipeline, one of the big outer-reef breaks that broke rarely and remained almost wholly untouched. He would go out in just about any conditions in his trademark black and white horizontal-striped trunks, his massive shoulders digging him into the path of the largest waves and sheer cojones getting him out again. Or not. He took beatings with apparent indifference. He eventually made films out of his exploits and the whole point of them seemed to be to place himself in the way of an express train and show that he could survive, against the odds. And so it was at Waimea too. It was a way of exorcising the ghost of Dickie Cross. Noll and a couple of friends had been looking at it, off and on, for years, thinking about it, trying to visualise what it would be like.

– We can make it, Noll said.

– Are you kidding? they would always come back. It's a deathtrap. Let's go back to Makaha.

And so they would drive west to Makaha. But the image of Waimea remained seared into their minds, never fully leaving them, teasing, provoking and seducing them. Until one day (it may have been 7 November 1957), Noll just paddled out – 'Fuck, I'm going,' he says – and his friends followed, and Waimea finally conceded. Waimea was the last and most formidable fortress to be taken by this band of fearless foreign legionnaires. Just as the earlier whalers and traders and sugar cane growers and evangelists began to land and impose themselves on Hawaii, so in the sixties others followed in the wake of those first explorers, men like Ricky Grigg, who became an oceanographer at Hawaii State University, Peter Cole, who taught mathematics at Punahoe School in town, José Angel, another teacher, who died diving too deep, Fred van Dyke who went on to write *Surfing Huge Waves with Ease*, and Pat Curren, who didn't seem to do anything much at all other than surf.

In Hawaii in the nineteenth century one Hawaiian eventually emerged from the internal power struggles as the unifying ruler of all the islands: King Kamehameha I. At Waimea at the end of the sixties it was Eddie Aikau. All others were welcome there – the permissive spirit of *aloha* reigned supreme – but all had to defer to and acknowledge Eddie's pre-eminence. But, just as the Hawaiian royal family was doomed to be outmanoeuvred and ultimately deposed by the colonists, so too Eddie's days were numbered. At the end of the seventies, just as plantation owners, traders and evangelists had done at the end of the nineteenth century, stealing Hawaii from under the noses of the Hawaiians, so Americans had once more colonised and annexed the island.

Or rather, one American in particular.

5

Foo-Foo

Snowflake-Melting-on-a-Maple-Blossom and Major Charles Foo first met on a railway station platform in Taiwan. It was like a scene from an Oriental *Brief Encounter*. She was on the run from her first husband, and he was a photo journalist (divorced) with a Bronze Star, attached to the American forces. It was snowing at the time, she was crying and he gave her a tissue, in fact he gave her an entire box of Kleenex.

Her name, 'Wu', in one form or another, meant (among many meanings): complete darkness, total absence of justice, no or not, impeccable moral integrity, flying squirrel, treasure, despicable, ballet, wizard, a fine mist, love, centipede, the sound of crying, a species of parrot, enchanting, insubordinate, warlike, alas!, and something to do with dialectical materialism.

Her family were descended from the Manchu dynasty. Her mother had lived in the Forbidden City and had become the second wife, or concubine, of a high-ranking Peking senator. They were a progressive family and their beautiful daughter no longer had to have her feet bound and was able to

complete a college education. But when the Communist
Revolution finally toppled the Nationalists in 1949, they had
to get out of China in a hurry and took ship for Taiwan,
smuggling out gold bars under their coats. Snowflake-Melting-on-a-Maple-Blossom, Mark Foo's college-educated
mother, Lorna Ling Foo as she became known, suddenly
found herself in an arranged marriage with a general, known
to be a torturer of prisoners, and with a similar attitude
towards his wife.

Snowflake didn't care if her marriage was a beneficial
political alliance for the clan. She kept running away and
her parents kept sending her back to her husband each time.
Then she would be beaten, kneeling on the ground in the
snow. No wonder she ended up hating her mother as much as
her husband. She understood why there had been a revolution in the first place and thought it was time for another. She
wasn't allowed to do anything. If she wanted clothes, a tailor
would bring in reams of cloth, laid out on a pallet. She
couldn't go anywhere. And the more they locked her up, the
more rebellious she became. She didn't care what anyone
thought or said. Snowflake had been educated partly in Japan
(before the Revolution her father had been ambassador to
Japan) and read Japanese novels and spoke fluent Russian
(they had lived for a while up on the northern border) and she
knew her own mind. She hated men, above all her husband,
but all men, she suspected, were the same: tyrannical and
cruel.

Charles Foo's father – Mark Foo's grandfather – had been
born in Shanghai, but was orphaned young. His only worldly
possession was an old towel, which he'd picked up in the
street and used by way of clothing (it made an excellent
loincloth or a short sarong) and even occasionally as a towel.

He was eventually found and adopted by Methodist missionaries from Michigan who took pity on him and took him and his towel back to America with them. They named him Charles. Charles Foo married a Canadian woman who was three-quarters Chinese and a quarter French and she gave birth to Charles Foo the younger, born and brought up in Michigan. 'Never forget you're Chinese,' his father told him. Which he didn't, but he was also a child of Middle America. He learned to speak Chinese, but only as a second language. His parents were frugal and conservative and always feared having only a towel to call your own. Charles Foo Jnr was a handsome boy, but he was quiet and kept himself to himself, even when he joined the military after graduating from college.

It was during one of her many doomed escapes from her marital prison on a bleak day in winter that Major Charles Foo first saw Snowflake in the snow at the railway station. She was sobbing and initially he tried to ignore her. But she kept on sobbing and he eventually spoke to her and was moved by her plight, so he gave her the box of Kleenex. When she got to the bottom of the box some days later she found money in it, and a note, encouraging her to escape again and promising help if she needed it. At last she had somewhere to go other than back to the less than warm embrace of her own family. Snowflake, Lorna Ling, and Charles Foo from Michigan found themselves on the same train together rushing through life. On the strength of his military rank she obtained a divorce and they were married in Taiwan, just a few miles from the station where they had first met.

Lorna Ling's first son, Wayne, Mark's older brother, looked exactly like her hated first husband, and she was therefore content to let her domineering mother take over the job of raising him. She loved her daughter, SharLyn, born in Michigan of her new husband, and she quickly became her favourite. When Mark Sheldon Foo was born in 1958 in Singapore (they were living in the British quarter at the time), looking exactly like his father, she made up her mind that she preferred girls to boys. Boys, after all, would ultimately become men. It took her a long time to discover that she and her son had many things in common.

When Mark was young he and his family travelled a great deal. His father had become an information analyst, an intelligence officer, attached to the foreign service. He was now Major Charles Foo (rtd). It was 1967 and Mark was nine and SharLyn thirteen when they moved to Hawaii. Major Foo had been posted to Saigon – it was the height of the Vietnam War – and the family could either stay on the mainland or go halfway – to Hawaii. They rented a house around from Diamond Head, in the district known as Niu Valley.

SharLyn and Mark felt as if they were being exposed to reality for the first time. There were plenty of bad influences to choose from – miniskirts, drugs, pregnant schoolgirls. Mark took up a paper round and soon expanded the business, brought in other little kids and took a percentage of their pay. 'He was an incredible entrepreneur even then,' SharLyn recalls. He was also suspended from school more than once. He found school almost too easy, and got bored, and then they would phone home to say he was misbehaving. He was fast gaining a reputation as a 'wild child'. Then a kid with polio took him surfing for the first time. Lee Wi Doo had withered legs but a good upper body and he liked to go bodyboarding at Waikiki. Some of the other boys scorned him as a cripple, but Mark liked him, perhaps because of their shared Chinese background. So one day he went along with him and soon they were going out together all the time, at Niu Valley or Waikiki. The waves on the south side of the island are generally broad, gentle and forgiving, nursery waves, good for learning the art on, and yet Lee Wi Du was amazed at how quickly Foo-Foo (as he liked to call him) took to the surf. From his first time on the borrowed board, Foo-Foo was on his feet, balanced, and riding. He was a natural.

Lorna took little interest in the activities of her younger son. She didn't even know when he graduated from high school. 'They tell me he's top of his class,' she said to SharLyn. When he told her he'd taken up surfing, she said, 'That's nice', having no idea what he was talking about. Lorna could barely swim. In the end he persuaded her to take him to the beach. She had very pale skin and would sit on the beach under a large parasol, occasionally glancing up to see what he was doing. He appeared to be standing up, riding on the backs of waves, like some kind of circus performer. It was absurd. She'd far rather be in New York, she said to SharLyn. 'Give me cement any day.' She was a night owl who squinted in the sunlight.

Dennis Pang, a few years older than Foo-Foo, was another of the Niu Valley surfers, along with Randy Rarick. He would be further out, riding the bigger, cleaner waves that broke on the outside, at Toes Reef or Picos. Foo – who christened himself 'the White Water King' – would watch him, longing to be like him. When Pang and the others finally cruised into shore, they would seek out this little wannabe and tip him off his board. It was good for his training. 'Why don't you get yourself some real waves, kid!' Pang and the others would yell at him. But he always came back. They respected him for that, even if he was flopping around in the mush.

At least it was all free. The waves didn't cost a cent. Probably thanks to the influence of his own father and that towel, Charles Foo was frugal to the point of fanaticism. He went about the house turning off all the lights (even when they needed them on). He conceded that showers were probably necessary but insisted on a three-minute maximum. He even hunted around the shops for cheap toilet paper (and impressed upon everyone the need to keep the number of sheets they used to a bare minimum). Lorna Foo, on the other hand, was used to having a lot of money and spending it. She liked money. She was brilliant with an abacus and could keep track of their accounts using it. She even carried a mini-abacus around with her and whipped it out at crucial moments.

The children were living a dual cultural existence. They were Chinese-Americans, but more Chinese than American. Their mother was a firm believer in Chinese astrology (she was a dragon), Buddhism, the Tao and money. Their father was not just stingy, he believed that they had to be better than perfect in order to represent China (and also to outmanoeuvre potential discrimination).

After only a year or two in Hawaii the whole family had to move back to the mainland, to Maryland. Mark was eleven and it was the first major trauma – he would have called it tragedy – of his young life. He hadn't wanted to go back at all. He sulked and threw terrible tantrums, locking himself in his bedroom and kicking the door, clamouring to go and live in Hawaii again. But America was pulling out of Vietnam and Major Charles Foo retreated to Washington while the family lived in Kensington, a suburb where everyone was well behaved and smartly turned out and the whole place was neat and tidy. When he was abroad, Charles Foo was given to moments of exceptional generosity and tenderness and grand gestures (as at the railway station in Taiwan), but when he returned to the United States he reverted to his narrowly abstemious ways. After Vietnam, he did more than retreat; he retreated into himself. He would never explain to his kids where the Bronze Star came from and how he had got the scar on his leg. (Mark and SharLyn speculated that maybe he was a spy, but nobody knew, and they knew that if he was a spy they probably wouldn't know.) Meanwhile Mark's mother couldn't adapt to life in Maryland. The longer she was in America, the more she reverted to her Chinese past. I have to do the dishes here? Culture shock in the kitchen. Similarly in the bathroom: in Taiwan Snowflake had been used to several separate baths, one for soaking, another for washing off, and so on. 'In America you don't do it that way,' her frugal husband explained. So much for America, she thought.

Foo-Foo was suffering his own crisis of water withdrawal. He wanted to live on the beach, or near it at any rate, not over a hundred miles away. The kid eventually talked parents, friends and the man who ran the Caravan Surf Shop into driving him the three hours to the nearest East Coast beach at Ocean City every weekend, without fail. He would pester people (including, eventually, SharLyn) for rides until they gave in, and then he was happy – until the next time. The waves weren't great and the water was cold, but it would have to do. For the time being.

At the age of fifteen, Mark, still wearing braces, on his own initiative worked out a plan that would enable him to stay close to the surf. He discovered a school in Florida that would take him and entreated his parents to let him go there. They didn't like the idea but SharLyn told them he'd just keep on bugging them till he got his own way so they might as well give in. She said if he didn't go she thought he might commit suicide. 'He is like a caged bird', she said, taking his side. 'We have to set him free.' She may have been over-dramatising, but it worked. Mark promised not to neglect his studies. The deal was that he had to go to school, get good grades and see the orthodontist. The great thing about this school was that it was five minutes from Pensacola Beach. He used to cycle to the beach with his board on a rack. And that's when he started competing in local surf contests and winning some of them. But maybe Mark was glad to get out of the family home anyway by this stage.

Mark's mother and father were always at odds with one another. For Snowflake there were no rules, she never said no to anything, she was consciously the opposite of her own deeply traditional and repressive mother. Mark wants to surf? Let him surf (whatever that meant). For Charles, with his military method, even in retirement there were plenty of rules to be observed. There was almost nothing but rules and regulations. Lorna was open, honest, gregarious; her husband was reserved, shy, sombre. He wasn't trying to be unlike everyone else. He wanted to fit in and conform. He cared what the neighbours thought. When SharLyn was a teenager he would say to her, 'Don't go downtown, bad things happen there. What are the neighbours going to think?' Her mother would say: 'Here's a credit card, do whatever you like.' Charles retreated further into the background. Which was when Lorna Foo came up with the idea of going back to Hawaii. It was halfway to China. She hated suburbia as much as Mark did. She told her husband to get early retirement and come and join them as soon as he could.

Mark went to live with his mother in Honolulu (the city this time, not Niu Valley) when he was sixteen while SharLyn was finishing high school on the mainland and her older brother, Wayne, the good Chinese son, was at medical school. They bought an apartment then a condo. Mark didn't miss Maryland, not even Florida, not for a second. He vowed never to leave Hawaii again. This was his home. It wasn't that there was no discrimination, no prejudice, against the Chinese in Hawaii. Hawaii was no utopia. It was rather that everyone was equally prejudiced towards everyone else. The Hawaiians hated the *haoles*; the *haoles* hated just about everyone except other *haoles*; and everyone hated the Hawaiians. West distrusted East and vice versa. Nobody knew if they were living in Polynesia or America. Everyone was confused. Everything cancelled out. Hawaii was everywhere and nowhere. It was a perfectly level playing field.

It was around this time, when Mark was in his early teens, that he and his mother finally began to hit it off, despite all her fears of him becoming a man. 'I want to be a pro surfer,' he told her one day. *Pro surfer?* she said. 'What is that?' He had to explain. 'So when you say "pro" you mean you can make money out of it? Well, that's fine then. And to think that all the while you were playing around in the water I thought you were just wasting your time. Now I see it all has a point. You'd better go ahead and do it.' His father would have urged him to find a steady job and fit in with the rest of society, but the major was several thousand miles away, which considerably reduced his persuasive powers.

Mark graduated from Roosevelt High School a year early and won a place at the University of Hawaii where his mother was studying linguistics and he ostensibly took law and economics while dedicating himself full-time to the study of surfing. It was the second half of the seventies and Foo was trying his hand on the newborn professional grand prix circuit. He went over to Japan to compete and was a big hit with the media. They had never seen a Chinese boy surfing before. Until then the Americans and the Australians and a handful of South Americans dominated everything. To the Japanese, Foo was a sign that Asians could surf too. He was a natural bridge between East and West. He was something like sixty-sixth in the world rankings, but suddenly Foo was in demand. Surfing was in demand. Foo was astute enough to spot a golden opportunity.

When he got back to Hawaii he set up his own company, Hawaiian Vibrations, got a bunch of board shapers to make him some boards, printed everything in English and Japanese and went back to Japan. He took his mother with him to translate and found himself a backer, the North Shore Surf Shop, in Tokyo. These genuine Hawaiian boards (and assorted surfing paraphernalia, T-shirts and shorts), signed by the great 'Maruko' Foo himself, were snapped up by the Japanese, at a significant mark-up. Foo made some money out of the deal, but more importantly he learned a lesson he would never forget: marketing was everything. There was no value to a commodity if you couldn't sell it. 'Unreal' was a term of approbation in the realm of surfing. But to Foo's mind it was literally true that surfing was unreal, it didn't really exist until it appeared in a magazine, as a photograph, a poster, a movie, a commodity. Only the simulacrum was the final guarantee of truth and profitability.

In 1978 Eddie Aikau died. Henceforth anything could happen, everything was permitted. Foo's dad had been an ace photographer; he had taken pictures of Mark when he was born, Mark the baby, Mark the growing child, Mark the teenager. So why not Mark Foo, surfer? Foo was born to be photographed. He cultivated photographers, took them to lunch, called them up when the weather forecast looked good, persuaded them to follow him around. Not that they needed much persuading. They saw in Foo what Foo had seen in Japan. Mark was a marketable kind of guy. Foo could be sold. There was a huge Asian market that had barely been tapped into as yet. Foo was the key. He was a good surfer, but more important than that he was different. Nobody else looked the way he looked, he was boyish, he radiated health and well-being, but he was Oriental too, with a mop of black hair and brown crescent eyes and fine features. Who cared what his ASP ranking was? The lens loved him. The magazines would pay handsomely to have this face on the cover. He became a favourite in particular of Bob Barbour, senior staff photographer at *Surfer*.

As a kid Foo loved to read. His main reading was surfing magazines. Foo was bewitched by magazines. While he was in Maryland, since he couldn't actually see anyone surfing, he was totally reliant on magazines and movies for his information. 'Whoever was considered number one or hot in each issue or movie was my hero . . . until the next month,' Foo recalled. He was sustained in his mainland wilderness on a hardcore diet of heroic tales, some of which were true, pitting weak but cunning men against mighty monsters. He pored over the stories of great waves and human courage and prowess. The men he saw in the photographs were his idols. Unlike me, almost from the beginning he had no shortage of heroes. Then, in the second half of the 1970s, Foo started to appear in the selfsame magazines. He was still a kid, in his teens, but in a way he had already attained the height of his ambition: to *be* in the magazines that he had been reading, to take the place of his own idols. Foo-Foo was no longer King of the White Water, he was an instant icon of surfing.

6

The Haole

After the long drive west the bus took the coast road south to San Diego. Transfixed, he stared out of the window at all the perfect waves, break after perfect break, like a youthful kleptomaniac gazing into the windows at Harrods or Bloomingdale's. It was 1968, Ken Bradshaw's own summer of love.

He didn't do drugs (he had got stoned one day, found it interfered with his surfing and vowed never to touch the evil weed again) and he wasn't too fussed about girls either, but Kenny was wildly in love, head over heels in love, madly, desperately, tragically in love with waves. He couldn't get enough. He never would get enough and that was his whole problem. The psychologist who tested him out and let him loose on the world might have warned him that Jacques Lacan, the cryptic French psychoanalyst, once said, 'The Woman does not exist.' It was the same for Bradshaw. For Bradshaw, *the* Wave did not exist, at least not the impossible, transcendent Platonic wave he saw breaking in his head all the time. Nothing real could ever match up to his imaginary, ideal wave. Which is why he had to keep on searching for it, keep on paddling right back out again.

Kenny had the good luck to arrive on the West Coast prior to the big winter swells of 1969 (which would be immortalised in the climax of John Milius's 1978 movie *Big Wednesday*, forerunner to *Apocalypse Now*). It was probably the biggest surf for thirty years, but he didn't know that at the time. Setting up base camp in Encinitas, north of San Diego, between Oceanside and Solana Beach, he tested out Swami's, Windansea, La Jolla Shores, worked in surf shops, pumped gas, bellhopped at the La Costa Hotel. He even went to night school to get his diploma, but it was the day school he was focused on. The names of the other surfers he remembers are: Tom Ortner, Jon Close, Cheer Critchlow and Alf Laws. He learned something from all of them. He was modest enough to know that he wasn't as good as they were, but arrogant enough to think he could be a lot better. Above all, he knew he was at home in big waves. The bigger the better. He loved the wipeouts, the beatings, as much as the rides. 'You'd pay good money to get that kind of dunking in a theme park,' I remember him saying once when I was moaning about some involuntary laundering I had undergone.

There was absolutely nothing he couldn't handle, nothing beyond his powers of grit and endurance. He would run down to Swami's, paddle out, get thrown, lose his board, swim in, swim right back out again, and get flattened all over again, and all the while he'd be humming to himself, 'The heavies at the Pipeline are OK . . .' At least his coach wasn't yelling at him the whole time and his father wasn't standing there saying nothing. There was no squad car waiting for him back on the beach. This was freedom. He could do anything he liked, but there was only one thing he really wanted to do.

But that big winter passed and left only memories which soon outstripped reality. Soon he was getting disillusioned with 2-foot mush and weeks and months of waiting for more of the heavies that he loved so much. One day one of the older guys came up to him on the beach and said to him, 'with the kind of lines you draw, you should go and surf Hawaii'. It was like hearing the voice of God. Everything else was just stepping stones to Hawaii. Texas, California, the islands – it was a natural extension, he was just going further and further west. *Go west, young man!* It had all been prophesied in *Ride the Wild Surf*. Bradshaw was re-enacting the trajectory of the entire American nation, going from the east to the west of the continent and then keeping on going, pushing the frontier ever further outwards into space. Bradshaw was America.

In the spring of 1972 he went to Hawaii for three months on reconnaissance, sizing up the terrain for the next advance. He only returned to California to collect his things. By October he was back on the North Shore and he's been there ever since. His parents never really forgave him. They'd agreed to let him go to California – but Hawaii? That was never part of the deal. By the time they knew about it he'd already gone. Sometimes Bradshaw felt that everything he did was wrong, from his parents' point of view, and that was fine with him. But he had the delicacy, the tact, not to hurt their feelings more than he absolutely had to. One time, going back to Texas on a sentimental visit, he wore a short wig hoping his dad wouldn't spot the shamefully long hair tucked underneath. But the shrewd old Special Forces operative worked it out and tore the wig off to reveal the true horror of what had become of the neat, tidy, polite and obedient little Kenny who used to do all his homework. His own flesh and blood – a *hippy*! One day, he suspected, he'd sniff out the drugs too.

Bradshaw's choice of himself, as a surfer, had been completely arbitrary. There was nothing in his genes, much less in his environment, that predetermined or induced him to become a surfer. On the contrary, everything was pushing him in the opposite direction, which is why he had exerted his formidable force of will, in a spirit of sheer perversity, to become what he was not. Just as he would go on to shape his own boards, so first he had to shape himself in his chosen image.

What do you think you are? his parents had said to him, scornfully. A surfer? A beachbum? Is that what you are? Is that all you want to do with your life?

And Kenny had replied: A surfer? Yes, that is what I am. A surfer.

He hadn't even realised it until then. Until that point he was just a kid who liked to go surfing from time to time. But the more his parents reacted against it, the more they despised him for it, the more forcefully he embraced and espoused his maligned cause. Yes, he would be a surfer, and to hell with everyone else in Spring Branch, and Houston too, and what if the whole of Texas went up in flames, so be it, what did he care, it was just one more confirmation of the rectitude of his calling. What had started as a double life, a role, became a destiny. The mask grew into his face, the baggy shorts became a permanent fixture, and it was too late to turn back. Now he would never make Sheriff, Mayor, Pipe Meister of Spring Branch or pillar of any community anywhere. And once he understood this, Bradshaw had the clarity of mind to follow the argument where it led. He wouldn't just be *a* surfer, he had to be *the* Surfer, the way his dad had been *the* Sheriff, *the* Mayor, *the* Father, *the* Commander. Dominant, supreme, unsurpassable.

Human beings suffer, Jean-Paul Sartre argued in *Being and Nothingness*, from a desire to be God. We want to be supreme and eternal: a waiter wants to be *the* Waiter, a philosopher wants to be *the* Philosopher, and a skier wants nothing other than to be *the* Skier, in the way that a mountain is a mountain, completely, unambiguously, through and through. Whenever I bumped into Bradshaw in Hawaii it struck me that he was the living embodiment of that existential fantasy. He yearned after becoming *the* Surfer. He was not really satisfied with being *a* surfer, someone who happens to be surfing, who could just as easily be doing something else, anything else. This is the realm of contingency, in which anything goes, and nothing has any meaning. Bradshaw had to feel justified; he wanted his surfing to be meaningful, but more than that, to be inevitable − not just an arbitrary option among others. He wanted to feel 100 per cent committed, as if what he happened to be doing at this particular moment were his whole life. A surfer and nothing but a surfer, so help me God. The great *I Am*. A pure and perfect being.

But the Surfer always fails. Not only can he wipeout and drown, but eventually he will have to stop surfing for a while and do something else. He can't keep it up for ever. The surfer is as evanescent and unstable and fragile as the wave he is riding on, which is doomed to collapse and atomise. To be *and* not to be, that is not even a question: it is just our fate. Being contains non-being, an inescapable trace of the nothingness we come out of, the void, an enveloping indeterminacy.

His original choice was absurd, but Bradshaw had to make it look as if it all made sense. Thus surfing is not fun for Bradshaw. Whenever he talks of 'having fun', you know he is lying. Bradshaw does not fear the suffocating pounding of the wipeout. Perhaps not even the non-being of death. What he is haunted by is the spectre of non-surfing, the age-old indelible *nada* that is represented for him by Texas and the other life, the other lives, he could have had but rejected. 'When you think about it,' Bradshaw says, 'it's almost sad, the opportunities I missed because I'm so obsessively addicted to surfing. I see myself as dysfunctional, I really do. Maybe you can admire me for enjoying my life, but don't *be* me. I don't have what most human beings want.'

By the time he reached Hawaii, Bradshaw's life had become radically simplified. He had found his exclusion principle. If Michelangelo wanted to sculpt an elephant, he would take an extremely large block of marble and simply remove from it everything that did not resemble an elephant. Bradshaw set about removing from his life everything that did not resemble a surfer. His realm of exclusion was massive indeed, almost encyclopaedic, from A to Z (but circumventing S). But having made the choice, there was no other choice left to be made. Being a surfer eliminated a lot of things, almost everything. Was it relevant to catching another wave? No, then consign it to the flames, let it burn. Surfing made sense of the world. What were London, Paris, Athens, Rome? Did they have waves? No? Let them burn! Bradshaw, when he finally arrived in Hawaii, puts me in mind of James Cagney at the end of *White Heat*, standing on top of a gasometer, just as it is about to explode and yelling his head off: 'Made it, Ma. Top of the world!'

It was 1972, the era of Eddie. Aikau was undisputed King of Waimea Bay. That left, out of the Holy Trinity of North Shore breaks, only Pipeline and Sunset Beach. Pipeline, superbly vertical and tubular, pirouetting like an extremely overweight ballerina, was too precarious, too mercurial, too rarefied for Bradshaw's broadside embrace. And the crowd there was too anarchic. He tried it out, rejected it as a 'zoo', never really surfed it. In reality, the heavies at the Pipeline were *not* OK, to his way of thinking. Whereas Sunset was the most consistent of all breaks, possibly in the world. It hoovered up every possible swell and grew large on the energy. It was as close to being a mountain right outside your window, reliably, every day, as it was possible for a wave to be. And there, unlike Pipeline, 'people have respect'; there was 'hustle' but there was also hierarchy.

Bradshaw rented a room just off the Kam Highway with a direct sight line to Sunset Point and set about taking possession of Sunset. Meanwhile he took a job as a bouncer, or 'doorman' as he was officially known, at a nightclub in downtown Honolulu, and commuted between the North Shore ('country') and 'town' on the south of the island. The job suited Bradshaw down to the ground. He would *be* one of the *heavies* that he dreamed of and sang about. And anyway it was hard to surf at night, except in very rare circumstances. So Bradshaw would shut up shop when it was sunset at Sunset, drive down south and impose himself on Honolulu and occasionally boot drunks out and then drive back and the next day go out and strongarm and wrestle Sunset into submission all over again.

Bradshaw was now 6 foot and weighed 185 pounds, with a square chin and a broad neck and a head that seemed to narrow towards the top. He put you in mind of lumberjacks and blacksmiths, something forged or quarried, hammered and chiselled. 'That corn-fed cowboy from Texas,' people would laugh behind his back. 'Who does he think he is? He doesn't stand a chance.' But hardly anybody laughed in his face. 'He had absolutely no talent,' Randy Rarick (Hawaii

Junior champion and Triple Crown director) once said to me. Randy Rarick lived just on the other side of Sunset to Bradshaw and had plenty of opportunity to make his assessment. He had no axe to grind. He had even sold Bradshaw his first board when he arrived in Hawaii. It was the closest possible approximation to a scientific, quantitative measurement of the Surfer's abilities. Bradshaw, it was clear, was absolutely devoid of all innate ability. 'He was not a naturally gifted surfer. I didn't give him a second thought.' Then Rarick left on an extended world tour out of which grew the original pro surfing circuit, the IPS (International Professional Surfers).

When he got back to the North Shore two years later, Bradshaw had miraculously become the main man, the maestro, the undisputed, at Sunset. Rarick couldn't figure it out. 'What's been going on around here?' he went about asking. 'How comes Bradshaw is stealing the show suddenly?' His friend and photographer Bernie Baker, who had been watching Bradshaw all the while and following his progress, replied: 'Sheer desire. He just wanted it more than anyone else.' Bradshaw was damned if a mere lack of natural talent was going to stop him, he just ploughed right on regardless.

Bradshaw was a Stakhanovite among surfers: he just never stopped working, he always overshot his quota and outsweated everyone else. He bootstrapped himself up into contention. The existential triumph of will over the facts. Nobody saw it coming. He had no natural advantages. But, in a way, that *was* his advantage. He was the dark horse, nobody was watching him. *Let them laugh*, he said to himself. They won't be laughing so hard when I'm in control. And it was true, nobody was laughing any more at the guy from Texas. Now they had to watch, he was on everything, he practically owned Sunset.

There had been a few incidents. Native Hawaiians especially didn't take too kindly to Bradshaw. He was a caricature of imperialism, marching in from Texas and trying to take over the place. They hassled him out on the break, got in his way, tried to intimidate him. *Where's your ten-gallon hat, cowboy? Hey, John Wayne, why don't you try lassoing yourself a wave?* Occasionally someone would break into a rendition of 'Home, Home on the Range'. Bradshaw just intimidated them right back. A Texan cowboy among the Polynesians. It was like throwing a Christian in with the lions. He was a big strapping healthy son of a gun but, on the other hand, there were an awful lot of lions. On the face of it, the nineteen-year-old Bradshaw was up against phenomenal odds. He grew a beard to make himself look older, more of a threat, perhaps even biblical, definitely hairier. That helped. But still no one in their right mind, looking at the form, would have put money on this guy to make it through.

What nobody knew was that Bradshaw had a secret trump card. He had nowhere else – and nobody else – to go to. This was *it* for him. He had completely cut himself off from Texas. Or had been cut off (his dad didn't give him a bean, 'and,' said Bradshaw, 'I thank God for that'). Either way, he couldn't go back, he could only go forward. This was all there was for him; it was Hawaii or bust, being or nothingness. Texas seemed to him – as it seemed to the Hawaiians – like another planet. It was as if he had been rocketed to Hawaii from Krypton and his whole damn home planet had blown up just after take-off. He couldn't back down because there was nothing left for him to go back to. 'I'm here, I'm not going away, I will survive, no matter how much you throw at me,' as Bradshaw put it.

Meanwhile, here, in the land of the palm tree, the pineapple and the mightiest waves on earth, Bradshaw had become invested with the magical power of the Outsider. From the Hawaiian point of view he was just another *haole*, invading their space, spreading his dogma, trying to take over just the way American missionaries and planters had done in the nineteenth century. But again, like a mirror image of the robust buttoned-up Puritans who first came to Hawaii, packing bibles, and frowned on surfing and other semi-naked native pursuits, Bradshaw had a similarly transcendental attitude. He was a missionary among surfers, and for him there was nothing but surfing: waves were the ultimate reality, and everything else was mere illusion and worldliness. 'Charlie,' he once said reproachfully of a fellow surfer, 'got into working, the working trip, and he's got a girlfriend. He's not into surfing.' Surfing was sacred, and anything that was not surfing was profane. It was not so much 'desire' that drove him on: it was belief, it was blind faith.

Bradshaw became known as 'the White Moke', a tough guy, a hulking bundle of trouble. When he went surfing, 'he essentially went to war' (as the sports writer Bruce Jenkins put it). It must have been around this time that Bradshaw developed his saboteur's skills in wrecking other people's boards, tearing off their fins with his bare hands, chomping great pizza slices out of the sides. Or, anyone who got in his way, Bradshaw would lie in wait until the guy was going into a turn, then he would ram him, drive his own board smack into the other guy's. Once he'd bitten his first board, Bradshaw realised he felt good about it. He got the taste for it. He expected to feel bad, at least a little remorseful, but he didn't. And the more he did it the better he felt.

But it wasn't that Bradshaw was an angry young man, or a borderline pathological criminal, or rougher and tougher than the average, he was just more virtuous than everyone else. He had a clear and calm conviction about the justice of his claims, of his semi-divine right to rule the waves. His word for it was *respect*. 'Once you establish something like that, people back off,' Bradshaw recalls. 'It gave me a place in the pecking order that is still accepted today.' He had a soft spot for those implausible western movie scenes in which everyone in the entire saloon slugs each other to a standstill, busting heads with tables and chairs and fists, and then has a drink together at the end, blood all over their shirts, with a respectful look in their black eyes, and rubbing their stubbly chins. 'Well, pardner, you sure know how to pack a good punch.'

There was one encounter which defined a transition. Bradshaw was out at Sunset, he was everywhere, hogging everything, just being Bradshaw. And then some local dude, a nobody, started calling him a *haole*. Bradshaw ignored him, just words after all, the guy was pathetic. But he kept it up. Every time Bradshaw paddled back out to the break, there he was again, this same guy, still calling him a *haole*, and he just wouldn't stop, like a dog that won't quit barking. Finally, after about half an hour, Bradshaw snapped. 'OK, mister, I've had it with you, just do something, so I can kill you.' At which point the little whippersnapper took his board and shoved it in Bradshaw's face. They grabbed each other, went under, and when they came up Bradshaw had the guy in a stranglehold. Game over, he's whipped, except that the next second his best friend was joining in and trying to spear Bradshaw. 'OK, I've had it,' he yelled out to the pair of them. 'Why don't you get all of your friends, whatever it takes, and we'll duke it out on the beach. I'll be there waiting for you.' And he caught the next wave in and stood there, bracing himself for the on-slaught.

Sure enough, the first guy, the one who'd called him a *haole*, was coming straight at him. Bradshaw's fists were cocked and loaded; he was ready to rumble. But it turns out the guy only wanted to shake him by the hand and apologise. Apparently he had checked with his friends and they told him Bradshaw was cool. So the pair of them shake hands then and there and break into a grin and laugh about it. Perhaps they even go off and have a drink together and one of them actually says, 'You sure know how to pack a punch.'

Bradshaw became largely accepted, acknowledged, by the locals. In fact, in his own mind he became a local. His boards, even his mailbox, carry the slogan: 'BRADSHAW – HAWAII'. This was integration. He was home, not just visiting; he had moved in and was even more protective of his property than the people who originally lived here. His beefs were now with mainlanders or hotshots from other countries. He hated Brazilians (too much 'macho culture'), Japanese, outsiders, the visitors, the casual tourists, all bad guys. Texans, for example, with their lack of respect. 'Would I wear muddy shoes and shit on the floor of your house? That's what it feels like. People come here for two weeks, take everything they can and leave all their trash behind because they're leaving and they don't care. I guess I grew up in a time when people were accountable for their actions.' Bradshaw would hold them to account. He was chief accountant on the North Shore. 'If you were a man of honour and were willing to defend it, you had a place here.' He came within a whisker of yelling out *Haole!* at visiting surfers.

Under this heading, Bradshaw had bust-ups with, among others: Tom Curren (top-notch pro surfer, soon-to-be world champion, matchless stylist) – knocked off his board; Mark Occhilupo (much-loved Australian power surfer, aka 'Occy')

– screaming match; Michael Petersen (another Australian) – grabbed in mid-drop, takes two solid punches to the head before they both go over the falls. And there were others who didn't even seem to fit this category but who just stepped out of line and trespassed according to Bradshaw's strict code of water ethics: Owl Chapman (longtime North Shore resident) – smashed once above water and once under; Charlie Walker (a stand-out regular at Waimea) – full-on brawl out on the Kam Highway with head-slamming which ended with them going off to have lunch together and they've been firm friends ever since.

Now, when I ask him what it used to be like on the North Shore, Bradshaw looks back to this period with fond nostalgia. It was the golden age of grievous bodily harm. 'It's all about litigation now,' he laments. 'If I break off somebody's fin or even threaten to punch him, it's "terroristic threatening". I've actually had the police pay some visits to my house.' Bradshaw is even a little outraged, like a veteran gunslinger regretting the decline of lawlessness. 'I've never been prosecuted, but it's changed the whole complexion of surfing. Discipline, that's all it was. We were disciplining the younger kids, and if it took a quick shot to the head to drive home your point, so be it.'

The funny thing was that, although Bradshaw was massively sensitive to any minor ethical deviation on the part of others (he denounced such notorious tough guys as Johnny Boy Gomes and Dane Kealoha), he was entirely oblivious to any faults on his side. There *were* no faults on his side. He was faultless, he was flawless, he was without sin (although plenty of observers queued up to denounce his aggression, his arrogance, his wave-hoggery). To be fair to Bradshaw, I almost agree with him. To put things in perspective, here is a bona fide transcript of a telephone conversation between one brooding, simmering

North Shore native (code-named 'Chico' for this purpose) and a
journalist friend of mine ('Bob'). Chico is famous for being two
things: one, a master of Pipeline; two, 'the meanest heaviest
baddest dude on the whole of the North Shore'. He has beaten
up a young woman who took his wave ('if you're going to surf
like a man I'm going to treat you like a man') and gone after a
reporter with a screwdriver. Bob called this conversation 'THE
WRATH OF CHICO'.

BOB: I heard a story that you told X he'd better not come back
    to Hawaii.
CHICO: Hey, Bob, listen. You going to talk about the contest
    or are you going to write some shit?
BOB: Um, well, I'd like to work it in if it's not bad.
CHICO: Don't.
BOB: OK, I won't mention it.
CHICO: Focus on the positive and not on the negative, you
    know what I mean, brah? I get sick and tired of idiots
    focusing on the negative. That makes me want to slap some
    head. You understand?
BOB: Uh huh.
CHICO: This pisses me off, Bob.
BOB: OK, I shouldn't have brought it up.
CHICO: Hey, listen, Bob, I'm getting tired of talking to you.
BOB: OK.
CHICO: Don't fuck with me, brah, OK? This year I'm not
    going to put up with no bullshit. If I hear any bullshit I'm
    personally going to fly up there and see you personally.
BOB: OK. No bullshit.
CHICO: Serious, brah. This year I'm not going to put up with
    nothing, man. I have tickets, brah. I'll come up there and
    take care of business myself, personally. You understand?

Chico was eventually sentenced to a long period of anger management. By comparison with Chico, Bradshaw was a saint. But an ornery, touchy, militant, fanatical kind of saint, intent on converting all and sundry. Conversations with him over the telephone only tend to become tense when you mention the name Foo. Also, he has a habit of referring you to a tape he allegedly made of his life story which he reckons he loaned out to some guy in California and has never been able to get back again ('hey, listen to that – you'll find everything you ever wanted to know on that tape').

In the time of Eddie, the great lifeguard would come along and calm things down and spread a little personal *aloha* around. Maybe Eddie succeeded (at least Bradshaw said he succeeded) in sandpapering down some of his rough edges. It was Eddie himself who introduced Bradshaw to Waimea. He had seen him out at Sunset, he smiled on Bradshaw, admired his take-no-hostages, gung-ho attitude, called him 'Brother Brad', showed him the way in at Waimea, the exact spot to sit in to catch the wave, passing on to him his personal Book of Knowledge and giving his blessing. 'Go, Brother Brad, I'll be on your inside.'

Bradshaw's debut at Waimea was on 25 March 1974, a late spring swell, a clean 15–18-foot day. When Eddie disappeared at sea on his doomed rescue mission in 1978, Bradshaw was perfectly poised and equipped to take his place. Eddie had been his hero, maybe the only hero for a man who didn't bestow admiration too freely. But now Eddie was gone. Bradshaw would have no one else on his inside. He would conquer Waimea, just as he had conquered Sunset, by sheer force, will and aggression. He would bite chunks out of the board of anyone who got in his way. He would bully 20-foot-plus monsters into submission. A *Surfer* magazine photograph of the period shows him eating a bowlful of nails for breakfast. There was something primeval about Waimea, it was a throwback, waves that put you in mind of dinosaurs looming up out of the Pacific, the Ocean that Time Forgot – and Bradshaw seemed to slot right in.

Around this time, the end of the seventies and the beginning of the eighties, Bradshaw, now in his late twenties, tried his hand at some of the professional contests that were starting to spring up. He ventured back to the mainland, but he never really felt at home on smaller waves. In truth, he hated small. He needed a big platform to show off his skills. Then the 1982 Duke contest took place at big Sunset in December. This was more than just another surf contest: it was a tribute to the late great Duke Kahanamoku – twentieth-century icon of surfing *par excellence*, Olympic gold medallist, Sheriff of Honolulu, Official Greeter, ambassador, evangelist, not to mention movie star (appearing alongside John Wayne in the 1948 *Wake of the Red Witch*) – and therefore, in some way, a celebration of the whole art of surfing. A hymn to the wave. It had been the first and was still the most prestigious of big-wave events. Bradshaw was on his home turf and it was his kind of day, a little stormy, but a west swell producing solid 8–12. It all slotted into place. Bradshaw took all the most significant waves that day and surfed them into extinction, finishing them off right on the beach (a ride of about half a mile). 'Going into the final I sat on the beach,' Bradshaw said afterwards, 'and thought about how many times I'd been here before and didn't make it. I started recalling all the mistakes I'd made in the past and I just decided there was nothing else to do but go out there and dominate this time.' He dominated. He won by a mile the way Eddie had won back in 1977. It was an intensely emotional moment for Bradshaw, 'one of the high points of my life'. He felt vindicated at last. *Surfing* magazine noted, 'when the final was over, tears streamed down his face as he came onto the beach'. His then girlfriend ran up to him and screamed, 'You made it!' When he held up the enormous trophy the still misty-eyed Bradshaw had a smile about a yard wide, displaying many bright white teeth.

The man of steel had a heart and the Duke contest proved it. Why did Bradshaw cry? He could never explain his original choice to become a surfer – that was beyond all possible explanation – but now at last he had some hard indisputable evidence of all the work he had put in. He had justified himself. He invited his parents over to Hawaii and showed off his trophy, the Duke statuette, with his name engraved on it ('To have your name engraved on that perpetual trophy is one of the greatest honours in surfing'), and the cheque (for $12,000). And his performance was shown on ABC's *Wide World of Sports* no less, broadcast the length and breadth of Texas.

He tried to explain the immense prestige attached to his victory. His mother thought it was enough that he was doing what made him happy. But this time even Ken Snr, confronted by all the visible signs of worldly achievement, said something like, 'Well done, son.' It was grudging, but it was acceptance all the same. Everyone had finally recognised Ken Bradshaw as *the* Surfer, even his own demanding parents. 'Made it, Ma. Top of the world!'

7

Cover Shot

Over more than a couple of decades there were really only two magazines worth reading. One was *Surfer*, the other was *Surfing*. *Surfer* was the first magazine to cover the field, founded in 1960 by John Severson, artist turned movie-maker who invented what was originally *The Surfer* to provide better publicity for his flicks. But demand soon outstripped supply, hence the advent of *Surfing* a few years later (ultimately the two would expand and multiply further still and spread around the world). *Surfer* liked to call itself the 'Bible' of surfing. But *Surfing* had at least equal credibility and claim to authoritative status. They had a similar circulation. Writers and photographers and especially editors from the two camps – located within miles of each other in Southern California – were often bitter rivals and constantly scheming and jockeying for advantage. The late seventies and eighties were the height of what had become known as the 'Ing/Er war'. But there was, at the same time, a kind of grudging camaraderie between adversaries. In the end they all wanted the same thing: to fix on the coolest stories and characters and images in the surfing arena and show them off to readers and thereby sell more magazines and pull in more advertising. They were always trying to scoop each other. But every now and then they just had to agree on what constituted an important item. Sometime towards the end of the seventies, Foo became an item. He was magazine-worthy.

In May 1974 *Surfer* published a couple of pictures of Mark Foo in action. He would have been barely sixteen. They were idyllic, almost innocent, pictures. The photographs, taken by David Skelton, show him crouching low and leaning into some semitransparent 4–6-foot ('clean, lighthearted') green walls. The waves were well formed but definitely not huge (Hawaiian-style), there were a few guys out there but not a dense and potentially aggressive crowd (California-style). These were the ideal faces for some explosive moves (the kind of radical attack that became known as 'hot-dogging', after the high-performance cars). 'With enough size to tuck into and enough speed to get you off. Good waves to be remembered by those who had them.' There was no drama. Nobody won anything. Nobody died. They weren't great waves. In a way the waves matched Foo's standing in the profession. He was good but not great, he was stylish, he was clean. He was not huge either, but he had potential. He was still young and 'lighthearted', unscarred by either Hawaiian heavies or Californian combat. He still looked like a skinny kid with skill.

February 1978, *Surfing*: it was just a one-page interview, but it registered a significant shift of emphasis. Foo had become first and foremost a *pro surfer*. He looked on the recently formed ASP circuit, the 'tour', as his workplace, a big enough platform not just to showcase his skills but also to provide a career path and a decent income. 'I'm totally committed to pro surfing,' he says, 'first because I love to surf and I like competition, and also because I like to live comfortably. So of course it would be the ultimate to live off surfing! I also know that that "ultimate" might become a reality, and if it does I want to be there. But, at the same time, I'm not being completely narrow-minded, and I'm also leaving other options open in case it doesn't.'

Foo forever cultivated the other options (money, women, media, real estate, pleasures). Like Bradshaw, he revered surfing; unlike Bradshaw he didn't think it had to be manically divorced from everything else in the world, kept sacrosanct: rather, it had to be traded, exchanged, transformed, translated, have all its latent value and meaning activated and disseminated. Where Bradshaw excluded, Foo included. 'The fox knows many things, but the hedgehog knows one big thing,' as the ancient Greek poet Archilochus once observed. Foo was a fox; Bradshaw was a hedgehog. Foo was into everything; for Bradshaw surfing *was* everything. Bradshaw lived by a single great organising principle, a prophetic vision that became a dogma; Foo pursued many goals, disparate and contradictory. It was the difference between monism and pluralism.

While the monistic, bristling, prickly Bradshaw wanted to keep surfing for surfers, the foxier Foo sought more pluralistically to put surfing up in lights and make it available and saleable to the whole world. He lived on a tiny island stuck out in the middle of the Pacific, but he was alert to the potential for globalisation. 'I want to be a professional athlete. I mean, to be a pro in anything you have to act like one, dress like one – everything. That's why pro surfing hasn't reached its potential, because most surfers aren't what they should be: professional athletes. Instead, they are just surfers or surf bums. So, it takes a professional attitude; but at the same time you can't heavy people out or alienate the average person. Some pro surfers are starting to think they're stars. They don't realise that this isn't rock and roll. It's surfing, which is still very insignificant in the world.'

Foo was intent on it becoming significant in the world. And, blasphemous though it was to say it, surfing could be upgraded, its image could be improved. 'It has been for you more than anyone that I had to prove that surfers were not bums,' he wrote in a birthday card to his mother. If he could sell it to his own mother, he could sell it to anyone. Foo wanted surfing to be as big as rock music. And he would be its Elvis, its Dylan, its Lennon.

Foo already defined himself as a North Shore surfer, but at this stage he was not attached to any one break. 'I say the North Shore meaning the *entire* North Shore. I feel versatility is really the key; so many people are just into one, or a few, spots so they are actually really limited and can only surf well at those spots. I'd rather be one of the better surfers out at every spot than *the best* at one particular spot. I want to be able to rip Chun's . . . or Waimea!' Maybe he was already thinking of Bradshaw, of how he had become synonymous with Sunset. Whereas Foo wanted to keep his options wide open.

At this stage, 1978, Waimea was just on the horizon for Foo. He hadn't really hit Waimea yet. Foo was described as 'promising' – one of the 'most promising' of his generation – but the interviewer admitted that 'it sounds like some big talk for a surfer not too many people have heard of'. Waimea was still only a distant ambition, a dream, not a reality. Ultimately, it would become his whole *raison d'être*.

Post-Eddie, June 1978: Foo appeared on the front cover of *Surfer* for the first time. This was his breakthrough. To some extent it was also his downfall. He is flying through the tube, crouching low, his eyes locked on the face, looking for his next turn, those enormous feet poised to change angle. He didn't really have enormous feet. The reason he looks so out of proportion is because, characteristically, he has a camera fitted to his board, fixed to the nose, so his feet come out looking massive. At the same time he was also appearing on the front cover of *Surfing* ('SPECIAL ALL-HAWAII EDITION'). Hit them all simultaneously, that was Foo's plan, and it worked. Here he is again, in the tube, low-slung, arms flung out, possibly at Pipeline Backdoor. He is getting maximum coverage.

In surfing terms, he was everywhere all at once. But to some this was a scandal, a disgrace, part of a sinister plot to take over the world. Who does the guy think he is? Barely twenty and already on every front cover? He lacks *respect* for his elders and betters. Almost immediately he became the object of ire and derision. Surfing was supposed to be for losers and rebels – so what did Foo think he was doing? He was betraying the whole ethos by getting so much exposure and threatening to become a success. Foo unleashed a storm.

His big sister SharLyn, who felt protective towards him, took him to one side: 'Mark,' she said. 'You're always going to be misunderstood.' She advised him to tone it down, to be more careful, but he was so self-confident, so bursting with ideas and energy that she knew he was going to go right ahead and be misunderstood anyway. The tide of bitterness that turned on Foo might explain why, the following winter, there was a shot of Foo in *Surfer* lying on the ground with all his boards pointed rather menacingly at his head, like missiles, poised to go off – but he still has an enormous grin, as if he is enjoying the joke at his own expense.

Like Foo, Bradshaw scoured the magazines, scanning them keenly, with a penetrating gaze, but always with a faint, abiding sense of apprehension, an anxiety that some unbearable injustice could be committed within their pages. He had grown to understand over the years that pictures always lied. They were invariably misrepresentations of the real thing. The experience itself, the contact between flesh and water, was incalculably, inexpressibly real; perhaps it was the only real thing left on earth, and yet everything in the magazines was unreal, artificial, reeking of technology and photographic apparatus and hype. Bradshaw believed that unless you did it yourself you would never get an idea of what true surfing really was, because all the photographs and all the words in the world could never give you an inkling of its scale and power and ferocity. So from the beginning the magazines were a farrago of fallacies, legends, and travesties from front cover to back. Everything they said was a lie, including the words 'and' and 'the'. They were part of a huge conspiracy of ignorance and misinformation. And yet, in an effort of will and generosity, he forgave them their inescapable fallibility. They were human, they were weak, they had not seen what he had seen. He who speaks does not know, that was Bradshaw's credo, He who knows does not speak.

All he asked, therefore, was a rough-hewn sense of fairness, a degree of correspondence, a faint resemblance at least between the True, the Beautiful and the Good of wave-riding and the poor, feeble allusions to truth that one came across in those plump, glossy pages. It wasn't much to ask, but it was a minimum. Bradshaw had become a fanatical fact-checker. He would write letters to editors, reprimanding them for any obvious deviations and discrepancies. Or give them a taste of the wrath of Ken on the beach. He found that he had to police the pages of *Surfer* and *Surfing* for veracity and accuracy just as he had to police the waves at Sunset and

Waimea. No one else would take on the job, and someone had to damn well do it.

When he saw those front covers with Foo splashed all over them, he thought he must be dreaming. And it was a very bad dream. In fact, it turned into a recurring nightmare: between 1978 and 1988 Bradshaw would have the same experience – of seeing Foo given front-page billing – no fewer than six times. 'What the . . .?' he barked, spitting out a mouthful of his carefully composed smoothie over the kitchen counter. He shook his head and looked again, but no, nothing had changed. It was as bad as he had thought. No, it was worse. The Kid was barely out of school (and possibly still at college, for pity's sake) and yet here he was on the cover again, all neon lights and bold typeface. You never saw him out at big Sunset, much less Waimea. He was strictly a small-wave warrior (hadn't he, indeed, published a small article, 'The Art of Small-Wave Surfing' in *Surfer*, February 1978?). The pictures were big but how big were the waves? And how big was he, for that matter? A beardless schoolboy, a skinny pint-sized kid. There was no way he could handle a wave of real scope and size and power; that was for real men. What the hell was wrong with these editors? Was Foo paying them or what? It was all Fooey.

Bradshaw cursed himself for one moment of weakness. It was in the winter of 1977 at Sunset. A morning of huge, devouring tubes. Some brash young kid had been out there, never seen him before, way out of his depth, smashed up two boards, and then he was out. And then he'd seen him again, sitting in Bernie Baker's front yard. It was just one of his old blue boards that he happened to have lying around at Bernie's, a piece of shit really, but still it had BRADSHAW – HAWAII branded into it. And he'd tapped him on the shoulder (he remembered seeing him look up and hold his gaze; not many people did that) and offered it to the kid. Felt sorry for him, a pang of sympathy, seeing him boardless. 'Hey, if you want to borrow that board, go ahead.' And the kid had said something like, 'Yeah, sure, thanks', and he'd paddled back out on it and caught some unreal waves. Bradshaw had felt protective towards him, almost paternal. That (he now realised) had been Foo – the Kid. Bradshaw had actually been responsible for *elevating* Foo. Well, he didn't feel protective any more.

The incredible truth was that, despite all his striving and achievement, Bradshaw hadn't yet had a cover shot. Even when, several years later, he finally fought his way on to the front page of these august and solemn publications, with a sense that the cause of justice had finally been served, still he couldn't put those early photographs of Foo out of his head. They rankled. They stuck in his mind and seeped through into his every waking thought, staining them with irreducible bitterness and resentment. The photos were, I suspect, the beginning of a lifelong grudge.

For Foo there was no radical split between being and appearing. If you looked good then you were good. It was a simple equation. If that was the way it came out in the magazine, then that's the way it was. There was no arguing with it, it was fate, you could only submit to it and collaborate. 'The bottom line,' he said in an interview, 'is that when the magazine goes to pick photos they pick the best ones, not necessarily the ones taken of a strong competitive surfer.' The ancient surfers of Hawaii had always had their surf-chanters, their personal bards, to hymn their exploits and turn a single wave into an epic, a saga of heroism and conquest. It was natural, in the order of things, that Foo should cultivate writers and photographers, and if they wouldn't do it for him then he would just go ahead and write the story himself if need be – become surfer and bard all in one.

Then, after getting what a lot of observers (Bradshaw was only one among many) considered too much exposure, he virtually disappeared, vanished off the radar of the magazines, became the invisible man. But he had not gone underground. Far from it. Rather, he had diversified. He knew that communication was the key to his new philosophy of surfing. So he started writing small weekly articles for North Shore newspapers and magazines. He branched out into broadcasting and got a job hosting a weekly talk show on a Honolulu radio station called *Rock Surf Hour*, when he would interview surfers and talk waves, technique, equipment, experiences, trade secrets, the latest gossip. Foo had turned himself into a pundit, a suave media operator, who, if he did not exactly control, definitely *influenced*, inflected, interfered with the words and images that defined and prescribed the great surfing universe. He turned up in small-scale surf movies like *Fantasea* (1978) and *Follow the Sun* (1982). He co-hosted a cable television show called H_3O (or *Heavy Water*). He started doing announcements and interviews at pro contests (which is how I used to run into him, on the beach at Sunset, when we were both reporting on the Triple Crown). Then – around the same time that Bradshaw was taking out the Duke contest – he flew to St Louis.

St Louis, MO, mainland US – and not an obvious top spot for waves. In fact he was going to the headquarters of Anheuser-Busch, manufacturers of Michelob beer, among others. Foo was a businessman. He was carrying a portfolio of his work in his briefcase: photographs, articles and a highly embellished CV (in which his 'photogenic looks and athletic prowess' had produced a 'spiralling media career as a print, radio, and TV personality'). Anheuser-Busch was only one company among fifty or more that he had written to suggesting that they might benefit from making use of his image. And they responded favourably. Managing directors, accountants and CEOs were suddenly sitting up and taking notice of Foo, 'surfing's consummate living legend' (etc.). Not just on the beach but in the boardroom, too, it was all Foo Foo Foo.

Mark Foo more or less invented mainstream sponsorship in surfing. There had always been plenty of internal support for surfers from shapers (*have some free boards*), surfwear companies (*have some free shorts*) and even makers of sunglasses (*look cool*). At different times, Foo benefited from a variety of such deals. But he set his sights higher or at least broader. He could see that there was something incestuous, tautological about this kind of insider trading. Of course everyone benefited, it was a reciprocal relationship. But Foo realised – and was certainly among the first to do so – that surfing had made such an impact on society in general, from around the sixties on the image was so pervasive, that even companies that had absolutely nothing to do with surfing could cash in on the feel-good, sun-kissed, beach lifestyle. A brewer of beer, for example, could associate his beer with surfing and expect to reap some semiotic enhancement from the liaison. In particular, Michelob and Foo could be seen out together, and above all in magazines and photographs, to their mutual benefit. And then he wanted to change the image of surfing too, to make it more mainstream, to get away from the whole slacker/drugs cliché – surfing was too hard for that and he needed to stay healthy (and on this point he would agree with Bradshaw: they both hated drugs).

Anheuser bought it. Foo sold the deal. It was a commercial breakthrough. He had two boards made up, one in gold, the other in silver, proudly bearing the name of Michelob. (It was said, at one time, that he even carried and rode a board shaped like a beer bottle, but this seems unlikely and perhaps technically unfeasible.) Foo developed a taste for cracking deals. He was a born haggler, with an instinctive feel for the fluctuations of demand and supply. Next it was real estate. In 1981, he bought an old house just east of Waimea and he fixed it up, doubled the size and opened it as the 'Backpackers Hostel'. It would make him some money, of course (he had to live too), but he would be doing a service to surfers at the same time. So SharLyn says at any rate. Many who came to the North Shore to shoot at the biggest waves in the world had nowhere to stay. There was the Turtle Bay Hilton a few miles up the Kam Highway, but not many could afford to stay there, or not for long anyway. The Backpackers was a cheap alternative. It was his good deed. But others point out that Foo, as always, had ulterior motives. He would offer special deals to photographers, in particular ('The least I can do for one of the greatest surfing photographers in the world, etc.'), in exchange for putting Foo on the cover of the next issue.

Foo was one of the first on the North Shore to acquire a mobile phone: it was massive, the size of a military-style walkie-talkie, but it meant he could talk real estate and compere radio programmes without ever leaving the beach. Then he acquired a second phone and became known, for a while, as 'Two-Phones (Foo)'. Foo had a weakness for new technology and accessories. Anything that could help him along in his career, he'd take it. It was all good, he wasn't proud.

He had his successes, the moments of glory, but Foo was restless. He hadn't yet found his niche. He was doing many things but not one Big Thing. When he wasn't doing deals or talking on TV and radio he went exploring, crisscrossing the world, a wanderer always on the look-out for the wave that would not so much make his name – he already had a reputation – but rather justify and extend it. He was seeking a goal, and he was still sporadically trying to make it on the world pro circuit, at the same time denouncing 'the politics, the subjectivity, the lack of money' of a 'Mickey Mouse' enterprise. The truth was, he was (as Bradshaw perceived) in a small-wave rut.

In 1981, *Surfer* magazine, having already been indirectly responsible for arousing Bradshaw's scepticism about Foo, took it upon itself to bring them together on a trip down to Mexico which Foo would record as 'In Search of Nuevo Wavo'. They knew of one another, but only from afar, via third parties. Mexico was a blind date: a fleeting marriage of convenience. Bradshaw, the big-wave hellman, and Foo, the new boy on the block. From a magazine point of view it was a natural, with all the scope for potential friction. It is certain that the editor of *Surfer* knew all about Bradshaw's resentment of Foo (how could he not when Bradshaw has been so vociferously complaining about all the attention Foo was getting?):

– Ken, we want you to go to Mexico with Mark Foo.
– What!? You mean that snivelling kid, the College Boy, the small-wave ripper who paid you to get on your front cover? *That* Mark Foo?
– Yeah, that's the one.
– Man, you have got to be dreaming! We're not in the same league, we're not playing in the same ballpark. Jesus, it's a totally different game. There is no comparison.
– Ken, it's all expenses paid.
– When do we leave?

They flew off together to southern Mexico and a newly discovered point break. It was a primitive far-flung place and the pilot had to buzz the village to get them to take down the goalposts on their field so that he could land on it. Then the landing was aborted when a pig ran on to the pitch. No electricity, no TV, but Foo was impressed by the locals and listened to their stories. He reproduced one legend that chimed with his own fundamental belief that waves can liberate you from oppression. The original founders of this village had been abducted from Angola by slave-traders. When the slave ship sailed into this Mexican bay to obtain fresh water it was hit by a massive set. Foo sees this event as a kind of miracle.

The first huge wave had swept the majority of the crew off the decks and into the churning ocean cauldron. The captain was powerless as the hurricane-driven winds pushed the ship towards the point. The next monster wave crashed into the bow, and suddenly he too was in the foaming breakers among the screams of his men, as their bodies were pulverised against the rocks. Miraculously, the vessel skirted the point and beached itself in the now serene bay. The ship's surviving human cargo came out from the holds, freed themselves of their chains, and quietly despatched what remained of their former captors. They then set forth to make a new life for themselves.

The waves wrecked the ship but freed the slaves who went on to build the village and live off the abundant land and lagoon. Waves could kill and waves could save.

Between waves, Bradshaw and Foo talked magazines. *How did you ever get away with those cover shots?* snapped Bradshaw.

Foo admitted to wooing photographers and editors. Bradshaw objected that the true surfer should let his surfing do the talking. Foo said that he, Kenny, ought to go out and sell himself, too; it would be good for surfing. It will destroy everything that is good about surfing, objected Bradshaw, maintaining a steely politeness. A surfer has to surf, nothing else. Then Foo really provoked him: How do you like my new board, amigo, the one with the beer bottle on? Cool, don't you think?

Bradshaw remained tight-lipped. The editor had warned him that he mustn't hit Foo because, moral issues aside, Foo was writing the story and it would make Bradshaw look bad. But it was a strain for Bradshaw, having to rein himself in, like having to keep up a smile for the camera – for days on end. One photograph of Bradshaw standing on the beach, looking resentful, carries the caption: 'Feeling slightly ill, Ken Bradshaw watches Mark Foo, who has found the right sand bar.'

Despite some good waves, 5 feet and fanned by offshore breezes, and tubes on offer at a place Foo calls 'Los Tubos', Bradshaw left early and went back to Los Angeles. Possibly he just couldn't stand the Kid's seemingly endless good humour and bounciness and fraternising. Possibly he feared the relentless mosquitoes ('so mean they would debate on feasting on you there or taking you home for dinner,' writes Foo), possibly the gay advances from the Mexicans he had had to swat away. What with a lack of women in the neighbourhood, Ken and Mark were welcomed with open arms. Naturally the Mexicans assumed they were queer. After all, they were two virile, muscular young men, with a habit of going around in wet shorts and openly wielding an immense phallic symbol. They were duly propositioned and only managed to repel boarders when Foo gave out that they were indeed a couple, sentimental sweethearts, and too much in love to consider any other contenders. The Mexican men nodded sympathetically and gave each other knowing looks: *¡qué romántico!* Bradshaw, as a lifelong committed heterosexual, didn't altogether approve of faking gay passion. Can't we just slug the damn faggots?

When he saw the article, Bradshaw couldn't help but feel that somehow, despite his best efforts, and truly heroic civility on his part, the Kid had managed to score off him. The kid had more fun than he did, got more waves, and now he was getting more than his fair share of attention too. And, to add insult to injury, he had his own by-line. Foo, for his part, was amused by Bradshaw, how stiff he was, how self-conscious, how dignified, as if he somehow had to represent the great Church of Surfing, and God was watching him all the time. He was only a few years older than Foo (six in fact), but he seemed to be of another generation entirely. Maybe it had something to do with the beard that he kept so fanatically trimmed and combed. Foo called the trip a 'dream'; for Bradshaw it was more a nightmare.

It was around the same time, the beginning of the eighties, shortly after Foo's explosive breakthrough in the magazines, that Michael Willis said to Foo, 'You ought to be coming out at the Bay.' Michael Willis was one of the shapers that Foo had brought in to make boards for the Japanese market. Foo would stand over his shapers like a maestro urging on and steering his string section, giving instructions and suggestions and sketching out possible innovations, another wedge out of the tail here, another fin there, extra rocker or 'V' for speed and manoeuvrability. Michael Willis always had ideas of his own. A few years older than Foo, he was a dreamy, barefoot San Diego exile who had transplanted himself to the North

Shore with his identical twin brother Milton in search of bigger and better waves. The pair of them were laid-back, easygoing characters, with melancholy utopian yearnings balanced by a buoyant, irreverent sense of humour. Bradshaw never took them seriously and would give them a verbal cuffing every so often on account of what he referred to as their 'antics', but they went out at Sunset and Waimea whenever they could, aspiring to higher things.

Now Michael Willis was inviting Foo to come out with them. And he shaped him a dedicated big-wave gun. 'If you want to make it big,' he said to him, 'you have to surf big waves.' The truth was that Foo had been out there before, although never when it was huge. And Willis was not the first to say this to Foo. Everything on the North Shore seemed to be saying it to him. In a way there was really no point to the North Shore if it was not to push you in the direction of the biggest possible waves. And, oddly enough, Bradshaw himself was saying the same thing.

It had happened in Mexico. Bradshaw, who rode only 'BRADSHAW – HAWAII' boards, heaped scorn on Foo's Michelob boards. Foo pointed out that Anheuser-Busch were partly paying for the trip, so that Bradshaw, despite his reservations, was in fact a beneficiary of the brewers. This riled Bradshaw, so he went for the White Water King's Achilles heel.

– So how come we never see you out at big Waimea, Foo-Foo? Scared? You look pretty, tearing up some of these kindergarten waves, but what about the Real Thing? I doubt you'd look quite so hot then. Why don't you come out with me on a 20-foot-plus day at Real Waimea? That should sort out the men from the boys.

– Funny you should say that, says Foo, I'd been thinking that myself. I've been gradually working up towards big Sunset and Waimea.

– Yeah, says Bradshaw, mockingly. Sure!

It was a chance for him to score off Foo for a change. It was his only chance.

Why don't you get yourself some real waves, kid! In the early eighties, this old message – whether from Willis or Bradshaw or Dennis Pang or almost anyone and everyone on the North Shore – started to chime fully with Foo's ambitions. He had already written the CV. He had had his picture on the front cover and everyone had said, 'Why him and not me? He was just lucky – in the right place at the right time', or, more conspiratorially, had cried, 'Fix!' Now Foo needed an extra card to play. In this sense he would back Bradshaw in saying that there was a disproportion between the coverage and his real achievements. He needed some big-wave notches on his belt, a few war wounds, to justify his prematurely heroic status. But there weren't that many really big waves to go round. And Bradshaw seemed to have his name on all of them. He owned Waimea – everybody said so and it seemed to be true. He was like a brick wall guarding and blocking out the inner sanctum. The Sheriff stood in the Kid's way like some monstrous immovable object, a colossus bestriding the waves.

Then that great winter of 1982–3 came along: the winter that Bradshaw won the Duke, the winter that Foo and Bradshaw first started sparring with one another at Waimea. The winter of El Niño. It changed everything.

8

The Brotherhood

He would go on to surf 20-foot Waimea and team up in Hollywood with John 'Big Wednesday' Milius. But in an article published in *Surfer* in May 1983, though almost certainly written months earlier, before the winter of 1982–3, Leonard Brady asked, 'WHATEVER HAPPENED TO BIG-WAVE RIDING?' He dared to ask the question, 'Have surfers turned into candyasses?' The way Brady put it, 'Twelve lets you enter the game. Twenty makes you a player. Twenty-five, thirty, and hardly anyone wants to play any more.' Brady wrote, elegiacally, as if big-wave surfing were an endangered species, on the brink of extinction. And he was heavy on innuendo, implying that masculinity itself were under attack by a creeping feminisation, a mass emasculation, as if the proud lions of surfing were turning into pussycats.

In fact, the way it turned out, this article sounded the opening shots in a new struggle for supremacy. In a way, it was already behind the times and the magazine duly acknowledged as much in a picture of Bradshaw at Waimea, headed 'MONSTER SURF!' and captioned, 'A couple of months ago we posed the question: "Whatever happened to Big Wave-Riding?" Now, with the help of the iron man of surfing, we have the answer.' Bradshaw had fought and he had won. He was the most consistent, the dominant force at the Bay, and he was always out there, whenever it broke. Bradshaw took over from Eddie, but he was the genetic descendant of Da Bull. He just wanted to be better than Noll, that was all, better than anyone. There were always going to be contenders, and occasionally he was going to have an off day, but, post-Eddie, it was Bradshaw's wave, if it was any-one's, everyone agreed on that.

That is, not quite everyone. Foo, for one, was looking at Waimea hungrily, like a young sea-lion prowling around and thinking about challenging the alpha male and muscling in on his harem. He probably wouldn't have admitted it to himself, but Foo was stalking Bradshaw. He was hungry enough, and confident enough, to know that he wanted to be number one at the Bay. Not number two or any other number. And the Bay was itself number one, the premier big-wave spot on the planet. Nowhere else got close to Waimea. If you could dominate here, you dominated, without qualification. You had no rivals. There was no dispute about it, no possible argument about 'self-publicising' or sniping about schmooz-ing photographers. Automatically, ex officio, everyone un-derstood that you were the pre-eminent surfer on the planet. Foo's entire vision of sponsored non-competitive surfing hinged on attaining this pre-eminence. And, in the first half of the 1980s, one man alone stood solidly, stolidly, in his way. Bradshaw.

Bradshaw knew it, too. He was smart enough to realise that, having attained domination at the Bay, he could not afford to relax and nod off after lunch; he had to remain perpetually alert and in shape and ever ready to defend his position. Bradshaw was jealous of Waimea and he didn't want to see anyone else fooling around with her. He developed a fanatical daily training regime for keeping himself on top, contributing an article to the 'Tuning Up' section of *Surfing* in November 1979, entitled, 'GETTING IN SHAPE: Ten Workouts for Winter Waves'. 'Your exercise programme can, and probably will, progressively become more strict'. He pumped iron. He stretched like a yoga adept. He did press-ups and sit-ups and chin-ups and crunches. He would simply surf more than anyone else. And when the waves were finally worn down and depleted and gave up the struggle, he would take to diving down, pick up some heavy boulder, then stroll along the bottom lugging it about. Good for lungs and upper body. Then he would go down to Sharks Cove (east of Waimea) and take a deep breath and prowl through long lava tunnels, underwater labyrinths, surprising scuba divers with tanks of oxygen on their backs. Sometimes he would swim a few miles out then swim back again; other times he'd take his board along for the ride and practise paddling, endlessly, like some virtuoso pianist doing complicated scales for hours at a time, always aiming to enhance his authority and speed and endurance and agility at the keyboard.

He knew that there would always be someone, some cocky young gunslinger, like the Kid, eager for his chance. Bradshaw knew he couldn't afford to blink or back off or weaken. 'Your dedication is the factor,' he wrote, 'because the more time you put into exercising, the better stamina you will have for *the day when you really need it*' (his italics). We can be certain that Foo read this article, drank it in, pored over it, and filed it away for future reference.

Foo had a fast-talking strategy of attack. He tried to psych Bradshaw out. He had access to the media after all. On his radio show he started to make smart and slighting remarks about 'the Men with Beards' at Waimea and 'Mad Dog Bradshaw' and 'Kong'. In his columns in the North Shore press he prognosticated about the forthcoming big-wave season, naming all the performers and contriving to omit Bradshaw's name completely or at least relegate him to the ranks of mere contenders. It was an attitude designed to wound, to draw blood and cause Bradshaw to hoof up the ground in rage and frustration. His time was up, the articles seemed to say. He ought to make way for the younger generation. Retirement and euthanasia beckoned.

Bradshaw was no fool. He had developed his defence shrewdly (he was a linebacker by training, after all). To be fair to Bradshaw, it was not a carefully contrived, coolly premeditated plot. It just happened to fall into Bradshaw's lap and he almost unconsciously worked it up into a system, a cordon sanitaire, a Maginot Line. More by luck than judgement he came to realise the advantages of a classic feudal coalition. The king could rule but only with the support of the barons. There were elements of compromise and concession in the arrangement. Bradshaw had to accept that he could never hope to monopolise – well, hardly ever – the whole of the Bay. As in the Eddie era, there had to be room for other players. But Bradshaw had to feel that he nonetheless remained in command, in control. He could let potential waves go by, he could generously donate them to others, he could display largesse. He could be good-humoured and tolerant. He didn't have to bite chunks out of anyone's board. In this way Bradshaw soon found himself surrounded by lieutenants, right-hand men, who operated with perfect freedom within the context of Bradshaw's overall regime. With a kind of natural cunning for survival at the top, Bradshaw came up with the concept of the gang, the club, the Waimea mafia.

'When it's a big day – twenty-five foot or better,' Bradshaw told *Surfing*, 'only a few of us do it, and we're like brothers in the water.' The band of brothers, the Brotherhood, with a little bit of the Inquisition thrown in too. 'A whole entity': that was what Leonard Brady called 'this little club', 'the gang', when he interviewed them one night, having dinner at Charlie Walker's house (still probably trying to make up for that crack about 'candyasses'). They were Bradshaw's neo-Napoleonic shot at a blockade.

There were different men at different times but back then, in 1982–3, it was Charlie Walker (a glasser with a strong mystical streak), Adam Salvio (from Florida), Beaver (aka Steve Massfeller) and Roger Erickson. Erickson was a maverick among mavericks. His name and his trimmed red beard suggested a certain Viking ancestry. And he had the military background to go with it. His father first took him out surfing at Playa del Rey outside Los Angeles, insulated and idyllic, and he would bike to the beach with his board on a rickshaw. He had a collection of posters taped to his wall, advertising all the surf flicks he had seen as a kid: *Cavalcade of Surf, Have Board Will Travel, Barefoot Adventure, Sunset Surf Craze, Tales of the Tube, The Angry Sea, Going My Wave, Surf-o-rama, Walk on the Wet Side, Wave Hunters, Big Wednesday* (the first one, by John Severson, from 1961, 'that was the one that got me').

When he came back from Vietnam in 1968 after two years in the Marines (he served at Khe Sanh during the Tet Offensive, occupying the dreaded Hill 881), his whole home-town had disappeared, gobbled up by the aggressively expansionist LAX airport. Erickson felt aggrieved. He had been defending the free world from communism, or trying to, shooting and getting shot at by snipers, blown up by land- mines, regularly laid low by contaminated water, his best buddy wasted, and when he came back everything he knew had been destroyed, bulldozed. The place he used to surf ('Hubbyland') had been dredged to make way for a marina. And his wife had left him.

'The world had changed,' he says. We are sitting on the veranda at Bradshaw's house. He still remembers everything vividly. 'It was like waking up from a coma.' He was only twenty-one. The next day he was taken to hospital with hepatitis. He never got over the mentality of the lost paradise. 'There's no Camelot, Camelot is gone,' he laments. One way and another, he was permanently wounded, a walking cat- alogue of injuries, physical and mental. He had a Bronze Star (like Ken Bradshaw Snr) and the haunted look of a man who has seen dark and terrible things. After a year in jail for fighting with a cop at Venice Beach (he argued strenuously that the cop started it, but that defence didn't go down too well), and a spell in hospital with a fractured skull (he brawled with a whole gang of Hell's Angels), he took off for Hawaii in 1972 and flung himself into the big-wave arena with an almost kamikaze sense of abandon, a manifest death wish, but with no thought of glorifying himself. He hated glory, he loathed glory and glory hunters. He thought of competitive pro surfing as some kind of tragedy, a betrayal of surfing. He felt like a fugitive, an exile. Then Ken Bradshaw let him know that there was a room to rent at his house.

'A guy like Roger,' approved Bradshaw, 'he'll paddle out there and sit and wait and wait, and then take off on the biggest fuckin' wave he can find. Make it or not, he couldn't give a shit about who's watching.' He didn't really need to add, shaking his head, with a look of disgust, as if he'd just found something unpleasant on the sole of his shoe: 'But Foo . . .'

Having Bradshaw around made it easier if you were part of the gang. 'It works better when we trade off the pole position,' Roger said that evening when they were all having dinner at Charlie's house. 'In the past it used to be pretty cut-throat. We've worked out a good system.' Beaver added: 'This doesn't happen any place else. Dog eat dog.' Adam Salvio called it 'love' or 'camaraderie' in 'the last spiritual sanctuary'. Despite the talk of love, Brady wasn't calling them 'candyasses' any more. Bradshaw used to drive them all around in his car, like troops, like his personal bodyguard. 'Five guys surfing Waimea Bay in 1983 alone,' Bradshaw rhapsodised, 'piling into a VW van at dark.' 'This is like the fifties!' he exclaimed as they were all bowling along the Kam Highway, with 50 feet of boards squeezed in there, and Roger Erickson hanging out of the tailgate. This was the way it used to be, in the beginning, and this was the way it always ought to be, men without women, pure, massive masculinity, for-ever, unceasingly, without alteration. Bare feet swinging in the breeze, Erickson, who was probably the most nostalgic of them all, but who didn't like to talk about it, growled, 'Shut up and drive!'

They were never really 'alone', as Bradshaw claimed. There was, for example, the figure of James Jones, a 'switchfoot' surfer who could lead with either left or right and had won the Duke contest in 1972 and 1976. He was the first to ride inside the tube at Waimea and the first to let everyone know about it. 'I think I'm the best big-wave rider in the world,' he declared. Jones was good but (born 1952) he was as old as Bradshaw and he wasn't subversive, not in the way Foo was. Bradshaw says he never really noticed Foo until around 1984.

Personally, I think it was earlier, much earlier, back in 1978, when he first saw the name 'Foo' up in lights on the highly visible front covers of *Surfer* and *Surfing*. Then there was Mexico. And then it was 1982–3, the El Niño year. That was when Foo was trying to make his breakthrough. In a sense, he had magnitude thrust upon him. It was a time when there were so many big waves there just weren't any other kind of waves available on the North Shore. Everywhere was big, from Haleiwa up to Laniakea, through Pipeline and Sunset and all the way up to Turtle Bay: but it was just bigger at Waimea.

Bradshaw's calendar for the first three months in 1983 show Waimea at over 10 feet no fewer than eighteen times, five of those days at over twenty (one of these rated as 'best in six years'), and one at thirty-plus. There is even one day at forty-plus ('STORM SURF'). In the margin Bradshaw has scrawled, intoxicated, as if he had finally found El Dorado, 'THIS IS IT!' and – underlined – 'THE MOST CONSISTENT BIG WAVE WINTER EVER'. Bradshaw had written off 1981–2 as 'the worst winter ever' and went off to Montana to take up skiing in retaliation; now there were more big swells unloading on the North Shore than anyone could remember. There was no end of waves, and they were all huge. Roger Erickson says that that winter was the 'golden age' of Waimea Bay, 'the Renaissance'. It was also, to his way of thinking, the end of an era. 'After that it wasn't worth a damn,' he said, mournfully. 'All the soul had gone.'

For once the supply of extra large waves on the North Shore seemed to be outstripping demand. Everyone was satisfied. The struggle to overcome the waves was as intense as ever, and yet there was a kind of mellowness, a degree of solidarity out on the break that hadn't been known since the days of Eddie Aikau. All human conflict arises out of the scarcity of resources. There is just not enough to go around and in the struggle to get fair shares there are always going to be winners and losers and blood on the sand. For once, in the winter of 1982–3, none of that applied. There was more than enough to go around. Everyone's cup was running over. There were no fundamental disputes any longer, harmony had been restored. When it came down to a narrow call as to who was going on which wave, courtesy prevailed. 'After you, sir.' 'No, sir, after you. I insist.' And then Foo came along and ruined everything.

Around this same time, after Bradshaw had lit up the runway, after Michael Willis had proposed big waves as a career path, after exploring all around the world and eventually coming back to base, in Hawaii, and then running smack bang into an El Niño winter, Foo made a breathtaking discovery. He was good on big waves. He didn't need to be scared of them. He had a natural feel for positioning and approach and entry and exit. And, above all, he knew how to make the most out of the ride and to turn it into something more than a Greg Noll-style do-or-die make-or-break hell-ride. All the evidence is already there in the 1983 film *Follow the Sun*, which contains the first footage of Foo at Real Waimea. When Foo paddled out at the Bay for the first time, in early 1983, he looked like a karate kid among a band of heavyweight pugilists. He was David to their Goliath, relatively slim, slight, sinewy, Oriental, boyish. And he surfed that way too. He didn't set out to do battle or wrestle with big waves: he danced with them, he finessed them, he caressed them. Foo had style. Foo was new.

Later, Bradshaw would speak of 'hot-dogging' big waves, of bringing to the big-wave stage the kind of high-performance moves that were the norm in small waves, the cut-backs, the off-the-lips, the tube rides, the tail slides. And maybe, every now and then, he had brought it off at Sunset. But mainly he was just out there slugging, he was just better at slugging than anyone else. He out-slugged them. Foo was something different: he had flair, imagination and he had the moves. He had an arched, low-slung stance that marked him out for photographic attention. Suddenly the small-wave manoeuvres that had gone unnoticed by the judges on small waves were coming into their own and getting noticed on the big-wave canvas. Bradshaw was, essentially, a classicist at Waimea. He knew the rules and he had the technique. He was still using the traditional single fin. Foo, experimenting with the tri-fin thruster beloved of small-wave performers, was a modernist, an abstract expressionist, displaying more subjectivity, improvising and inventing, making it up as he went along, always coming up with new lines and angles and strokes.

And Foo was amazed by it, too. He realised that he felt comfortable in big waves. It was the only place he felt really comfortable and at home. He was sick of small waves. This was his natural habitat. He was afraid of a lot of things, he once said: he didn't like fast cars, he hated heights, he would never have made it on the high wire or clambering up Everest; hell, he couldn't even take a rollercoaster ride without getting the shivers and shakes. He wasn't an Evel Knievel-style daredevil or thrill-seeker. In truth he thought of himself as a bit of a wimp. But, when it came to waves, the bigger they were, the cooler and more laser-like he became. All that natural high-octane all-purpose energy, that almost manic electricity, that had him forever ducking and diving, bobbing and weaving, wheeling and dealing, forever on the lookout for the next profitable opportunity to come along, all of that channelled into his big-wave style and came out well-formed, sculpted, precise. One of his friends called him 'the Transformer' (after the children's toy which could convert from a robot into a weapon or a vehicle and vice versa). 'Every day I wake up I pray it's twenty feet', he said to me one time when we were standing looking out at the Bay.

At last, he had found his métier. This was what he had been born for, he realised. He was a capitalist, an entrepreneur, an exponent of the free market; but at the same time he found himself harking back to an Eastern sense of fatalism, where big waves were concerned, as if there were some big script out there, already written on the water, and he was just fitting into the grooves. This was what he began to call his 'Foo-losophy' of life. Everything he did, everything that happened to him, all was inevitable. It was fate. All he could do was surrender. That was what it said in the *Tao Te Ching* (his mother kept a copy with her in the original Chinese):

Nothing in the world can be compared to water for its weak and yielding nature. Yet nothing is more powerful than water. The hard and the strong cannot stand against it.

And

The highest goodness is like water. Water is beneficent to all things but does not contend. It stays in places which others despise. Therefore it is near Tao.

Foo was just following the Tao, the path of water: his dream was not of dominating the waves, but of becoming one, being a wave, yielding and flowing.

Foo was a threat. There was no doubt. From Bradshaw's point of view, it was not to be tolerated. 'Two-Phones Foo', the publicity hound, the would-be media mogul. 'No photos, no Foo', that was Bradshaw's crack. He was not a true believer, one of the chosen, one of the elect. He was guilty of 'a lack of respect', all those gibes of his about the 'men with beards', all those sponsors' stickers on his boards. 'Some guys,' Bradshaw chided, during that dinner at Charlie's, rallying his troops, 'some guys think all they have to do is take respect outright, not earn it.' That was Foo all right. He didn't have respect and he wasn't going to get respect either. He was merely a performer, a stuntman, a careerist, a glory-hunter – none of which could ever be said of Bradshaw. No, Bradshaw stated for the record, emphatically, we are 'unlike those who want to glorify themselves. Who're out there for the glory. We try to think we're into it just to ride the biggest waves. We've become a tight bunch of guys because we have the common desire.' Foo, on the other hand, was an outsider, an intruder in the hallowed halls, a hurdy-gurdy man in the studious cloisters of Waimea Bay. Which is when Bradshaw swung his big guns around to meet him head-on.

Bradshaw, contrary to the recommendations of the Tao, believed in contending. Contending was his mantra. The gang, the mafia, the henchmen, the veteran troops, the Brothers – Roger, Beaver, Charlie, Adam. Each of them was focused on what he was doing and yet all of them served Bradshaw's cause. They crowded Foo, they hustled him, they manoeuvred him out on to the shoulder, they strained to keep him away from the crown jewels. He wasn't ready, he wasn't deserving. They were the inner circle and Foo was forced out on the edge, on a long elliptical orbit, where nobody would notice. Thus, in the winter of 1982–3, 'the best there ever was' (Erickson), the time of plenty, Bradshaw and his crew managed to gang up and block Foo and maintain a hold on Waimea. 'We had the Holy Grail,' Erickson says. 'And we didn't want anyone else discovering it.'

None of which prevented Foo from putting it about, and disseminating the view in print and on air, that he was now the stand-out performer at Waimea: Foo had become (did his CV not say so?) 'surfing's pre-eminent big-wave rider'.

9

As Famous as Mickey Mouse

Bradshaw was even-handed, fair-minded and didn't just pick on Foo: absolutely anyone who got in his way was liable to receive similar treatment. Like Ace Cool, for example.

Ace wanted everything that Bradshaw wanted. But Bradshaw was never less than completely serious, verging on solemn, whereas Ace (aka Alec Cooke) seemed to him like a joker in the pack, a court jester, a fool, a blundering narcissist. 'I want to be as famous as Mickey Mouse,' he once said to me, sitting in the shadow of the great monkey pod tree that still stands outside the Coffee Gallery in Haleiwa, his bleached hair gleaming in the sun. 'Or Snoopy.' He had a weakness for outrageous utterances: 'The wave is my lover and she gives me the ultimate orgasm.' Bradshaw says that 'mostly' he would just laugh at Ace: he had the guts, he had the desire, but he didn't have the requisite skill (in Bradshaw's judgement): he might fluke the occasional big one, but he didn't have the consistency to challenge him. But, in truth, Bradshaw didn't laugh that much out at Waimea and that 'mostly' still left him a lot of scope. Deep down he frowned on this kind of crudely reductive approach to the complex business of surfing, and above all he disapproved of Ace Cool's explicit egocentricity. Bradshaw had a severe, monastic aversion to anything that smacked of profanity and impurity. Ace caused him the same kind of distress, acidic grumbling, and tight-lipped disapprobation as the offer of a bottle of Coca-Cola would arouse in a connoisseur of fine wines.

Maybe it had been too long a day. The whole day it had been only Ken Bradshaw, Ace, Charlie Walker and Roger Erickson. By the end of the afternoon each had had his fill of waves, the most perfect waves imaginable – huge, well formed, rideable. And yet, shortly before sunset, when these four dedicated tillers of the ocean, now weary after hours in the water, were starting to think of harvesting one last wave to take them in to the beach, a wave appeared that seemed to outshine all those that had passed before it.

It was not the biggest wave of the day, but it was possibly the shapeliest, the most seductive, a siren wave, one that seemed to call out, to anyone with ears to hear and eyes to see, to be ridden. Only Bradshaw and Ace were in position for it. They both elected to go for it. The history of what happened next can never be fully established. The evidence is minimal, the hype immeasurable, the opinions inexhaustible. The way Ace tells it, twenty years later, the memory still vivid: 'Bradshaw started pulling a Texan linebacker on me. I was committed. He was trying to drop in on me.' Bradshaw's recollection is different. 'Alec never had a chance of making it. He was way out of position. He was just clowning around.' Ace argues that he was always in there with a fighting chance. It was not a percentage wave but he was in just as good a position as Bradshaw.

A photograph demonstrates the simple fact that it was Ace

who took off on this particular wave. Bradshaw only appears at the very top of the frame, pulling back; or not even appears really, only the trace of where he could have been had he driven forward, the ghost of Bradshaw. But even the ghost looks distinctly furious. The distance between Bradshaw and Ace must have been minimal because, as the photograph reveals, Ace effectively takes the line that Bradshaw would have taken anyway. But the second undisputed fact is that Ace doesn't make it. In the photograph Ace is already doomed. The wave is almost vertical; Ace's green board is almost vertical; Ace himself is perpendicular to the board, and his hair is flying upwards, and yet there is something in his oblique stance, which runs counter to his whole trajectory, which suggests that he is falling with style rather than really riding the wave, and about to lose contact with anything that is not water, heavy water.

Ace's board was smashed into three pieces. Ace himself was intact. Bradshaw paddled over to him. He was not pre-eminently concerned about his fellow surfer's well-being. 'What the fuck are you doing stealing my wave?' he yelled at Ace.

'Fuck you,' Ace retorted. 'That was my wave. You were too late.'

Bradshaw wanted to continue the argument and resolve it, forcefully if need be, right then and there. At that moment a wave came though and Ace, even though his board was in pieces, managed to latch on to it on the back of one of his fragments, and hightail it out of there, even (so he claims) 'getting barrelled' on the way, wrapped up in the embrace of the wave as if the ocean itself were protecting him and acknowledging that he was in the right.

Later that evening, Ace was round at Charlie Walker's

house. Charlie thought that Ace deserved that wave just as much as Bradshaw and he liked Ace for sticking to his guns and not letting Bradshaw intimidate him (although one of Bradshaw's Brotherhood, Charlie didn't always subscribe to the dogma). Charlie had developed this special training technique, which consisted of walking up and down (very slowly) wearing 'gravity boots', the kind of heavy lead-lined boots that deep-sea divers wear to keep them on the bottom. He got Ace to try them on and Ace was testing them out, laboriously lifting one foot then another, each encased in its own boot-shaped coffin, trudging and thumping along the wooden floor, holding on to a wall for support. Which is when Bradshaw chose to come through the door.

Bradshaw wasted no time on formalities. He marched straight up to Ace (who could not move for all practical purposes) and grabbed him by the throat and forced his head back against the wall. 'What the fuck do you think you are doing taking my fucking wave?' said Bradshaw, getting down to business.

'Kenny,' said Ace, 'like I already told you, that was my wave.'

'It was my wave,' maintained Bradshaw. It was starting to sound like a pantomime routine, they could go on and on like this all night. Someone had to cut the knot.

Bradshaw was about ready to pop. All the veins were standing out on his neck and his face was crimson. He balled his right hand up into a fist and pulled it back into the loaded position.

Charlie, meanwhile, who was high at the time, was enjoying the scene. He could have tried to calm things down but he didn't. 'Scrap! Scrap!' he yelled, dancing around, as if to urge on the two combatants, an *agent provocateur*, encouraging them to draw blood.

'Listen, Bradshaw,' said Ace — and I think it was brave of him, in the circumstances, to point this out to Bradshaw — 'who the fuck do you think you are coming over here from Texas and saying it's your wave? You're a football player. I'm an eighth-generation Hawaiian. Your ancestors were cowboys. My ancestors were missionaries. What special fucking right do you have to say it's your fucking wave?'

Bradshaw paused to think about this for a moment. It was a reasonable question and it deserved a reasonable answer. 'Ace, I'm going to tell you why it was my wave.' He paused again, purely for rhetorical emphasis this time. 'BECAUSE THEY'RE ALL MY FUCKING WAVES!' Bradshaw owned the Bay. It was as simple as that. There was no room for argument. He might graciously allow some of his serfs a few crumbs from the high table, but essentially all waves belonged to him just as all deer used to belong to the King of England and all swans still (theoretically) belong to the Queen.

And with that he finally pulled the trigger and threw a punch at Ace. His fist missed the side of Ace's head by a centimetre and slammed into the wall behind him. Bradshaw left Charlie's house, rubbing his knuckles. 'My guardian angel was standing right there on my shoulder that night,' says Ace. 'But also — you know — I think Bradshaw has a heart. He just couldn't bring himself to do it, not to me anyhow.'

Even if he didn't seriously think he owned the whole of Waimea Bay and every single wave that ever broke there, Bradshaw nonetheless knew that he had marked out one particular spot as his own. Eddie had passed it on to him like a baton, a legacy. The Bay was vast but when the swell was just right there was only a narrow take-off zone that put the surfer in optimal position to get into the wave. 'X marks the spot,' says Bradshaw. He thought of it as his secret, but it was a secret everybody knew about. He lined up the spot by reference to the Catholic church tower to the east and a particular tree up on the cliffs, like looking through the crosshairs of a rifle. Unlike Eddie on his last ride, he only had to navigate within sight of land. It wasn't rocket science, but Bradshaw was nothing if not methodical. It had been Eddie's spot and now it was Bradshaw's. The 'X' was his. And Bradshaw often had the idea that people were following him around to wait and see where he would sit, just in order to grab his spot (sometimes this was true, but mostly not). He was convinced that this was exactly what Ace was doing.

Bradshaw decided he couldn't hit Ace: it would be like tormenting a cripple and tipping over his wheelchair. But he could scare him, take the wind out of his sails a little. So one day he positioned himself 10 yards deeper, closer to the curl, than he generally would, and waited until Ace came over to join him. Then, when a particularly outsize set came in, he feinted to go for it, then pulled back and cheered on Ace. 'Go, Ace, your wave!' he yelled encouragingly. Ace fell for it (dreaming of the guardian angel on his shoulder and how Bradshaw couldn't bring himself to do anything really mean to him) and got smacked on the head by the lip of a 20-foot-plus wave – and the deluge that came after it. And then Bradshaw did the same thing all over again until Ace finally figured out that this was not the 'X' at all, but something like 10 potentially lethal yards east of X, way too deep. He shook his head and came to the conclusion that Bradshaw was not infallible after all, that he had miscalculated.

I'm not sure he ever understood that Bradshaw was being flat-out mean and cunning and vindictive. And territorial.

Bradshaw was instinctively territorial and he would defend his ground to the last drop of blood.

But, in the end, maybe Ace was right. Bradshaw didn't really have it in for him. At heart, he was sympathetic to Ace. Maybe, at some level that would never be fully articulated, he realised that Ace was a caricature of Bradshaw. Nearly everyone who ventured out at big Waimea wanted to *be* Bradshaw. Paradoxically, what Bradshaw resented more than anything else was not someone invading his patch and pretending to be him, but rather someone who didn't even bother to try to invade, who didn't really want to be Bradshaw at all, but who somehow succeeded, despite Bradshaw, and traced new lines, located new take-off zones and did everything differently. *Not*-Bradshaw. That was the ultimate insult. That was Foo.

10

The Unridden Realm

Foo had flu. He was in bad shape. By 18 January 1985 he had
been battling against flu for ten days and he couldn't shake it.
He had only been in the water once in all that time. He was
feeling rusty, below par, and altogether unfit. It was a bad day
to wake up to what he later described as 'a date with destiny'.

Bradshaw, on the other hand, was optimal. He was always
optimal. He showered in the outside cubicle with the slatted
wooden door, singing 'It takes a lot of skill and courage
unknown, ha-ha-hum . . .' He was clean, he was healthy, he
didn't have a germ on him. He slurped down his smoothie,
with an extra dose of wheat germ and ginseng, put on his best
shorts, took his best big-wave board, the tangerine-coloured
one (that logo, 'BRADSHAW – HAWAII', still made him
feel good every time), and strapped it down on top of his car,
hopped in and drove off, whistling. He was cool, he was
composed, he was anticipating great things. It had only taken
one look out of the window that morning, as the sun came
up, to tell him that this was going to be a special day. Sunset

was already maxed out, a chaos of breaking waves and an immense meringue of white water. There was only one place that would be working today. One place that *he* would be working. It was his place, the Bay he had made his own.

Foo yawned and dragged himself out of bed. Stupid to be out partying the night before when he was already ill. But he felt it was all part of the job once he'd finished recording one of his radio shows. He opened the door on to the balcony and gazed out across Three Tables, just around the point from Waimea. Twelve-to-fifteen-foot waves breaking on the reef. He knew, like Bradshaw, that there could be only one place worth looking at today. Amazing, he thought to himself, that it takes so much energy to make it show. Places like Sunset, Pipe and Haleiwa can all be totally out of control with close-out second reef sets – and still Waimea is barely aroused. It was truly a sleeping giant. And, in his judgement, it was probably still half asleep. The swell was not quite large enough to make the Bay break, as it ought to, in its classic big-wave form. So, in the light of all these considerations, Foo felt justified in taking a pill and sipping a glass of honey and lemon and slumping back on his bed for a while longer. After all, it had been a late night last night.

Bradshaw smiled as he got out of the car and took his board off the rack. He congratulated himself on getting to bed early the night before. He liked to describe himself as a 'space cadet', disciplined, with good habits, and therefore ready and able to meet any challenge. He had become a vegetarian – a 'lacto-ovo-vegetarian', to be precise (and he was never less than precise) – suspecting that too much meat slowed you down and made you too bulky. He looked down at his sculpted chest. Lots of hair, but not an ounce of fat on it, lean and mean, fat-free. It was not vanity, it was just pragmatism; you had to be in perfect condition to stand a chance of grappling with the biggest waves on the planet and coming out on top. He just prayed it would hit twenty today, the magic marker beyond which Waimea turns into the majestic and ravenous beast known as Real Waimea.

Foo snoozed. When he next looked out of the window it was around midday. He had to admit, the swell had been building, the sets were heavier, and he was pretty sure that the surf would meet the 18–20-foot minimum requirement. He wolfed a bun, a banana and two cups of coffee before grabbing his 9-foot Lundy and crossing the street and walking the last few hundred yards down to the Bay. He could hear the noise of thunder. Every now and then the earth seemed to tremble beneath his feet as another wave hit the beach and exploded. He could still back out without losing face, he told himself. It would all depend on the conditions. They had to be right, because he wasn't. But as soon as he saw Waimea, as he came around the point, his mind was made up. As he wrote later in his article 'Occurrence at Waimea Bay', 'I was far from being in the most prepared state, but Waimea was doing it and there was only one guy in the line-up. I was out there.'

The one guy in the line-up was, of course, Ken Bradshaw. Foo knew it had to be Bradshaw; he was the only one with the balls to be out there when it was like this. It was not classic Waimea, with waves like pyramids chugging in out of the Pacific and gradually walling up and folding. No, today Waimea was *untraditional*. Extreme west swell. The recent storm had dumped a lot of sand in the middle of the bay, making the place shallower, like a sand bar beachbreak, but much much bigger, so that the waves sucked up suddenly and pitched around precariously and toppled over. And the rip channelling out all the surplus water was working overtime as if a sorceror's apprentice had switched on an assembly line and cranked it up to maximum. It was made for Bradshaw, with that broad-shouldered muscular physique of his. But Foo knew he had to go out there and mix it with him. He kept on going, going down the concrete steps that led on to the beach. He could see the swell was still building: it was already beyond twenty, with some 25-foot sets at roughly twenty-minute intervals. Timing would be crucial.

While Foo was still thinking about things, checking timing and going through his loosening-up routine on the beach, Bradshaw had already been out for around three hours. He just couldn't help but think of the words of that good old song, 'it takes a lot of skill and courage unknown to catch the last wave and ride it in ALONE . . .'. And that's just what he was: *alone*. Last man out. There had been a small crowd to start with, but everyone else had been gradually burned out. No one else could hack it out here. It was just too huge and unpredictable. People were being cleaned up and washed right in. Everyone, that is, except for one man. If anyone had caught the wave of the day, it had to be Bradshaw. He was on to everything that was half makeable, and he was making it. And now, since there was no one else left, everything was his for the taking. God, he loved Waimea. He thought of it as a giant toilet flushing away all the shit in life. Cleansing, purifying.

Sometimes he thought to himself, when he was out here, that no one else really existed. All those strange people you saw walking around town, doing things, well, they were just phantasms, illusions, they weren't real human beings at all;

maybe they were androids, designed to test him in some way, to see if they could weaken him, distract him from his mission, cause him to swerve when he should be going in a straight line. It was the kind of insight you had in massive surf. Bradshaw felt a sense of enlightenment sweep over him, flooding him with knowledge and power. He checked his positioning, lining himself up with the church tower and the tree on the cliff. What was the word? *Omniscience*. That was it. He savoured the idea. Sometimes – for a moment or two – he had the sensation that he had finally attained it. He could do no wrong. He had the feeling he was invulnerable and he was immortal. It was a good feeling. Today it struck him so clearly, so forcefully, that he knew it had to be right.

While he was being rolled around underwater – who knew which way was up any more? – Bradshaw was put in mind for a moment of that scene in *2001: A Space Odyssey*, in which an astronaut, venturing outside the vehicle, has his lifeline severed (by Hal the deranged computer) and tumbles chaotically through space until gradually he runs out of oxygen, his movements finally cease and he is encompassed by the infinite cold and darkness of the universe. His limbs jerking wildly as if controlled by an insane puppet master, Bradshaw struggled to comprehend what had gone wrong. His positioning had been perfect, nobody could fault him on positioning. He was right in the driving seat for anything in the 20–25-foot range. There was only one conclusion: he had been caught out, or rather caught inside, by a 30-footer, and spanked like an errant schoolchild. That was *interesting*. So the swell was still building. He continued spinning for a good long while, thinking to himself, hey, this is a heavy hold-down, must have been a serious 30-footer all right. This kind of rough treatment doesn't come around too often. Ah well, might as well enjoy it. It was sent to test me. *Go on, hit me again!*

When he finally popped up into the world above, Bradshaw had no idea where his board was. Then he saw it, or rather a part of it, and there was another part over there, and another. His best big-wave board had been shattered into orange shards. *Far out!* – that had been a tough old board, a three-stringer, built for endurance and resistance above all, and now it looked as if it had been fed through a woodchipper. Well, there was nothing for it now but to swim in. He could no longer 'ride the last wave' but he could swim through it, bodysurf maybe. Bradshaw wasn't about to make the kind of elementary error Woody Brown and Dickie Cross had made in the 1940s and try to come in through the channel. That was out of the question. The rip was just enormous. Anyway he liked to come in through the breaking waves; that was the only way to have any fun when you'd lost your board. A bit of ducking and diving. You'd see turtles and dolphins doing it all the time at Waimea so he saw no reason why a human being couldn't do it as well.

He knew there was only one way in – the narrow exit lane along the rocks at the east end of the Bay, wedged between the point and the beach. All Bradshaw had to do was keep powering through the shorebreak. He charged it, head down, full throttle, maximum power. To his surprise the surging rip current kept on tugging him around, away from the beach, towards Coffin Corner, the great shipwrecking rocks to the west at the far end of the Bay. He kept on churning his massive steam-shovel arms, kicking those thick tree-trunk legs, but it was no good, he was going sideways and backwards. That damn rip had more of a pull than he'd encountered before. There was no point trying to fight it now. Eddie had said: 'If you can't make it through before the river [some 100 yards from the rocks], you're not going to make it through.' He'd just have to go round and try again.

So Bradshaw angled out with the channel – that was easy, you could hardly help swimming that way! – and then geared himself up again for the swim in. He took a couple of medium-sized waves on the head, floundering a little, then came up and, blowing hard, drove for the way out. Again, incredibly, he felt himself sliding away in the wrong direction, as if being towed off by an invisible hand. Again Coffin Corner beckoned. With a perfectly justifiable sense of *déjà vu*, he steered for the channel once more, paddling out into the immense and inexhaustible Pacific again.

It was about now that Bradshaw started to feel a faint sense of fatigue. It didn't happen to him too often. He realised that he had been surfing for several hours even before swimming a couple of times around the Bay. It came to him then, and the idea was shocking, that he actually had limits, and that he was starting to run up against them. *Fascinating*, he said to himself, like an alien observing some eccentric human trait – this sense that he was running out of gas, running on empty, never had *that* before! His whole life was built on the twin pillars of absolute strength and unquenchable stamina. The idea of defeat entered his mind for the first time and he fought to hold it back. Was this what fear was like? Well, there was nothing for it now but to go through the whole procedure again. His third lap of the Bay. He had no better idea. There was only one way to go so he had better go for it.

A couple more big ones drilled him down and drove him forwards. He came up in the middle of a lull. For once the great heaving, howling, bay-sized Suds-o-matic that was Waimea paused in mid-cycle, gathering its strength for another onslaught. Bradshaw put his big bull head down and windmilled his arms around one more time and tried to hug the rocks. Again he felt the gut-wrenching drag of the rip sweeping back into the middle of the Bay. He was low on energy but he dug for shore, grinding out the strokes, like a man pulling himself up a rope, hand over hand, up and away from the yawning abyss under his feet, but all the while aware that the rope was fraying and unravelling under the pressure.

People on the beach had begun to assume Bradshaw was a goner. It was like seeing Houdini go under for longer than five minutes. Banzai Betty, who rented me the room at Backyards, stood watching him and thought, 'No one has ever swum more than twice around the Bay in conditions like these and survived. It is just physically impossible.' She felt a twinge of sympathy for Bradshaw, even though, when she had once courageously paddled out at Waimea on a big day, he had seen her coming and raised a sarcastic eyebrow: 'You're coming out? I'm going in – it must be too small!'

When he dragged himself up on the sand, a lifeguard came running up to him. To shake him by the hand? Bradshaw pushed him away. He didn't need oxygen, he was alive, wasn't he? He strode up the beach, for once rather enjoying the feel of solid stuff beneath his feet, amid applauding spectators. It was probably one of the most epic feats of endurance ever witnessed at Waimea Bay, a saga of the will to survive. Bradshaw gritted his teeth, sucking in air through his nose, and stuck out his chin, as if to say, *Look, no problem, business as usual, that wasn't so bad*. At the same time the look he gave everyone defied anyone else to go out there and give it a whirl. Then he saw the Kid doing his stretching routine on the dune.

There was something about that warm-up routine that never failed to rile him, this big public display, as if Foo were saying, *Hey, look at me everybody, here I am, Mark Foo – the great Foo! – I'm getting warmed up now, I'm getting ready to go out.* Surely nobody was going to go out now. He, Bradshaw, had proved that it was too big to handle. If he couldn't make it, nobody could. End of story.

Foo looked up again to see if Bradshaw was OK. He knew that he was going to make it. He hadn't even begun to worry about him drowning out there. As a combination of experience, water knowledge and sheer guts, it was an impressive display, he had to admit. He would have put money on Bradshaw making it through, though. He always did, that was the way he was. He was solid, dependable, rugged. He just lacked imagination, that was all. He was like an old warhorse that bullets and cannonballs seemed to bounce off. That was Bradshaw's Law – survival. Foo always felt that even if he came up quietly behind him one day and walloped him over the head with something good and heavy it would do no more than rile him.

But Foo's instinct told him that you had to do something more than just survive out there. You had to do it with style, with finesse, with a degree of savvy and sophistication that was surely beyond the wit of the old warrior. So what if Bradshaw hadn't been able to make much of those waves? Foo glanced at the ocean again. He was confident he could get inside some of these big fat juicy smokers and get the hell out again unscathed. And now Bradshaw, that great obdurate, stubborn obstacle, was safely out of the way, there was nothing and nobody to stop him. This was his big chance to make it count and rebrand himself as a big-wave maestro. No more 'small-wave specialist' jibes. No more 'Kid'.

'Where there is an opening at Waimea,' he would subsequently write, 'you have to make your move.' This was his opening. It was destiny calling. He didn't particularly *want* to go, he just knew he *had* to go. He was far beyond any idea of choosing.

Foo knelt down, picked up his board and went down the hill to the edge of the water. James Jones and the bodyboarder J. P. Patterson were already paddling out just ahead of him. He flung himself into the steaming broth of the shorebreak and paddled forcefully into the channel and Ace Cool followed right behind him, trying to stay in his slipstream. Ace had been watching Foo: if Foo was going out, he was going out. The funny thing was that Foo had never really checked the surf at close quarters. He was concentrating on his own moves. He didn't like to watch the waves too much in case it stopped him going out. So when Foo was followed out by Ace it was the blind leading the blind. Now there were four men out. Bradshaw shook his head up on the dune and looked grim. They were all dead meat. If he couldn't make it, nobody could. Of that he was certain. It was curtains for Foo.

Bradshaw never admitted to fear. It was a point of principle with him. He always said if he was afraid he'd never go out (but since he was afraid of nothing he always would go). Foo, on the other hand, regularly acknowledged fear. Especially at the Bay. Now, as he paddled out, he was starting to regret not having checked out the surf properly. He could taste the faint, bitter tang of imminent peril on his tongue and he could feel the fluttering of the great void that loomed up inside him as a reminder of the immense nothingness that awaited him somewhere down the line. Maybe not too far down. Foo took his regular slow wide-angled course around the back of the break, through the middle of the Bay, so as to prepare himself for what lay ahead.

Now he would have to look at the surf, from very close

quarters. Sometimes too close. 'We all quickly realised that this was no ordinary big day.' All the waves were ledging up, hitting a fully vertical angle, as perpendicular as lighthouses, far too soon. There seemed to be no chance of getting into any of them, no ramp, no entry lane. The four men remained wide, out in the channel, not even on the shoulder, apprehensive of the sheer refractory trickiness of these waves, with a geometry none of them had seen before at Waimea. Not one of them seemed in the least rideable. And even then they had to keep swinging out and around crazy, lumbering, lopsided waves, the kind of waves that defined 'gnarly', that were jacking up and pitching over in an area that would normally be considered 'the safety zone'. What they all quickly realised was that, on this day, there was no such thing as a safety zone at Waimea. The field of play had had all its lines washed out, erased. Twenty-five-footers were springing up almost at random and taking over the entire Bay, leaving no breathing space. It was the kind of day that Woody Brown and Dickie Cross had once encountered and found beyond their powers.

The interval between the biggest sets was going down all the time. In other words, the number of extremely large and terrifying breakers was going up. There was one solid 30-foot wave that had all four men scratching to get up the face and over the top before it went into meltdown. As it lurched by under him Foo had the opportunity to see it break, seemingly in slow motion: 'It was a moment I will never forget. The monster pitched up and out and turned into the biggest tube you could ever imagine. On other days at Waimea, Sunset, Pipeline or Honolua, I've seen some big holes . . . but nothing like this. It looked like a huge cavern with half the ocean as its roof and sides.' This trembling, thundering sine curve seemed to Foo so overwhelmingly powerful that he had the impression that the water was no longer a liquid element at all but rather something solid and hard, 'like concrete'. *The hard and the strong cannot stand against it.* The wave was cemented into his imagination like architecture. It was far far in excess of anything that could reasonably be attempted and brought off.

All four men looked back respectfully, and with an enormous sense of relief, at the wave as it rolled on by. James Jones turned to Foo and said that he had taken off on a wave like that on the morning of the 1974 Smirnoff contest (also held at Waimea), got tumbled and held down and had almost died, and that he would never try one like it again. Foo nodded in agreement. Jones was right. He realised then that 'there was no way to ride such a wave, no matter how long a board, no matter how early you got in, there was just too much energy and moving water'. Perhaps by way of easing the tension, Jones hollered out to Ace, 'Hey, Alec, if you had caught that one you would have had the record.'

Ace Cool, everyone knew – he had made *sure* that everyone knew – was fixated on capturing the biggest wave. That was his one aim in life – claiming the undisputed big one. Sheer size mattered to Ace, as it mattered to all of them – it was just that he was more outspoken about it. And yet, when it had come along, he too had been glad to get the hell out of the way of it. The desire to score the mightiest wave ever ridden by man constantly battled against the flickering desire for self-preservation. Yes, he would have had the record if he'd ridden it, but there was no way he was even going to touch a brutal bucking rabid maniac of a sidewinding wave like that one. It all came down to selection.

It was shortly after that colossus passed them by that Foo heard screaming on the beach and the massed honking of car horns. He looked towards the crowd that had gathered there – it seemed a long way off, almost like another dimension, although only half a mile or so distant – and they were pointing out over his shoulder. There was a 25–30-foot wave behind him and Foo scrambled to get over the top of it. Is that all? he said to himself. Piece of cake. What were they getting so worked up about? And then he looked up at the horizon. Way up at where the horizon used to be.

What Mark Dambrowski saw a couple of miles away made him reach for the phone in the lifeguard tower. Aged thirty-one, he had trained under Eddie Aikau and thought he had seen it all at Waimea – until approximately 3 p.m. on the afternoon of 18 January 1985. 'Get the chopper in the air,' he screamed down the phone, 'there's four guys in the water and not one of them is going to get out of there alive. You're going to be picking up bodies.' In those days there was a rescue helicopter based at the fire house opposite Foodland, less than a mile to the east of the Bay.

Foo called it 'the beast' or 'the thing'. It made all the other waves that had passed them by that day look feeble by comparison. The effect it had on Foo was this: it made him laugh out loud. It was a freak, the mother of all freaks: an impossible wave, unbelievable, insane, a caricature of a wave drawn by a lunatic, straining up into the sky. A King Kong among waves. Technically this was a 'rogue' wave, resulting from the union of two or more waves; but this one was not so much a rogue as Public Enemy No. 1. Call it what you will – it was coming straight at them. Estimates of its size vary. Foo called it more than twice the size of anything else they had seen that day, which would make it around 60–70 feet from base to toppling crest. Others called it eighty. All agreed that they had never seen anything like it on the North Shore. Perhaps it was comparable to the wave that

Woody Brown and Dickie Cross had seen and had claimed to be 100 feet. It was still a good couple of hundred yards away and already it was standing up and feathering at the top. It was impossible to see anything else. There was nothing but this immense wave. To Foo the sky had become liquid, the sheer presence of water filled his whole perceptual field. He began to feel that he did not exist any more, he was nothing, nothing existed, nothing except this all-encompassing immensity.

James Jones was already steaming for the horizon, with a view to making it over the top. He saw it first. Foo was in the worst possible position: he was the furthest over, on the inside, more exposed than anyone to the severest forces. He knew as soon as he saw 'the thing' that there was no chance whatever of getting to it before it broke, so he turned towards the centre of the Bay and paddled for the channel, reckoning that the aftermath would be at its least potent in this area. What he didn't know was that this megawave was about to break from top to bottom across the entire width of the Bay. It was the biggest close-out at Waimea that anyone had ever seen.

Standing up on the dune, shading his eyes from the sun, Bradshaw gazed out to sea with mixed feelings of admiration, reverence, sorrow and satisfaction. The ocean was playing fair, without fear or favour. Everyone who had foolishly, vainly, ventured out there, despite the warning that his own experience had offered, was about to be erased from contention. He turned to the white-haired, one-eyed Peter Cole, sitting on the bonnet of his car and timing the set intervals, and said, 'That is undisputedly the largest wave anybody has ever had to deal with.' Cole, at fifty-four a tall, loping, James Stewart figure, one of the grand old men of Waimea, who had delivered a eulogy at Eddie Aikau's funeral, thought he had seen everything – the massive swells of 1969, the Smirnoff in 1974 – now he had to revise his 'everything' significantly upwards. Even he, temperamentally conservative in his estimations, had to admit that 18 January 1985 was an exceptional kind of a day. His single functioning eye followed the surfers like a telescope and registered the not very surprising fact that they had all just disappeared, steamrollered by the great wave.

'The beast' had metamorphosed from a lumbering, towering cliff-face into 'a thundering avalanche of white water' (in Foo's words). You couldn't surf it: there was no way over or around it. The only way through was under. Wherever they were going, all four souls bailed, sucked in their last mouthfuls of air and dived immediately for the bottom, fugitives from the thrust of the primal wave. Wedged on the seabed, Foo looked up and watched in wonder as an extremely large inverted tornado ghosted by above him. The thing he feared was what would come behind it: a second successive hold-down, on this scale, would surely finish them. All four men had been wearing leashes, attaching their boards to their ankles, like a prison ball and chain. But when, almost miraculously, they floated up to the surface, still breathing, only the leashes remained – all the boards, bar one, had been swept away. The exception was Foo's. His leash had held. That had been one all-time mother of a rogue wave – but only one. He slid gratefully back on to his gun.

'What kind of leash you got on,' said J. P. Patterson, resentfully, 'a chain?' The other three, Jones, Patterson, Cool, had no cards left to play; they struck out for shore, leaving Foo all alone in the middle of the Bay.

Foo was the last man out, just as Bradshaw had been earlier in the day. Then it had been Foo who was watching from the shore; now it was Bradshaw. Their positions had been precisely reversed. It was the Kid who was living out Bradshaw's fantasy for him – to catch the last wave and ride it in alone. Bradshaw could no longer delude himself into thinking that he was the last man left alive in a world which had been flooded by the great oneness. He had to concede that now there were two men at least, two who moved upon the face of the deep.

The helicopter had taken less than five minutes, after Dambrowski's call, to get in the air and race over to the Bay. They knew that the wave had eaten everyone up, so they were relieved to see all four men below, still alive. James Jones, with fifteen years of big-wave experience behind him, didn't hesitate: as soon as they lowered the basket he hopped right in, grateful for the ride. Ace, too proud to take the easy way out, opted to swim in, but got trapped in the shorebreak and was being tugged around towards the rocks. The helicopter lowered the basket to him again. *D'you want it this time?* Ace wanted it all right, and was reaching up to pull himself in when another of the outrageous close-out sets barrelled on through and smacked right into him. The crew kept on lowering the basket and every time Ace tried to climb in another wave dragged him off again, sucking him towards Coffin Corner. Finally he did the only thing he could do: he clung on to the basket by his fingertips, yelling, 'Go on, get me out of here!' As they were reeling him in another wave, as if reluctant to let him go, smashed into him and rocked the basket and shook up the whole helicopter. But this time the leash held and Ace was airlifted out, dangling and spinning on the end of the basket. The helicopter dropped him off and came back for Patterson, who had retrieved his board but had nowhere left to go.

That left only Foo. The last man out. The crew called out

to him to grab the basket, his ticket back to safety and sanity. But Foo ignored them. He was scared, but he was still alive. He was still on his board. The Kid waved them away imperiously. He was surfing all alone in closed-out Waimea and, having seen what he was up against, was fully aware of the seriousness of his position. But how often did opportunities like this come along? So this was what destiny felt like. He'd often wondered. Being part of 'the Plan', some higher cosmic irony. Big Waimea and no one else out, not even Bradshaw. Bradshaw, he knew, was marooned on the beach, bereft of an operational board. Foo had to admit that this was an additional incentive. Any wave he caught now would be like a dagger into the heart of Bradshaw. He would naturally feel that it was his wave, part of his personal collection, one of his harem, and that Foo had stolen it from under his nose. It was the thought of Bradshaw pacing up and down on the beach, grinding his teeth in frustration, that suddenly made Foo feel like a thief, casing the joint. He was stealing waves and it felt good. His only anxiety, at this point, was that the security measures at Waimea were severe and potentially lethal. There were good reasons to keep your hands off and behave. And, meanwhile, that helicopter basket being dangled in front of his face looked mighty tempting.

Foo had an idea that it would be advisable, in the circumstances, to get back to the beach. But he knew he had to do it on the back of a wave, not cradled in a basket. That was his vocation, his duty, his fate; he couldn't shirk it. Anyhow, he had a point to make, no matter that there might be a high price to pay for making it. For years he had been aiming for just this moment, never quite knowing if it would ever come, and now it had come and he was ready. The flu didn't seem to be bothering him any more. He had come out from under 'the beast' in one piece, in good shape, and this was his big chance. Foo had worked out a reasonable cat-and-mouse-style plan (in which he was the mouse). He was going to keep a sharp weather eye out for the big close-out sets and paddle out over them (if he could) and then scoot back to the line-up in the hope of picking up a wave of more manageable proportions.

It was a good plan and it might have worked on any other day but this. More homicidal waves kept him sprinting for the horizon, but the intervals between major sets were now so short that Foo had no time to get back to the line-up before another big one forced him way outside all over again. The sets just kept on coming. There was no stopping them. The helicopter came back for Foo. He had no choice. There was no way he was ever going to get in; even he had to realise that now and throw in the towel. It was no loss of face. Everyone would agree he had been a plucky little devil, but this was the end of the road. They lowered the basket and shoved it in his face. Foo flat out ignored them. He stuck to his damn plan, even though he knew it was stupid and there was not a chance of it ever working out. He ought to take the ride, he knew. It was the only sensible course of action. But he couldn't back down now. The rational self-preserving side of his being cried out to him to hop into the basket. That basket was as tempting as a bouquet of flowers to a bee. But Foo willed himself to shut it out of his mind. The irrational wave-accumulating side of his personality asserted itself: *Forget the chopper! Damn the basket! Find a wave to hitch a ride on!* The helicopter continued to hover overhead, as if to remind him of everything he was missing.

If he couldn't get an inside wave, he would have to go outside. Foo was somewhere in the middle of the Bay when a set approached. He drove for the first wave in the set, a certain left. But it started sucking out and going over before he could get on to it, so he pulled back. But he knew there was another one behind it. He calculated that even if it was bigger than the first wave in the set, it had to be breaking in deeper water after the first wave had broken and that might just give him a shot. Part of his theory was correct. The wave was big all right, but it held up and didn't fold over too soon. He had a window. He steered into position for take-off. The wave lifted him up towards heaven. Then he saw the whole thing hollowing out under him – as the last one had done – and going concave, bending right over like the sting of a very large scorpion. But now he had no choice – he had to keep on stroking, driving forwards. He had gone past the point of no return, too late to back out now. So he did the only thing he could do, which was to push up with his arms and spring to his feet.

He knew what was coming: a freefall drop. When a wave is this concave there is no chance of the board sticking to the wave or the surfer sticking to the board; one of them has to give, or both simultaneously. Foo launched himself over the ledge and took off. He was in flight, riding his board as if it were a wing. But he wasn't exactly glued to it in the first place. And now he was coming unstuck. He and the board flew through the air, aiming at reconnecting with the face further down, at a more rideable angle. They both flew well, Foo and the board, over the best part of 25 feet in a downward direction, but they parted company somewhere down the line. 'Technically and mentally', Foo wrote, 'I kept it all together', and maybe so, but unless he could actually walk on water, Foo was sunk, since he no longer had anything solid under his feet to ride on.

Somehow he managed to hook up with the board again,

but he couldn't hold it. He crash-landed. That strange vision of Foo's — of the wave turning solid — seemed to have come true. Anyone who has gone off a high diving board knows: the faster you hit water, the harder it becomes. So it was that instead of penetrating the surface, Foo just bounced along it, skimming and skipping like a stone spinning across a lake. If only he could keep going like this all the way to shore, it would have been the next best thing. Then the wave folded over and 'a good portion of the Pacific started to collapse on me'. Foo felt the lip explode and he was right in the middle of it. He heard the sound of snapping — it was not his own body but the sound of his cherished 9-foot three-stringer Lundy giving up the ghost. Then, as if in slow motion, he saw the watch on his wrist being hoovered off and sucked into the maw. Finally he felt himself getting slurped up and spat out and hurled down — and this time he stayed down, a long way down.

For a while — a time hard to calculate, probably only half a minute or so, but played again and again endlessly in his memory — 'Things turned grey'. When he resurfaced, the helicopter was still there waiting. His board was gone. The chopper had won. The basket beckoned.

When Foo came to write the history of that day, he recalled each particular episode and element — 'that gigantic tube', 'that monster close-out', 'that take-off', and so on. But what he emphasised more than anything else was a shift in his perspective. He used words on the page — for the first time, so far as I know — like 'destiny,' 'fate', 'the Plan'. It is a strange sense that afflicts nearly everyone on the North Shore at one time or another: that of being caught up in something infinitely larger than themselves and yet not being an entirely meaningless chunk of debris, but rather an integral, functional entity within this great system. Suddenly it seemed to Foo as if contingency, the random realm of chance, had come to an end, and history, the orderly domain of the inevitable, had begun. Everything had a purpose. Raw, chaotic nature had been transformed into a meaningful, providential narrative. The way things happened was the way they were meant to be, the way they had to be. Foo had to be there, henceforth big waves were his domain, the Bay was his backyard. Telling the story was another part of 'the Plan', too.

In 'Occurrence at Waimea Bay' − syndicated in surf magazines around the world, from the US to Australia and Japan − Foo also coined a new phrase that gained a certain currency: 'the unridden realm'. That was Foo's name for the kind of wave he had taken off on, 35 foot and beyond. It was not meant to be. Certain waves cannot be ridden and that's that. To the question, 'Who has ridden the biggest wave?' Foo answered, rather modestly: 'Nobody.' When he read Foo's story, this is the one part that Bradshaw definitely agreed with, especially the word *UNridden*. Some people were calling it 'the biggest wave ever ridden'. Well, that was just hype, the usual kind of propaganda and mystification you found in the magazines. As soon as Bradshaw tracked down the editor who had quoted Sir Edmund Hillary at the top of Foo's article − 'Challenge is what makes men' − and added a totally spurious comparison between Foo and the mountaineer ('For Mark Foo, that sentiment manifested itself in this heroic ride'), he was going to straighten the guy out, harshly. It was time for some *rectification*.

The plain fact was, Bradshaw grumbled, 'he never even *rode* the damn thing'. He just took off on it. There's a world of difference. He was just showboating. It was the biggest wave *never* ridden. And he had to be picked up by helicopter. There was no way the Kid was going to swim three times around the Bay, he was too much of a ballerina for that, he expected to be chauffeured back home. Bradshaw read the 'epilogue' again: 'Since the events of this extraordinary afternoon, an unprecedented amount of media and public interest has been generated.' *Damn right*, he thought, *and mainly by you*. Foo had engineered the whole story, and sponged up all the glory, and now he had the bare-faced audacity to speak of 'destiny'. It was yet another travesty.

There is a photograph of Bradshaw greeting Foo, shaking his hand as he returns triumphantly to the beach, 'in a poignant moment of camaraderie'. But the caption also suggests there is something other than pure camaraderie: a note of ambivalence: 'Bradshaw congratulates Mark Foo not so much on his performance as for the fact that he made it in alive following the most intense session ever witnessed.'

But whatever Bradshaw thought about it, from this day on Foo would always be categorised as, above all, a big-wave rider. A hellman, a fire-eater, one of the elite. Pretty soon he would be pronouncing in *Surfer* on the subject of 'late take-offs' in heavy big-wave situations ('So much of surfing is mental, and heavy take-offs are more so than any other manoeuvre'). His name and reputation, his 'destiny', were assured.

For the first time, Foo now started to talk in public about the realistic prospect of dying. He mentioned it one night at Sunset Beach Elementary School when he gave a speech to the kids. I couldn't help mentioning it to him myself from time to time in the years that followed the 'Occurrence' article, the strong possibility that he might eventually run out of luck. He tended to reply: 'If you want the ultimate thrill, you've got to be willing to pay the ultimate price.' That was the rational capitalist in him speaking: he saw it as a fair exchange, a wave for a life. But he also thought that it would be better to die doing what he loved doing anyway. Another Foo-ism: 'To go out surfing a monster wave – that would be a glamorous way to die.' That was the applause-milking exhibitionist in him: he imagined dying, swan-like, on the biggest possible wave, spectacularly, with a final bow and a kiss to the audience. But behind all the bravado and the calculation, there was a deep and persistent sense of fatalism.

'You know I could die out there,' he said to SharLyn, shortly after 18 January.

'Then, don't do it,' she said.

'Yeah, but I have to die sometime anyway,' he replied.

In truth Foo was fond of the idea of going out with a bang rather than a whimper. 'When the *Challenger* blew up,' he said to me one day at the Bay, 'everybody said it was a tragedy. But I thought: this was the moment they lived for. They died happy. That is the way I want to go. You can die at Waimea as easy as Outer Space.'

Peter Cole, sitting on the bonnet of his car, looking at his watch, timing the sets and electing not to go out, said that what they had witnessed that afternoon was, more than anything else, 'a lack of judgement'. Bradshaw would have agreed. Perhaps even Foo would have conceded the point, but he would also have said that, if it was a mistake, it was nevertheless a mistake that had to be made. It was in the order of things to make precisely this mistake and no other. That was the way the cosmos was shaping that afternoon, so there was nothing to be gained in struggling against it and debating the point.

Cole also made two contradictory assertions. Firstly: 'Big-wave surfing is one of the only applications of sport where records aren't broken as time goes on.' The biggest waves he and Pat Curren had ever ridden, twenty years earlier – they were no different from these waves; it was scientifically impossible to surf anything bigger. And, secondly, in conclusion: 'But who can say? The biggest wave ever hasn't been ridden yet.' Both Foo and Bradshaw thought the same way. So did Ace Cool.

That night, the night of 18 January, Foo ended up at Ace Cool's house on the other side of Waimea. They watched a sketchy video recording of the afternoon's event and they agreed that neither of them had yet surfed the biggest wave. Nor had Bradshaw. It was still out there somewhere, still up for grabs. Everyone was still in the race. And yet there was a new degree of respect from Ace towards Foo. Maybe he had just been lucky, the way his leash had held, maybe it was fate; either way, Ace needed some of it. One thing he noticed that Foo had been using – and he wondered if it could have given him a slight edge – was webbed gloves. They were supposed to help with paddling faster and, therefore, potentially, pulling off the bigger, faster waves.

The next day Ace went out and bought himself some webbed gloves.

11

Foo's Brazilian System and Bradshaw's Revenge

'In terms of performance, I don't think anyone surfs Waimea better than I do,' Foo had been bragging to *Surfer* (December 1986). 'To me, good surfing is making it look easy. Kenny's approach has always been a make-it-look-hard approach.' It was around this time that (a) Foo was invited by the Hawaiian Department of Education to speak at a careers fair on the subject 'Surfing as a Career'; and (b) Bradshaw attacked Foo in the water on the 'perfect day' at Sunset, dunking him and biting chunks out of his board. But Foo laughed it off – he could always get himself another board, it was sponsored anyway.

Bradshaw was not laughing: he still had to balance the books. Foo, like some charming con-artist, had managed to finesse the numbers, to fraudulently make out he had more credit to his name than he really had or deserved. All Bradshaw was doing was making the crooked straight, doing God's work. In fact, in later years, he would deny it ever happened. Ken Bradshaw denies a lot of things. All he allows now is, 'Yes, I've heard that rumour. It's funny. I can't even remember what they're talking about. She wasn't even Foo's girlfriend. Not so far as I knew.'

It is one of the great myths of surfing that surfers are somehow sexier than the average human being. And that surfers have more sex. If you believe all the newspapers, they are the incarnation of the pleasure principle. Ted Deerhurst, for one, knew it was a myth. I first ran into him on the contest circuit in France, when he surfed in the European equivalent of the Triple Crown, on the Atlantic coast, at Lacanau, Hossegor and Biarritz. He used to be known as 'Lord Ted', which was almost justified, because he was a viscount, the son of the Duke of Coventry and an American mother. His full name was Edward George William Omar Coventry; family motto, *Candide et constanter*: candidly and constantly. He did well as an amateur, and represented Great Britain, but he never really made it on the pro tour. A few good results (he once made the semis at 10–12-foot Sunset, knocking out the highly rated Australian Cheyne Horan) but nothing consistent.

The year he came 229th in the world, I was talking to him at the annual end-of-season ASP dinner at the Royal Hawaiian hotel in Honolulu. He had been reading a book called *How to Increase Your Self-Esteem*, but he didn't really need it. In his never-say-die way he had set his sights on the Most Improved Surfer of the Year title. 'I only have to get up to 139,' he said, 'and I'll blow everyone else away.' He had a theory as to where he had been going wrong. He put it all down to the lack of a good woman. He vigorously rejected the concept of sublimation (chastity is good for you): he had been sublimating for years, he argued, and it didn't work; now he was going to try the exact opposite. *His* theory was that if only he could get a girlfriend to accompany him on the tour and keep him in a permanent state of well-being and satisfaction, his results would improve. But he was very specific about the kind of girl it had to be. 'When she walks down the street and you're looking at her from behind, you still have to be able to see her breasts.' 'From behind?'

I had the idea that it was because he was so damn specific, so exacting about the kind of girl who would make the perfect girlfriend, that he didn't have a girlfriend at all. No real woman could possibly match up to that description. Every now and then, as a good-looking woman walked by, I would find myself turning around to see if she could possibly match up to Ted's requirements. None of them did. I thought it was just another of Ted's crazy ideas. He would have to scale his ambitions down a bit. But he didn't want to scale down. He wanted girls to scale up. It was a tall order, but in the end he found his perfect woman: her name was Camille and she worked in an exotic dance club in Honolulu and he had to pay her $50 every time she sat on his knee and whispered in his ear. Ted once introduced me to her. As she walked away, I watched her. Even in the shadows I could see that she comfortably fulfilled Ted's exigent criteria. 'She's in love with me,' he said. He was only paying her the money, he explained, to keep management off her back. As I say, the surfer as sexual superman is a myth. But it is a myth that most surfers seriously believe in: they want it to be true, they do their best to make it true, and, in some cases, it even becomes true. It was true of Foo and it was true of Bradshaw.

Surfing has been mixed up with religion and politics and romance since the beginning. Ancient Hawaiian legend tells of a man sharing a wave with a woman and then making love to her on the beach, as if riding the wave was a prelude to riding a woman. There was a general sense that the ocean was feminine and the wave was a woman. Surfing was already symbolically sexual, an apparent enactment of coitus in its obsession with the tube. Getting in the barrel was, in effect, coupling with a wave. It was a Freudian fantasy that happened to be real, an outlandish erotic dream that could sometimes turn into a nightmare as the wave folded and crushed the victim within. There was no pleasure without pain, the experience seemed to say.

The image of surfing was defined by an early woodcut of shapely Polynesian women cruising naked towards shore, poised on top of waves, like Venus on a half-shell, like voluptuous statues on pedestals. William Anderson, the young ship's surgeon on board Captain Cook's *Resolution*, witnessing surfing for the first time in Tahiti in 1777, called it 'the most supreme pleasure'. In the nineteenth century, buttoned-up Puritan evangelists from America's East Coast came to Hawaii and denounced the 'evil pleasures' of surfing. Its brazen hedonism brought it close to extinction. But the neo-pagan twentieth century rebranded the beach and sold it as the platform *par excellence* of rampant, youthful sexuality. The beach became the scene of Dionysian frenzy. For modern surfers, machismo came with the territory. It wasn't an option, it was an obligation. The sociologist Jean Baudrillard once described masculinity as 'an eccentric and exhausting condition'. Bradshaw might have agreed with him.

He saw girls as a distraction. He almost invariably had a girlfriend. But ever since I've known him he has manifested an extreme ambivalence towards women. 'They're always asking you to choose,' he said to me once. *Choose between me and surfing.*

'And what do you choose?' I said.

'If I have to choose, I'll choose,' he said, unhesitatingly, 'to go surf.'

He picked girls up easily and he tossed them away even more easily. They were like waves. There would always be another one along soon. They were soft and yielding and would succumb to his power. It was his form of compromise. In an ideal world, he would probably jog along perfectly well without women. Become a monk, take a vow of chastity and dedicate himself full-time and exclusively to the pursuit of the waves. But, for one thing, the waves weren't always around. You felt with Bradshaw that if only there had been a constant supply of extremely large waves on tap the question of women would never even arise. But, in reality, even in Hawaii, there were always flat spells, intermittences, voids, and they had to be filled somehow. And then there was the risk, remote but nonetheless potent for all that, of being considered gay. Surfing has always been highly sexualised, visibly homoerotic in tendency, but at the same time, from Sydney to San Francisco, resolutely homophobic or at least heterocompulsive. The beach was straight with no deviations or detours allowed (one Australian surfer, rumoured to be gay, lost friends and sponsorship and rushed to deny it). The truth was that Bradshaw needed to have a woman, *had* to have a woman, to compensate for all that time he spent in close proximity to large numbers of semi-naked men. In surfing circles, it was his passport to respectability. It went with the job.

Bradshaw embraced the logic, the necessity, of having a girlfriend, but he always felt a certain relief when it was over. He didn't have to exert himself that hard. He didn't go out of his way to pursue anyone. He was a well-built, good-looking guy, and he bumped into a lot of women on the beach or just walking along the street and going into shops. 'Aren't you Ken Bradshaw?' they would say. He was a celebrity. They had seen his picture; what was it like surfing those massive waves? Bradshaw was willing to tell them.

Once he reeled off the names of all the notches in his belt for me. There was Kate, and there was Suzy: Diane, Shirley, Bridget, Luciana, Lily, Julia, Felicia . . . And more. I forget. Even he forgot. There were a lot. But one encounter, bizarre and incredible though it is, sums up a lot of Bradshaw's experiences.

Bradshaw – and this didn't happen very often – was dancing. When it came to nightclubs, he was more adept at kicking people out than getting down and grooving on the dance floor with them. It was not really his style. Required too much lowering of defences. And this particular episode proved the point. It was an old friend's birthday and he wanted to celebrate by going to a nightclub in Honolulu. Against his better judgement, Bradshaw went along. He checked the surf forecast before he went out: nothing doing the next day. He could risk one late night surely?

The funny thing was that he couldn't even remember the girl's name afterwards. Or rather, he couldn't understand it in the first place. Something like Veronica, or Vesuvia, or Versace, he wasn't too sure. The music was too loud, for one thing, and for another, being Brazilian she spoke Portuguese. She was one of that generation of female Brazilian bodyboarders who flooded the North Shore in the second half of the eighties and the early nineties. She had been brought up on a diet of Latin American surfing magazines (such as *Fluir* and *Ride It!*) and, although Brazilians got top billing Bradshaw nevertheless still appeared regularly alongside them, admired from Floranópolis to Rio de Janeiro, under the heading 'Hawaiian hellman' or 'Master of Waimea' or 'Lord of the North Shore' or something equally imposing in Portuguese. And now there he was, this invincible god, this icon of surfing, standing right in front of her, recognisable even in the dim lighting of the club, swaying in time to some visceral rhythm. How could anyone resist?

She introduced herself. 'Hi, I'm Ken Bradshaw,' said Bradshaw. He didn't really need to, but it gave him something to say. He leaned over. 'What did you say your name was again?' He still didn't get it. She was dancing smoothly and sinuously, and made Bradshaw feel stiff and awkward by comparison, and she seemed to be getting closer and closer to him, closing in, until he found himself matching, or trying to match, all her moves, and she fitted snugly right around him. She was a few inches shorter and he could see she had a great head of dark wavy hair and there was a scent of something fresh and natural – coconuts, maybe, or pineapples – that reminded him of surf wax. It wasn't until the slow dance that he really got the hard-on though.

She was clinging to him like ivy round a tree, coiling around him like a python. He was wearing some sharp Chino pants, fairly tight cut, and now they were even tighter. She could feel him expanding, pressing against her, thrusting out to meet her, and Bradshaw put her in mind of a surfboard, all taut and shiny but at the same time supple as it moved across the face of the wave and cranked out an acute bottom turn and smashed off the lip. That was when she unzipped him and bent down.

It took Bradshaw completely by surprise. He was not exactly a veteran of public fellatio. As luck would have it, the lights were so low and furtive on the dance floor that no one around them seemed to have noticed what was going on. He was aroused but not exposed. He was sweating and his breath was coming out in sighs and grunts and he could feel himself melting like an ice-cream cone in the noonday sun. He couldn't stand it any more.

'You want to know the real problem with her?' he says one day when we're discussing the 'occurrence at Joe's Bar'.

'Tell me,' I say.

'I couldn't understand a word she was saying.'

'Was she saying anything?'

'Sure she was saying something, every now and then, when she'd stop for a breath. And I couldn't figure out what it was. Her English was terrible.'

Bradshaw pushed her away abruptly, zipped up and backed away into the darkness. 'What is problem?' she said, uncomprehending, as if what she was doing was the most natural thing in the world and Bradshaw was behaving eccentrically. She didn't understand that Bradshaw couldn't take too much zealous phallocentrism. It made him feel vulnerable and uncomfortable. He broke through the crowd and vamoosed. He didn't like to feel so out of control, at least not in public.

As it happened, Mark Foo was also involved with a Brazilian girl. In fact, with lots of Brazilian girls. But before I get into that I have to explain about the day I was mistaken for Kelly Slater. (There is a connection.) I was on the beach at Pipeline, one day in the early nineties, looking for Foo. Two young Japanese women came up to me and asked, 'Are you Kelly Slater?' The point about Kelly Slater is that he was then the coming man in the ranks of professional surfing (and has since won the world championship a record seven times). He was a young, tanned Floridian who was making some of the most innovative and eye-catching moves on the faces of small-to-medium waves ever seen (notably floaters, aerials and his trademark tail slides). I, on the other hand, was not quite so young, and definitely not world champion; my only plus was that my hair was whiter than his. We were anything but surf clones. The two Japanese girls were gorgeous and definitely qualified for the two highest accolades in the surfing lexicon, 'honeys' and 'zowie mamas'. They were slim but perfect and slotted into extremely small bikinis. Either they were high, or they had the sun in their eyes, or they were insufficiently acquainted with Kelly Slater. Nevertheless, it was one of the proudest, most electrifying moments of my entire life. The next moment was probably the stupidest of my entire life. I said, 'No'. Then I gave them a thumbnail sketch of Slater and sent them off in his general direction.

I spent the rest of that day and most of the night in semi-mourning, paralysed by regret, desperate to get in a time machine and go back and replay the scene. The next morning I had a date with Foo. He was expecting me for breakfast at his house, the two-storey A-frame that sat on top of the bluff overlooking Waimea Bay, and provided him with a perfect advance warning system for any incoming giant swells. I was still wondering what had become of the Japanese girls when I walked in. And then I found out. They were making breakfast for Foo. Foo was still lazing in bed and they were beavering around in the kitchen, cooking eggs and squeezing orange juice and slicing bread for the toaster. They had spent the night. They hadn't been able to find Kelly Slater, but they had found Foo. Foo would do. It was his destiny.

There was a side of Foo that was relaxed, fatalistic and blissfully indifferent. And there was another side that was as fanatically interventionist as a man with a system playing the tables at Las Vegas and intent on cleaning up. So it was in matters of the heart. He was, as I've said, a little like Bruce Lee, only better-looking. He was a movie star among surfers:

smooth, suave, chiselled, with boyish charm. Perhaps he could be classified as 'irresistible'. Ace described Foo, with a touch of envy, as 'the boyfriend of all women'. Certainly a lot of beautiful women dated him. I once saw him dancing at a disco at the Turtle Bay Hilton. He moved with the grace of a snake gliding up out of a charmer's basket. He did not leave alone that night.

It was like a dream. And yet this was not enough for Foo. There had to be more, there had to be better, everything could be improved on. It was Foo and Dennis Pang who developed the scheme, but it was all Foo's idea. 'It was his vision,' says Pang. Foo was always sensitive to the fluctuations of demand and supply. He was one of the first to become conscious of the great Brazilian influx of that era. Every now and then he would go out with a Brazilian girl. It never lasted long. But the arrangement was too erratic and intermittent, in fact there was no arrangement, it was all pure chance, a matter of dumb luck, a throw of the dice, a spin of the wheel. This is where Foo brought his great entrepreneurial skills to bear. There had to be a way of maximising rewards. There had to be an angle. He spent weeks on the problem. And then he cracked it.

Pang was, initially, baffled, incredulous. 'You mean, find a Brazilian girl and DON'T sleep with her?' Was Foo mad? It was almost like a breach of etiquette. A North Shore scandal in the making. 'STOP PRESS: MARK FOO DOES NOT BED A BRAZILIAN.' It didn't sound good and it would surely undermine his otherwise impeccable reputation. 'Yes, that's the plan, you'll see, it'll work out.'

Foo took on a Brazilian girl called Serena to work at the Backpackers Hostel. She was desk clerk, cleaner, manageress, depending. She had to be versatile. She didn't have a place to stay. In those days none of the Brazilian girls had a place to stay. They invariably ended up staying at the houses of surfers – those who had houses – and paying for their board and lodging with sexual favours. It was a crude, primitive form of bartering, it was ruthless, it was immoral, but nobody complained about it too much. It took a visionary of the stature of Foo to see that it was also a criminal waste of resources. He invited Serena to stay at his house. And she accepted. But he stressed he didn't want the usual *quid pro quo*. It was strictly business. Maybe she could clean and tidy around the house and cook a bit? Was that a fair deal? She nodded her agreement, while not really believing it.

What was he, a monk, celibate, gay? Did he have a very tough and vindictive girlfriend? Serena checked herself in the mirror. What she saw was right up there with the Girl from Ipanema. So she was all the more shocked, as the days went by, that Foo stuck to his guns. He didn't lay a finger on her. He had no expectations. He would wish her goodnight and at most, like a favourite uncle, give her a benevolent kiss on the top of her head. She couldn't believe it. It was like heaven at Foo's place, he didn't even ask her to do much cleaning and cooking. And, into the bargain, he didn't mind who she invited over. 'Treat the place as your home,' Foo said. 'What is mine is yours.' She told all her Brazilian friends. They were open-mouthed in amazement. The guy was some kind of saint. And good-looking too? *Enigmático!* They just had to come over to get a look at this paragon of virtue. They flocked *chez* Foo, all those gorgeous young Brazilian bodyboarders, who were otherwise strung out along the entire length of the North Shore, scattered, submerged, hidden. They came in carloads, they came in busloads. They all piled out at Foo's house. His house was crammed full of Brazilian honeys craning their heads just to catch a glimpse of the best employer on the North Shore and the most virtuous landlord in Hawaii, possibly in the world.

Which is when Foo and Pang swooped. It would not be fair to describe them as foxes in a chickenhouse. But it was close. They had the pick of all Serena's friends. At one time or another just about all the Brazilian girls on the North Shore passed through Foo's place (and at least two Japanese). *Increased throughput* would be the technical description of the net effect. Such was Foo's ingenious if utterly ruthless 'Brazilian system'. Pang was blown away by the simplicity and sheer brilliance of the scheme. 'I guess he was some kind of genius when it came to women,' he says. Foo swore him to secrecy. He didn't want anyone else getting wind of the system; they'd all want to use it. And remember: the key thing was that you mustn't sleep with Serena. She was sacred. Everything hung on that.

Around this time, Bradshaw was still furious with Foo. It used to be that everyone was talking about Bradshaw at Waimea. Now it was all Foo, Foo, Foo. And he hadn't even ridden that damn wave, it was just a feint, he knew he was never going to make it. It was a typical Foo stunt, choreographed for the cameras. There had to be some way to get even with the Kid.

Bradshaw's first plan was simple, efficient, but, he soon realised, utterly pointless. To seduce Foo's girlfriend. He couldn't help noticing, as he drove past, the knock-out Brazilian woman who worked at the Backpackers. He soon picked up that she was living at Foo's house as well. The old bartering system, Bradshaw assumed. He'd done it himself from time to time, but it tended to lead to complications: it was easy enough to get them in, but how did you get them out again? He'd had to give one or two lodgers the old heave-ho – 'And don't come back again or I'm going to get my gun out.' (Bradshaw really had a gun – it was a long-barrelled rifle which he used to shoot wild chickens roosting in the trees outside his house which dared to disturb his beauty sleep.)

In truth, Bradshaw was surprised that Foo would stoop to something so primitive. He thought he was better than that. No matter: all Bradshaw had to do, then, to put one over Foo, was grab his girl and run. That would seriously rile him. Maybe even put him off his stroke the next time they were both out at Waimea. It would give Bradshaw his old edge back again.

Bradshaw had it all worked out, like something out of *Mission Impossible*: in, steal the jewels, and out again, and nobody the wiser, kind of. And then it all fell apart: he heard the astonishing news that Foo was not in fact shagging the Brazilian chick. It came as a blow to Bradshaw, and a shock. It was like some kind of back-to-front miracle. Foo had scored again by *not* having sex with a Brazilian bodyboarder. It was unheard of. The kind of thing that Bradshaw himself was tempted by, but nobody noticed when he did it, everyone expected him to be a kind of monk anyway. Bradshaw fumed, smokily.

But in his heart of hearts, he never really believed it. Foo and chastity didn't add up. It was like his big-wave exploits; it wasn't real, it was all done for show. It was good publicity, but it was faked. Like a conjuror who seemed to know exactly what cards you had in your hand. Bradshaw knew it was a trick, he just couldn't work out how it was done, that was all.

And then he overheard the conversation in Foodland. He was checking out the ginseng and wheat germ when he caught the sound of a familiar voice in the next aisle. Whispering. He didn't hear all of it, but it was enough. I'm not saying who it was giving away all Foo's secrets. I don't even know for sure. But it had to be an insider. And he was spilling the beans. He might as well have broadcast it on Foo's radio show.

– System . . . Brazilian girls, heaps . . . but you can't sleep with her, that's key.

– NOT sleep . . .!?

– the beauty of it.

– Genius . . .

– master . . .

– man!

So *that* was how it worked. Bradshaw had penetrated the Magic Circle. Now everything clicked into place. It was obvious, he should have seen it before. He drove out of the Foodland exit as if he were going through the gates of enlightenment and before he'd even made it back to Sunset he had figured out the weak spot in the whole system, Foo's Achilles heel. Serena. So maybe Foo was abstaining, and getting back tenfold what he was giving up. But that didn't mean that everyone else had to.

Bradshaw laid siege to Serena. Foo had her well guarded, fortressed at both the Backpackers and his own house across the way. But – Foodland, running errands, going for a dip at Three Tables, just crossing the street: there were times and places, the guard would be down and she would be un-defended. Bradshaw was always around, waiting for his chance. But it never really happened until that small day at Sunset. Bradshaw never even planned it, it just fell into his lap. It was a training day, more to do with getting wet and paddling out than getting any serious waves. And she was out on her boogie board. The pack didn't really approve of bodyboarders at Sunset. It wasn't kosher. So Bradshaw gave her a personal cordon sanitaire to make sure she could get a shot at a wave. He lured her, corralled her (as he had done with Ace) smack into the path of a bigger set. He just knew she wasn't going to make it.

– You OK? he said sympathetically, coming to her rescue.

– No problem, she spluttered, spitting up a lungful of the Pacific and rubbing her eyes.

– Why don't you stick with me? I'll find you a good wave.

– Thanks. Aren't you Ken Bradshaw?

Admittedly he had to do some pretty fancy talking to explain how come he and Foo were supposed to be at loggerheads. Mark and me? Yeah, I've heard the rumours. It's a media thing. They like to exaggerate this stuff. We're like brothers. Comrades. Buddies. And even brothers have their squabbles from time to time, you know how it is. He didn't mention Cain and Abel. Turned out she had a younger brother, back in Brazil. She knew how irritating they could be.

The great thing about Serena was: at least she could speak English.

It took about a week. A week is a long time in the sexual politics of the North Shore. A week and then she moved out of Foo's place and into Bradshaw's. Of course, she had to sleep with him. It was the only way he could get her out of Foo's evil clutches and into his own. Foo hadn't fully calculated quite how ripe she was for the taking. She couldn't be expected to remain a holy virgin for ever. That was the weak spot in the system. She too had desires, like Foo, like Bradshaw. Perhaps, ultimately (I can only speculate), she may have regretted the whole thing and might even have agreed with Foo that everything depended on her remaining intact, sacrosanct.

Bradshaw had destroyed Foo's Brazilian system, without really meaning to do it. He would gladly have stolen the system too. The whole thing came apart pretty quickly after that. No more Brazilian bodyboarders, not en masse anyway. Consider Foo's reaction – and Pang's. Much knitting of brows and clenching of fists. Bradshaw had won. But after the smoke of battle had cleared, Foo liked to think, in retrospect, that maybe there were going to be diminishing returns anyway, that they had probably started to exhaust the reserve of raw material. He would have to think of a new scheme. He knew that Bradshaw had moved in and stolen his talisman, his lucky mascot. Without her the system just wouldn't work any more. He took a fatalistic line. It was destiny, after all. Bradshaw was just one of the myriad forms of fate.

Foo's consolation, when he stopped to think about it, was this: Bradshaw may have got his hooks into Serena, but he didn't have the system. He had simply destroyed the system, in his bull-in-a-china-shop way. He hadn't really understood the infinite subtlety and voluntary passivity required to make it work. You had to refuse, and then everything would come to you, without trying, effortlessly. Bradshaw laboured harder for lesser results. It wasn't a good exchange.

Serena was everything a Brazilian bodyboarder should be. She had skin the colour of cappuccino, hair as long as the Amazon, and brown eyes so deep you could dive in, swim around for a while, then drown. Bradshaw really enjoyed having her in his house. For a while. A few nights. But in the end he was left wondering how to get her out again. Let's face it, he had never been that crazy about bodyboarders in the first place. Had had to deal with a few of them who got in his way. Now Serena was threatening to disturb his space-cadet time-table and throw off his strict training regime. He hoped he wouldn't have to resort to the old chicken gun again.

12

The Eddie, Part 1

So Bradshaw had won. But he also knew that he had lost. There was no more simple, unequivocal, undisputed numero uno. No more last man, on the last wave, all alone. The lone surfer, *the* Surfer. Maybe he was still God out there, but now he knew he had a rival. Foo had made it past Bradshaw's blockade. He was now a fully certified contender at the Bay. A *Surfer* magazine article of 1986 pictures Foo standing on the cliff above Waimea, like Zeus presiding over Mount Olympus, his giant gun, twice his size, poking up right over the horizon, and the camera is looking down on the church tower far below, and Foo is planted solidly on a chunk of volcanic rock. It is obvious that Foo is staking his claim. He owns the Bay.

'Mark Foo is now known primarily as a Waimea man,' notes the writer, Matt Warshaw, an old friend of his from those early half-hearted pro circuit days, the era before destiny beckoned. 'At Waimea, he's fast becoming a legend.' (I could imagine Bradshaw's derisive reaction: he's only a legend *in his own mind.*)

In the picture Foo stands alone. The image is misleading. In reality Foo was never 'alone' (as Bradshaw said of 1982–3). There was no more 'alone' at Waimea. There was always a small crowd out there. Not just Bradshaw and his buddies, the men with beards. There was always someone else trying to muscle in on the act (that young whippersnapper, Brock Little, for one). Foo accepted this. It was the destiny of the Bay, to attract more attention, just as it was his destiny to be there and attract more attention than anyone else. Reality and appearance were one.

Ace Cool, who followed in Foo's wake on 18 January 1985, was always out there trying to trump Foo. His whole act was geared towards the pursuit not just of big waves but of the biggest wave, period. If he didn't quite have the skill and finesse to choreograph a vote-winning routine across the stage of giant waves, he nevertheless had a grudging awareness of his own limitations, and therefore picked on the one thing about which there could be no dispute: sheer brute size. Quantity not quality, that was the thing. Ace was laughed at and scorned, not just by Bradshaw. 'Hey, whatever you do,' Foo said to me, and he was more sympathetic than most, 'don't mention my name in the same paragraph as Ace.'

Ace was still foaming with a torrent of wild talk: 'It's God's playground out there. I want to assume the throne of the big-wave maniacs. My rightful place is at the top. Yea, though I walk through the valley of the shadow of death I have the biggest surfboard ever built.' Crazy guy? The evidence is all there. Anywhere else he'd probably be certified and locked up and sedated. And yet. I couldn't help feeling, every time I ran into Ace, that he was being unjustly scapegoated, because in many ways he typified and expressed all those things that everyone else was thinking but was just not quite so upfront and out loud about. Didn't they all want to be 'Chairman of the Board', as Ace put it neatly? In truth, everyone on the North Shore, and especially Foo and Bradshaw, all wanted one thing: to hold the record for the biggest wave. Nothing else really mattered. It was a simple, clear-cut and seemingly impossible ambition.

Ace had actually had a T-shirt printed – and produced in volume – bearing a photograph of him on an enormous man-eating wave that goes right off the edge of the picture, stating flat out: 'THE BIGGEST WAVE'. A video appeared, entitled, a touch more modestly, *In Search of the Biggest Wave*. And yet Ace was never really satisfied. He could not rest on his laurels. He didn't even have any laurels. Not everyone accepted his claims. In fact hardly anyone did. I was probably one of the few who bought the T-shirt and listened sympathetically to him. To me, if it looked the biggest, it was the biggest. And it was obvious to me that just about everyone wanted the biggest wave; they just weren't owning up to it. This was where I somewhat parted company with Foo. If you were going to accept that being and appearing were one, then you had to stick with it, all the way, and not make an exception in the case of Ace.

Ace sought me out specifically to tell me about it. He knew I was writing some articles for *The Times* and he wanted to make sure that *The Times* got it straight, not as smeared and distorted and traduced in the second-hand coffee-bar gossip of the North Shore. That was just hearsay; I was getting it straight from the horse's mouth, I was getting the truth, the only story that was fit to print. Listening to Ace, who speaks at about 100 mph, I sometimes felt as if I was standing under Niagara.

It was 5 January 1985. A couple of weeks before the Biggest

Wave Never Ridden. And it was a full 35 feet if it was an inch. Ace had arranged for a helicopter to drop him and his board (all 12 foot 6 inches of it) off at what he was calling Fifth Reef Pipeline, an outer reef, the kind of place that could conceivably go beyond Waimea. You had to have a helicopter, Ace argued, it was too big to get out there any other way. The fact that it was also more spectacular and high-profile that way was the icing on the cake. He was paddling around, looking to get into position when the mother of all waves, the one with his name on it, reared up out of the void, licked him up and spat him right out. I had no doubts. I was already wearing the T-shirt. I had sent the postcards. I had watched the video. Still Ace insisted, looking around for a point of comparison. 'It was as big as that tree over there.' The tree was a huge monkeypod, spreading out like a cloud, ballooning out over a two-storey building, disappearing into the night sky, probably a good hundred or more years old, and which I would have called a good 40 or 50 feet high.

If anything could be called a mountain among waves, this was it. I wouldn't even put a figure on it. It looked like an infinite green wall, topped off by an avalanche, with an extremely small man, Lilliputian in scale, scribbling a line down it. That man was Ace. There was no argument about that. But absolutely everything else was contentious. 'I was laughing to myself,' Bradshaw recalled when I asked him about 5 January, 'because I could see Ace out there paddling around and it wasn't even twenty feet.' According to Bradshaw, that's why there was no one else out there that day, not because it was too big but because it wasn't big enough. Other hardline sceptics maintained that the picture distorted the true size of the wave because it was taken from above – from the helicopter – and you couldn't see where the base was. Where did you start measuring from? The aerial perspective doubled the size of the wave *at least*!

Ace had been hoping that after his monster ride the helicopter would pick him up again and whisk him back to the beach where, given a hero's welcome, he would be surrounded by jubilant crowds, beautiful girls would kiss him and tenderly place fragrant leis around his neck, and small boys would ask him for his autograph, and movie moguls would be falling over themselves and saying, 'Sign here, son!' But it didn't quite work out like that. The helicopter was worried about running out of juice and vamoosed, leaving him to paddle a mile or so in to shore where he was greeted by precisely no one, and eventually ran into a great tide of derision.

There was an element of tragedy in Ace Cool's story. 'I had done everything I set out to do,' Ace lamented, 'and nobody took me seriously.' Most people thought he hadn't ridden the biggest wave, he just had the biggest mouth. Bradshaw heaped scorn on Ace's use of technology. He was a purist. If you couldn't swim out there, you didn't deserve to be out there. A man on a board on a wave, that's all there was. Everything else was just theatrics. OK, take a helicopter, take a ship, just make sure he has a submarine to scrape him off the bottom too! (In fact Ace had recently taken to paddling out with a two-minute miniature oxygen tank strapped to his trunks just to be on the safe side.)

Ace hadn't earned the respect of his peers and he still wasn't as famous as Mickey Mouse or Snoopy. But he had a plan. 'I'm aiming for forty-five feet this time,' he announced to the world, 'that'll settle the argument.' He had a theory that Kaena Point, at the extreme west end of the North Shore, beset with rocks and cliffs and swirling currents, would tee up the right wave at some point. He called it 'the final frontier'.

There were other melancholy cases of good decent surfers who nevertheless failed to register on the North Shore Richter scale. Lord Ted was one of them. He took time off from his relentless pursuit of the perfect woman to found a board-making company called Excalibur. He rented out one of Foo's cabins in the new Backpackers 'village', walked down to Waimea and rode boards decorated with a flaming sword of truth and justice. He funded outings to the beach for under-privileged kids. His slogan was 'Spreading the Spirit'. And he railed at not being taken seriously. He was probably the most serious surfer ever. Brought up on a diet of Winston Churchill and the *Dam Busters*, he used to restage battles from the Second World War on his bedroom floor, using toy soldiers; and when he went out to surf he was surfing to save the world from tyranny. Like Foo, like Bradshaw, he never really made it on the pro circuit. He was convinced that the judges didn't really want a British aristocrat to score too highly. He suffered from being over-privileged. Surfing big waves represented a kind of salvation to him: there could be no ambiguity or subjectivity in that. He didn't need judges, just the respect of his peers. He enrolled as a law student at Hawaii State University down in Honolulu, but that was just a cover and he set up camp on the North Shore and focused all his attention on Waimea Bay. 'It's like jumping off the top of a three-storey house,' he once told me, 'and then having the house chase you down the street.' But, in Ted's case, the house was winning. Unlike Foo, unlike Bradshaw, he never really made it there either. Not many did. Like Ace, he was seen as an amiable eccentric at best, in other words, a loser. But he refused to accept this judgement and struggled heroically against the consensus, the opinion of the majority. What did *they* know anyhow?

There was, in short, endless debate up and down the length of the North Shore (there was no breadth to speak of), discussion, bickering, squabbles, disputes, duels being fought, about who was in and who was out, who deserved to be taken seriously, who was a serious contender and who was just faking it. And who really had surfed the biggest wave? What the place needed was an arbitrator, an overseer, an ombuds-man, to sort it all out. Quiksilver ('Surfing's biggest, richest, and most successful company according to *The Encyclopedia of Surfing*) deserve the credit for coming up with one. Just as Eddie Aikau, when he was around, strove to resolve all quarrels, so too the point of *the* Eddie was to settle the argument, once and for all, and provide a clear and author-itative judgement.

Around the time I first started turning up regularly on the North Shore, the word 'Eddie' acquired a new meaning. It no longer referred to a particular human being, recently de-ceased. It now denoted a surfing contest. Quiksilver named it 'The Quiksilver in Memory of Eddie Aikau': if it was going to be shortened to anything, they felt, it should have been known as 'The Quiksilver'. But 'the Eddie' it became, revered, idolised, just as much as the man himself. The two were one; the contest became not just a commemoration, an act of surfing nostalgia, but a sporting reincarnation of the spirit of Eddie. The Eddie *was* Eddie. The whole thing had a slightly mystical feel about it. And it was as elusive as a ghost.

'Psst. The Eddie's on tomorrow. It's definite. Get ready.' These words, when whispered around the bars and cafés of the North Shore, used to send me into raptures. It was the greatest contest in the world, bigger than the World Cup, or the World Series, or the Superbowl, or all of them bundled together into one. It was unique, it was the ultimate. It boasted the richest prize in surfing ($50,000, soon raised to $55,000). It could only take place at Real Waimea, during a waiting period from November through to February, whenever the waves had attained a minimum height of 20 feet – nothing less would do. (There had in fact been a premature, inauthentic Eddie contest held at Sunset in 1984 in mere 6–8-foot surf with a derisory $5,000 going to the winner: the *real* Eddie upped the ante on all fronts.) Each contestant in the thirty-man field had two shots at it, two windows of forty-five minutes each, with four men per slot. It was fair and it was final. I lived, like so many others on the North Shore, in a state of perpetual anticipation, waiting for it to be called on. But whenever I was ready the Eddie was not. I turned up and the waves turned down. It always happened just before I flew in or just after I flew out. But all the time I was there the talk was always of the last Eddie or the next one. And the less it happened the more talk there was about it, flooding in to fill the vacuum.

Not everyone was happy about it. There was only a finite number of 'invitees'. And not everyone who thought they ought to be there was invited. The Willis Brothers, for example, Michael and Milton, they didn't even get a look-in, not even as 'alternates' (the back-up list of replacements if the A-list didn't turn up). They weren't being allowed to get to the starting line. 'All I want is my shot,' Michael said. The whole thing was just a sham, they thought, an advertising scam designed to put Quiksilver guys up front. It wasn't a real contest, it was fixed from the beginning. 'I've been hosed,' said Ted Deerhurst. The Nazis hadn't won the war, they had just taken over at Quiksilver instead, it was all part of the plan.

Ace Cool managed to sneak into the first contest (and tied for twelfth place), but only that first one, and after that he was in the same boat as the Willises and Ted: the boat of the damned, the excommunicated, the outsiders and marginals, not taken seriously enough by the big corporation. Which only served to justify the righteousness of their original claim.

The first Eddie took place in 1986. It was 23 February, barely a week before the end of the holding period. Everyone agreed that Bradshaw and Foo were the main contenders. All the smart money was on one or the other, with Bradshaw having a slight edge. They had been out training, preparing, thinking about nothing much else. This was what they had been born for. And the event itself seemed to be bearing out the judgement of the punters. Waimea was massive, stormy, architectural that day: great hunks of water, blocks like pure stone, wedge-shaped pyramids, were ledging up out of the turbulent Pacific, seemingly crafted with draughtsmanlike precision. They could have been designed for a couple of big-wave graffiti artists to scrawl their signature all over them.

Going into the last few minutes, Bradshaw was in the lead and he knew it. 'It was all going according to plan,' he said. 'I honestly thought it was all over. I was first and Foo was second. That was fair.'

But maybe Foo didn't think it was fair. Maybe he didn't want to be runner-up. And, more to the point, in his clear-sighted materialistic way, he certainly hadn't given up all hope of winning the $50,000 first prize. It would be the biggest-ever single payout in the history of surfing. But he was running short on time, which might explain why Foo took off on an obvious close-out. It was big but it was never going to be a rideable wave. Bradshaw saw it, evaluated it and dismissed it. It wasn't even worth paddling for. For Foo, on the other hand, it could be his last chance of glory and a small fortune. He got to his feet, got down the face and managed to cling on while the 25-footer exploded right on his heels, threatening to engulf him. Foo straightened out to stay ahead of the raging white water, and eventually went down on his chest and wrapped his arms tight round the rails just to avoid being blown off. So he came in prone, lying down, on his belly, not proudly upright, towering over the maelstrom. And *still* the judges liked it.

Bradshaw could never figure that out and always assumed there had to be some kind of pro-Foo, anti-Bradshaw conspiracy going on right under his nose. Had Foo paid these guys money? What was the deal? But, in truth, Waimea was not an ordinary wave. It wasn't so much a question of getting in a high-performance ride, the way it was on lesser waves, at the typical pro contest, even at Sunset. It was just a question of doing it, being there, not pulling back, and mingling with madness, come what may. I think the judges had a legitimate point. Bradshaw didn't see it that way though. 'They overscored him,' he asserted point-blank (he said exactly the same thing straight after the contest and many years later: any other opinion just bounced off him). 'I don't know why. Because he's Foo, I don't know. There's a lot of subjectivity in judging.' Bradshaw had a legitimate point here: the judges were probably seduced by Foo, bewitched, bedazzled, beguiled into giving him higher marks than, objectively, analytically speaking, he really deserved. That was the way Foo was. It was like a Brazilian system, applied to judges.

Whatever the explanation, the fact was that Foo was ahead. It was the penultimate ride of the day. History allows only one more wave to be successfully mastered and ridden on that afternoon in January 1986. If there was any justice in the world it should have been Bradshaw's wave, his chance to get back at Foo and prove once and for all that he still had the edge. But it didn't work out like that.

Clyde Aikau was sitting on his board, dreaming, half-waiting for a wave, drifting off, not really thinking about the contest any more. He had already given up any serious hopes of winning, he was somewhere in the pack. It was between Foo and Bradshaw now, everybody knew that. Clyde was Eddie Aikau's older brother and riding a ten-year-old board that had once belonged to Eddie. In 1978, after the *Hokule'a* had capsized, he had spent days out in the channels between the islands in a helicopter, trawling up and down, fruitlessly searching for any sign of Eddie. It was he who had spotted Eddie's board. Now he looked back at the old orange lifeguard tower and he couldn't help thinking about the way it used to be at Waimea when Eddie was still around and they would come out here and catch the biggest waves ever and there was no such thing as a contest, and no money either. It was funny, in those days he didn't feel poor, now he scratched a living as a beach boy in Waikiki, hiring out boards to tourists and occasionally taking out honoured guests for personal instruction. He'd never really seen that coming, but then he hadn't really looked ahead to anything in particular, he'd just enjoyed the waves and being out there with Eddie without ever really thinking about the future. Now he was bigger and heavier and older, he had a beard, and the world seemed to be passing him by, and he didn't really care two hoots anyway.

He looked out to sea. There were a couple of giant turtles way out beyond the line-up, ducking and diving. Clyde couldn't help being impressed by their indifference to the proceedings. No Eddie contest for these guys. They were calm and composed in the midst of what seemed to Clyde to be potentially life-threatening waves. Surely if they got in the wrong spot the wave could take them and dump them and rip their shells right off and chew them up and tear their defenceless bodies to shreds? And yet here they were, swimming around, ruminatively poking their wizened, ancient heads up, checking out the surfers, waving a flipper, gliding away again. *Cool turtles*, Clyde said to himself. What the hell am I doing in this stupid contest anyway? I ought to be doing what the turtles are doing, they weren't worrying about who was first and who was second and whose name was on the cheque. Then, as they came up again and went through their routine, Clyde got the crazy idea that maybe these turtles were waving their flippers at *him* and him alone: *Hey Clyde!* they seemed to be saying, *Get your big fat ass over here.*

That was what Clyde thought. And as he looked at them more closely they put him in mind of a couple of people he had known: one of them looked like Eddie and the other one bore a strange resemblance to José Angel. Angel, the fearless Angel, the schoolteacher and surfer who had died in Hawaii while diving several hundred feet down, looking for pearls, and whose body, like Eddie's, had never been found. Clyde didn't see turtles any more; all he could see was Eddie and José, come back to haunt him and taunt him. *What's the matter, Clyde?* the two turtles-that-were-not-turtles were saying to him, *Don't you recognise us?* He recognised them all right. It seemed to Clyde that the *mana* (the soul, spirit or 'force') of the two men had somehow entered into these turtles, that they were, in some way, none other than Eddie Aikau and José Angel. And then he realised that they had become his *aumakua*, or spiritual guardians, his guardian angels. Do I need looking after? Clyde thought. Am I going insane? But the Bay permitted madness. More, it *required* it: so you *had* to be crazy to paddle out here in the first place. Waimea was a lunatic asylum, you might just as well embrace the madness. Surrender. Why struggle?

Follow us! It was the turtles again, talking to him. OK, so he was nuts, maybe it was all in his head, and he was hearing voices, but he didn't have any better ideas right then, so he went ahead and followed them. Clyde was, to all intents and purposes, in a trance. He had been hypnotised by a couple of large cranky old sea turtles (temporarily possessed by the spirit forms of two dead surfers) who were leading him – or maybe misleading him – either to salvation or perdition.

Clyde paddled out beyond the line-up, far away from the three other men in his heat, far from Foo and Bradshaw. Which showed he had to be crazy, because he knew they knew what they were doing, if anyone did. By rights he ought to stick with them. Clyde knew full well that he was way out of position for the kind of sets that had been coming through, but he didn't care. All he was doing was following the turtles, messing around with Eddie and José the way they had always done in the old days. To tell the truth, he had virtually forgotten all about the waves, didn't really know why he was supposed to be out here any more, no reason other than communing with turtles. So when the horizon rose up and moulded itself into a whale, a great turquoise humpback, Clyde looked at it at first with a kind of amazement, bewilderment, incredulity. What the hell was that coming at him, blocking out half the sky?

Clyde, Eddie said to him, *it's your wave, big brother. It was meant for you and only you.*

It's going to lift you right up to heaven, said Angel.

Clyde turned his board around and started stroking. He had

an unusual sense of inevitability about what he was doing that day. He didn't really have to look over his shoulder to position himself. The wave was coming just for him. It was his wave and nobody else's. He felt it slide under him and lift him up towards heaven.

A hooter sounded, like a trumpet, the last trumpet. It was the end of the contest. Clyde Aikau was judged to have ridden the biggest wave of the day. It pushed him right up through the field. Foo and Clyde were tied on the same number of points. For a while there was confusion on the beach. Could you have a tie in the Eddie? Would they share the cheque? Then the judges starting 'counting back' (nobody had the slightest idea what that meant) and, lo, Clyde Aikau had won, by a whisker, from Mark Foo, with Ken Bradshaw in third place.

Clyde was too emotional to speak at first. Finally, with tears streaming down his cheeks, he stutteringly dedicated his victory to Eddie, his little brother. 'He was with me out there,' was all he said. He didn't mention the turtles till later.

The head judge, Jack Shipley, spoke as if he had had nothing at all to do with the final result: 'To have it come out that way . . . It was almost too much to bear. That Hawaiian *mana* stuff is pretty awesome.' What with the spirit of Eddie running around and all those turtles, it couldn't have come out any other way. It had to be an Aikau. As Stuart Coleman writes in his lyrical biography, *Eddie Would Go*, 'to this day, Clyde still believes the turtles were the guiding spirits of José Angel and Eddie – together, they had won the contest.' It was a beautiful story, a fairy tale that had come true in a tough, ruthless world.

13

Judgement Day

There is a more cynical interpretation of Clyde Aikau's victory that day. Nobody doubts that he was an outstanding surfer and perfectly capable of winning the contest on a good day. He was not a nobody at the Bay. He was a serious contender. But it was also true that certain people wanted him to win, and they made sure that he did win. And we are not talking about Eddie and José here, not *mana*, but real, living people, the kind of people capable of influencing the outcomes of real surfing contests and spinning them around this way or that. Nobody said it at the time, but a lot of people thought it.

Fix! If anything had ever been fixed, the first Eddie had. It had 'fix' written all over it: it was like one of those pseudo-democracies where everyone turns up and votes but in reality who gets to be President is a foregone conclusion, a done deal signed and sealed long in advance. All the guy had to do was turn up. Quiksilver, rumour had it, secretly wanted to give the money to the Aikaus. And, in fact, a lot of other people thought this was all fine and dandy, it was the correct

Hawaiian thing to do, it showed 'respect' to the family. I have no way of knowing or determining which of these two versions of history is true — the turtles/guardian angels or the fixers swinging it back on the beach for Eddie's big brother. What I do know is that Clyde should never have been given the title, because it made it look as if it was a fix. The contest not only had to be fair and square, it had to be seen to be fair, too. But it wasn't.

Surfer magazine got around the problem by simply air-brushing Clyde out. Clyde may have received the cheque but he wasn't really the story. The cover shot of Foo (wearing a white Eddie contest jersey with the number 1 printed across it) and the headline 'WINNING MOVES' implied that (a) Foo could have won, maybe (b) Foo should have won and (c) who really cared about one result anyway (which would be uncool), it all comes down to style and attitude. Clyde was a symbolic winner, a kind of mascot and icon for the whole contest, the token native Hawaiian. But the main mover had been Foo. With Bradshaw coming up behind.

Either way, Bradshaw still didn't like it. By 1990 he was ready to get things straight. No turtles this time, no fixing, no nothing. Nothing but the truth, the whole truth. Waimea Bay was the ultimate courtroom, the supreme court, in which the guilty would be punished and the innocent set free. Bradshaw had kept his faith in Waimea, despite everything. It had taken four long years for another Eddie to come around. That was the way the Eddie was. Majestic and unpredictable. The Bay had been firing off and on; Darrick Doerner (who worked as a lifeguard at Waimea and occupied Eddie's old tower) had ridden a wave some reckoned at 35 foot in 1988; all the riders had been gearing themselves up for the main event: but it was never consistent enough for the contest to be called on. And now, at last, on Sunday 21 January 1990, the day of judgement had finally dawned. As usual, at this precise point, I was on the wrong side of the planet, having spent December and half of January on the North Shore in a permanent state of wild anticipation.

It was big and it was mighty, the biggest swell, everyone was saying, to hit the North Shore in over a decade, and today the truth would be out, beyond appeal. Bradshaw was at his peak. He had been training fanatically and preparing for just this day. He was confident. He was ready. In truth, he had been ready for years. Maybe, as he said later, he was 'almost too ready'. Too confident.

In the days leading up to the Eddie – as I knew only too well – there had been some substantial swells at Waimea. One 18-foot day – Christmas Day, to be precise – had taken out one of the bookies' favourites, Titus Kinimaka from Kauai (who not only played in a rock band but looked as if he was carved out of rock), after he was clubbed down by the lip and sustained a fractured femur and had to be rescued by surfing samaritans like the Willis Brothers and was finally pulled out in agony by a chopper. There were some 20-foot-plus episodes, not sustained, not quite Eddie-worthy, but significant enough all the same to bust a big-wave board. Snap it in two, like a femur. It could have been anyone's but, in fact, it was Bradshaw's. It was his favoured big-wave board, the 9-foot 10-inch, the one he had been planning to win the Eddie on; and now it was garbage. It wasn't just the board that was shattered – it felt almost like a bereavement to Bradshaw. He laid the old board to rest in his backyard; he couldn't bear to part with it completely.

Bradshaw set to work, feverishly sculpting and planing a fresh blank. He worked all day and the next to produce a couple of boards (he couldn't rely on just one), one shorter, one longer. And he stayed up most of the night sanding and fine-tuning and caressing and glassing and making it right. At the end of it all he had two rock-solid brand-new boards. But smashing up your favourite board is not like breaking a string at Wimbledon, picking up a new racket and going straight back out again: it's more like bringing a new being into the world. There has to be bonding between man and board. Trust, communion, mutual adjustment – all these considerations enter into this obscure and precarious liaison, and more: and it all takes time; and Bradshaw didn't have a whole lot of time.

So he went out the next day, tested out the smaller board. It was wobbly, it just didn't feel right. Was it him? Was it the board? He couldn't quite put his finger on it. 'I didn't like the way it felt,' he says. The day of the Eddie dawned – the very next day – and Bradshaw had only one board, a 10-foot-6-inch, and he had never ridden it before, not once. A virgin board, completely untried, untested. Bradshaw hadn't had time to get to know it, didn't feel relaxed with it. It was like a first date. He was nervous. What if she didn't like him?

And one more thing: he was 'stressed' about his house too, not just the boards. He had been shaping his house off and on like a maniac – had stripped it, taken the entire roof off, planning to make it bigger and extend upwards, all on his own. It had to be at least as tall as one of the waves at Waimea; anything less would be too small. And the next thing he knew he was in a heat for the Eddie. He knew he should have finished the house before winter. So he was half-desperately waiting for a big swell, half-panicking that a storm could blow his house down. He was preoccupied, jittery, torn. The old Bradshaw wouldn't have let a house get in his way. Now the house, in its stripped-down, disassembled, defenceless form, was like an allegory of Bradshaw and big waves. He wanted it bigger than ever – small was definitely not beautiful – but at the same time he was not quite 100 per cent prepared and geared up for the job. His timing was all out of whack.

Foo, in contrast, had been preparing by *not* preparing. It hadn't always been that way, of course. The winter after 1985 he was as honed, toned, cut, smooth and sharp as a new card. And the one after that. Coming that close in the last Eddie, he was determined not to blow the next one. The Eddie became (in Dennis Pang's words) 'Foo's mission'. Apart from anything else, he could really do with the fifty grand. He had the sense that his moment of destiny had come at last. Everything pointed that way. All he needed was to give destiny a slight nudge. Maybe, he thought, after all the hassles with Bradshaw, and the big wipeouts, and the perpetual struggle to attain the biggest waves, he had been too light. Here he was in his late twenties, nearly thirty, and he was still built too much like a boy. So, together with Dennis Pang, he would go along to North Shore Neck & Back, up by Velzyland, to get himself in prime shape for the final showdown. That time the Old Man had ducked him and bitten chunks out of his board, he just wasn't ready, that was all. He had taken him by surprise. Well, he was going to be ready this time. Bradshaw was never going to get the drop on him again.

Pang just did a little loosening and flexing: he was happy to be slim and sinewy. Foo, on the other hand, was tooling himself up, racking up the ammunition. So he kept on pumping and pounding on the veranda at Neck & Back long after Pang had given up and gone home. He did press-ups and chin-ups and crunches, he worked his way right up through the weights, homing in on arms and shoulders and pecs and biceps and triceps and deltoids, even glutes, everything, anything that could give him an extra push, add another weapon to the armoury.

'If I want to surf big waves,' he told George Cromack, 'I have to be big.' It made sense. Cromack was a chiropractor who sponsored Foo and Pang and wrote articles as 'Doc Surf' for H_3O, the magazine Foo co-edited. According to Pang, Cromack 'was a shitty surfer but he knew everything about nutrition, alternative medicine, and body-building'. Following his advice, Foo bulked up, but he balanced it out with a regime of sauna, ultrasound, regular chiropractic manipulation, and pineapple smoothies with extra iron. Foo loved the idea of taking extra iron. He thought it would make him the Iron Man.

And then another winter came and went and still no Eddie. One time it looked as if it was going to happen. George Downing, contest director and old-school big-wave virtuoso, called it on, then he started wavering. Maybe it was too big and out of control. He didn't want to lose anybody. Foo was impatient to get out. He went to see Downing. 'You've got to let us go,' he said. 'Why?' asked Downing. 'Eddie,' said Foo, 'Eddie would go.' As usual with Foo, there were a couple of journalists around, tuning in. He gave an instant interview; they picked up on the phrase, then Quiksilver picked it up, and it soon became the official slogan of the entire contest. 'EDDIE WOULD GO' was everywhere, all over town.

There were ironies: (1) Foo didn't get a penny for it. 'I shoulda got paid for that,' he said. But he'd signed a waiver. There was some small print somewhere which said that Quiksilver never had to pay anyone anything if they didn't feel like it; (2) Maybe Eddie would go, but George Downing wouldn't go. The year Foo came up with that now proverbial statement, the Eddie didn't take place yet again.

And it kept on not taking place. It was mystifying. Some said Quiksilver didn't want to pay out all that dough. They wanted the kudos to be gained from theoretically holding the contest, but they were saving on any outlay involved in it really happening. The fix had gone in. The rumours were endless. And then Foo, the new, more muscular Foo, finally worked it out: he was overdoing it. The more he prepared for the Eddie, the more he visualised and anticipated and pumped, waking up every morning and running to the window and looking out for signs, the less it was ever going to happen. So he pulled back, he stopped going to North Shore Neck & Back, he blanked the Eddie out of his mind, and tried concentrating on other things.

Mainly Brazilians. That was when I used to run into him at discos, grooving the night away. And I used to marvel that he could be so relaxed when he might be surfing for his life the next day. I didn't know then that it was all part of his secret plan, his Eddie strategy. The more indifferent and utterly unprepared he was, the more he danced and wrote articles and did radio gigs and fronted TV documentaries and floated new deals, the more he was surreptitiously intent on closing out the Eddie. By day he did anything, everything, except the Eddie. By night he still dreamed of the Eddie. And his scheme worked, almost too well: just at the point when he had almost succeeded in scrubbing it from his brain – 'the Eddie?' he said to me, one evening at the Turtle Bay, 'What is that?' (he thought I was too obsessed, I didn't understand the subtlety of the Foo theory then) – it *happened*. Finally, Eddie Went (Again).

So it was that Foo and Bradshaw were level on the starting

line: neither of them was ready. They *had been* ready but history and destiny had not; now history and destiny were ready, and Foo and Bradshaw had their pants down. That was the way history and destiny were: unforgiving. And 21 January 1990, the day of the Eddie, was no more forgiving than any other day.

Heat 1

It was a flaky and unpredictable kind of day. Stormy and overcast. Grey. John Callahan, the *Surfing* photographer, hated it. 'You wait years for the Eddie and it finally comes off, traffic stacked up both ways on the Kam Highway and two thousand spectators on the beach – and the light is terrible.' He hiked up to the *heiau* on the cliffs and prayed for the clouds to break.

The first heat hit the water at 11 a.m. The swell was very up and down – inconsistent. Bradshaw was not certain they were ever going to get a really good set. Not to get the waves, that would be the worst thing, not to have a canvas to work on. Not to have his shot.

Then a big, beefy, bruiser of a wave finally came through, a full 30-footer, virtually designed for Bradshaw, with Bradshaw's name all over it. It was the best set of the day, no question: his due, his just reward, and he was in pole position. Everything had come together just the way he always knew it would. He saw it coming with plenty of time, lined himself up, got in early, stood up – and, suddenly, there was Brock Little, Brock fucking Little, 10 or 20 yards over on his inside, yelling out, nice as pie, 'OK, I've got this one covered, Kenny.'

Aged twenty-two, from Bradshaw's point of view, even

from Foo's, Brock Little was still a kid. He had been their collective blind spot for a few years now. When Waimea was going off in 1982–3, he was living up on Pupukea Heights, up behind Foodland, just a cycle-ride away. Waimea, even at 20 foot, was the only place that was conceivably surfable then. He was only fifteen at the time, but he didn't have any other options, he had to do it. His dad was a teacher at Punahoe (like Peter Cole), but Brock wanted to be a firefighter and he looked on Waimea – although it was the exact opposite – as a fire blowing up and he had to go in with his big hose and blast it. Maybe he'd get singed in the process, but he didn't care. He was spontaneous, with a loose-arm, straight-back style. He was what they called a 'charger'; 'all *balls*' is how Roger Erickson described him. Many years later Brock would realise this about himself: he was actually a full-on masochist. He really liked the pain. For example: once a whole bunch of bigger kids set on him and beat the bejaysus out of him – and every time one of them would hit him or kick him, he would laugh or give a crooked, blood-spattered grin – and eventually they fled in fear of this kid who was even crazier than they were. It was true, he really liked the pain, it gave him some kind of an immense buzz. 'I don't mind bleeding,' he once told *Interview* magazine, 'and I don't mind getting held underwater. If I get into a radical experience – getting into a fight, or driving fast, or riding a huge wave – and live through it, I'm totally stoked.'

His attitude gave him a tremendous edge in big-wave surfing. Whereas everybody else looked as though they were doing something dangerous and potentially life-threatening, almost suicidal, but were in fact (like Bradshaw, above all) being careful, cautious, calculating, selective, only going when there was a reasonable chance of making it (even

Ace didn't *deliberately* do anything stupid), Brock really was being semi-suicidal; he was knowingly putting himself in the way of harm, and still laughing as he went down yet again and took another massive beating. This was his idea of fun: 'the funnest thing ever'. Everyone feared the 'close-outs' at Waimea, where the face folds and clenches up into a giant fist: everyone except Brock, who actively set out to 'catch a close-out'. It didn't matter how heavy the wave was or how badly it mauled him, walloping him into the reef, thumping all the air out of him, Brock was convinced he was flying in some kind of flaming chariot and his head was resting on a pillow of clouds. For Brock, everything bad was good. The more insane, the more sensible. Gradually he had been working his way up the Waimea ladder. He was given his shot as an 'alternate' at the first Eddie. Somebody dropped out, George Downing had seen this kid surfing fearlessly before the contest, and he stepped in and – right out of the blue – placed fourth behind Aikau, Foo and Bradshaw. He was a mere nineteen at the time. He couldn't go out and buy a drink (of the alcoholic kind) but he could sure go and try to get on top of a lot of it (of the saltier kind) or have it come rushing irresistibly down into his lungs. He may not have registered on the Foo/Bradshaw barometer, but many more detached observers saw him as the coming man. Naturally, this time around he was on the A-list, given his designated spot in the Eddie, not among the alternates or rank outsiders. He was in as of right. And he had a strategy: be a hassler, watch Bradshaw and then get inside him. He'd done it before.

All of which might help to explain what Brock Little was doing here, 10 or 20 yards over on Bradshaw's inside, and Bradshaw didn't even notice him. Not, that is, until he was saying to him, 'OK, I've got this one covered, Kenny.' Then

Bradshaw really sat up and took notice, possibly for the very first time. In fact, he took a little too much notice. The truth is, Bradshaw could have gone, he was already standing, and in the Eddie it was legitimate: you could have more than one guy on the same wave at the same time. But, all the same, Brock was way over on his inside and that gave him a big edge; he was going to get a higher score. And then coming up behind there were at least a couple more waves in the set, with every chance that the next one or the next was going to be even bigger. This was the moment of choice for Bradshaw. Should he go or pull back?

In the end it was probably more surprise than anything else that prompted his decision. *You're dropping in on me?! You're stealing my wave?* Bradshaw had a strange sense of *déjà vu*, and he didn't like it any more the second time round either. For a moment he hesitated, bewildered, disgruntled, perturbed, incredulous, as if suspended in space. But not in time: the next instant he was going backwards, flying off the rear end of the wave, and down into the trough. You could say he pulled back, but it was more as if he was being pulled back, dragged backwards, blown off by Brock's unexpected intervention. Brock rode away all alone, perched on the head of a dark, stumbling, foaming behemoth as if bestriding an extremely large pint of Guinness.

The next wave was, as predicted, even bigger than the first. Bradshaw had been right. The trouble was, having traced the first one as far as he had, having stood up, almost taken off, he was now emphatically out of position, too far forward, and the wave was already on the verge of collapsing. So he had to work hard just to paddle over this next one: he got 90 per cent of the way up the face then forcefully shoved his way out through the back. He made the mistake of looking over his shoulder, only to see, to his astonishment, that a Japanese guy *was* on it: first Brock, then a Jap (Takao Kuga by name). Not the sort of start he was ideally looking for.

The third wave of the set really was perfect: the biggest of the bunch, wave of the day for sure, the kind of wave that would erase the memory of all the others before it, and Bradshaw was definitely on this one. He locked on, lined himself up, stroked forward with those massive unstoppable steam-engine arms of his, stood up and took off. He was set. He was already visualising the laurels, the applause of the crowd, the surreal outsize cheque cradled in his arms.

But as Bradshaw was forcing his way down, a tremendous man-hungry wind was sweeping up the face to meet him. The wind threw itself at him and Bradshaw braced himself, crouched low, and kept on striving, struggling forwards. He kept pointing the nose down the face, in the direction of glory. There must have been an instant in which all the forces were perfectly balanced and Bradshaw was frozen, looking and willing himself forwards, but going precisely nowhere, still standing, but as if paralysed, stopped dead, like a single frame in a film – and then frail flesh yielded and the blast hurled him backwards right up and off the crest, crashing down into the abyss.

'Yeah, I blew it,' Bradshaw says. The fact is that he was 'blown'. 'Then it was over.'

As Bradshaw discovered later – and this hurt him more than almost anything – Brock, having taken off on Bradshaw's wave, the wave he should have gone on, fell. He got down the face but then wiped out on the bottom turn and vanished, probably laughing as usual, under a solid 30-foot wall of water ('It was kinda cool,' he says). It was as if a thief had stolen your Van Gogh in the middle of the night and then pissed on it. It was obvious Brock was never going to make that wave. He was too far over. Bradshaw had been right all along. He could have gone, he could have made it, he could have had it all to himself, with Brock dumped in the soup somewhere. As if that wasn't bad enough, Little somehow got his teeth stuck into a mighty tube later that day, dug into it and came out again intact, almost as if he was being rewarded for stealing Bradshaw's wave.

Heat 2

The second heat was nothing. Well, maybe not nothing exactly, but the swell had tapered off, it was fifteen maybe, but *nothing*, so far as Bradshaw could see, that was going to get him back in contention. He was sunk. The dream was over. It was like a ghost of Bradshaw: 'by the time the heat was over, I hadn't done a thing. My spirit was broken. It's like I wasn't even there.'

Meanwhile, what had become of Foo? According to his theory, the more he was ready, the less he was ready; therefore the less he was ready, the more he was ready. Well, he got the 'less' part of it right. If the world was only tailored to fit the paradoxes of the Tao, then Foo would have been perfectly positioned for total victory by virtue of being out of shape and indifferent. But, in reality, Foo blew it, too. The great wind, whether real or allegorical, tore up all the plans and schemes of Bradshaw and Foo alike.

He came in with his board in three pieces and all the fins ripped off. It was worse than being worked over by Bradshaw. He went out again with a back-up board but he had lost his rhythm. Back in England, I got a letter from Banzai Betty, who had been watching the whole thing: 'Mark Foo set an example. He ate shit so bad that when the other competitors saw him they slacked off and moved over to the shoulder.' Foo putting the scare on other surfers? The Handsome One? Had he too turned into some kind of monster? The hunchback of Waimea Bay. The only one who wasn't scared was Brock Little, who was fundamentally unscareable, and just laughed at the sight of Foo screwing up. He had been laughing at the feud between Foo and Bradshaw all along. Brock laughed when he took second, too. It was no big deal. Foo was given fourteenth.

The Willis Brothers weren't in the least bit sympathetic towards either Foo or Bradshaw. They weren't sympathetic to anyone. 'Hey, at least they had their shot,' they said. 'We didn't even get a shot. We're the biggest losers of all.'

But the really bitter thing about this day? Just six months earlier Quiksilver had signed Bradshaw up as their big-wave rider. He was now officially the icon of big-wave surfing, the cover boy, getting paid big bucks just to do what he was already doing, what he always would do, infallibly, obsessively. It was the kind of deal that Foo scarcely dared dream of and Bradshaw had swung it. And the best thing about it: *they* had asked *him*. He hadn't had to go out and sell himself, hadn't had to brag and print up some fancy CV and fly to St Louis with a portfolio in his briefcase. None of that. Never had to take his shorts off. It was more a kind of respect and reward for everything he had done. And, what was more, it was the ideal omen for the future. Bradshaw was the Quiksilver guy and they were running the Eddie show – how could he lose?

But he did lose. He didn't just lose, he lost big, he lost huge, he lost spectacularly and publicly. He got spanked. He came in thirtieth out of thirty-three. It was almost more of a talking point than who actually won (in fact it was Keone Downing, son of contest director George). Quiksilver could have been cruel, but they weren't: they were tolerant, indulgent, understanding, compassionate.

– Hey, they said, it's just one contest, Kenny! Don't sweat it, brother! We're in this for the long term. Do you think we don't realise that anyone, even the great Kenny Bradshaw, can have a good day or a bad day? It's one of those things. No big deal! You'll do it next time.

And then a few months later he got the call.

– Kenny? How are you doing? You know that little conversation we had a while back? Well, all of that still applies, nothing has changed. Except, well, we've got to pull the plug. Nothing personal, you understand. It's just a redistribution of resources in the company. We have to pull back on some of our sponsorship deals.

Pull back? Nothing was said, but the implication was there. Pull back the way he had pulled back on that wave. Whatever was or wasn't said, Bradshaw knew and everyone else knew: he was being punished. He had a mortgage, possibly two mortgages, on his house, the house didn't even have a roof, and now he had no income either. He had been cut loose by the company, dumped, ruthlessly, the way he dumped girls, the way he dumped people who got in his way off their boards. It was his biggest wipeout yet. Bradshaw had willed himself to be King of Waimea. But the world had not shaped itself in accordance with his will. Somewhere there was, in all probability, a universe in which everything Bradshaw craved, he had achieved: dominion, peace, law, justice and endless great waves. But this universe was not it; it had signally failed to cooperate in Bradshaw's quest.

Meanwhile, Brock Little – who had never cared about going pro – was swimming in sponsorships (notably Gotcha) and regular pay cheques and all-expenses-paid trips to Tahiti, Fiji, Australia, Brazil, Nicaragua, Alaska, Easter Island, Ireland. (In fact even Brock felt a little bit bad about the whole deal. 'It's unfair how much I get,' he said. 'It's way more than other guys who surf big waves and I feel sort of guilty about it. It's not right. I shouldn't get so much.') The irony: Bradshaw had shaped Brock his first board when he was twelve. He had actually helped Brock get started.

Some might have been disheartened by this turn of events. Not Bradshaw. It only stiffened his resolve. He decided that his mistake all along had been to be too easygoing, too permissive, too benevolent. He just hadn't been competitive enough. Well, that was all in the past now. No more Mr Nice Guy. 'There's going to be a new Ken Bradshaw from now on,' he fumed, talking about himself in the third person, as if observing his own ego from afar, while still trying to fix the roof back on his house. 'He's going to learn from the arrogance and brashness of competition surfers.' He had a bunch of nails poking out of his mouth and took one out and drove it deep down into a beam. 'I didn't get any respect from Brock Little or Richard Schmidt [who placed third and got the *Surfer* cover], and if that's the criteria they want to create in contests, the hell with respect.' Waving his massive hammer in the air like Thor, Bradshaw blamed Eddie; it all went back to that damn *aloha* spirit, that was what had stopped him winning. 'What Eddie Aikau showed me, all that stuff about Waimea camaraderie – that stuff doesn't hold up any more. When I surf now, God help somebody if they're gonna be on the wave with me.'

Bradshaw would never back down or slack off or soften up. 'It's kind of a war out there now, and if you give up, they win.'

14

Beyond Waimea

The following winter. Bradshaw and Clyde Aikau found themselves out on the same line-up. It was some outer-reef break, not Waimea. No one else around, just the two of them. Clyde wanted to know what Bradshaw thought of the Eddie.

'It's cool,' said Bradshaw, swallowing his resentment at Quiksilver's kick in the teeth. 'You know, it's Eddie's name. It's the Aikau family.'

Clyde wasn't satisfied. 'Yeah, but what do you really think, Ken?'

'You want to know what I really think?' Bradshaw said. 'Yeah.'

Bradshaw paused. 'No, you don't want to know what I really think.'

Clyde was getting exasperated. It was worse than waiting for a good clean wave to turn up. 'Brah, we know each other a long long time. I want you to tell me. It's just you and me out here, nobody else. I want the truth.'

In vino veritas. It is one of the strange things about surfing that waves are very much like wine in this respect – and in a few others; despite all the hype and theatrics, they tend to elicit fundamental truths. 'Well,' said Bradshaw, 'I'll tell you. I think the second this contest comes to an end, the surf will come back. I don't know if this contest is right, because all it's done is to overglorify and overcrowd Waimea Bay. That's how I honestly feel, Clyde.'

Bradshaw had been right. Clyde didn't really want to know how he felt, he just thought he did. He was upset with Bradshaw, furious in fact; it was like an insult to him and his entire family, and, worse, to Waimea Bay itself. It was a kind of heresy. Aikau paddled a hundred yards away from Bradshaw, and sat there all alone, nursing his hurt feelings. Bradshaw, who knew all about hurt feelings, felt sorry for him. After a while, he paddled over to Aikau. 'I'm sorry, Clyde,' he said. 'I didn't mean any disrespect to you or your family. It's just the way I feel. But don't worry, I'll always surf in the contest, come what may.'

The second Eddie wasn't the end of the Eddie, and it certainly wasn't the end of Waimea Bay. It's still there, it still looks beautiful, when it doesn't look terrible and sublime, it still occasionally cranks out huge and shapely waves. And yet, Bradshaw had a point. That was why Aikau was hurt. He felt exactly the same way but he just didn't dare to admit it; he and his family had too much staked in Waimea. There was a sense in which the high tide had peaked at Waimea, and it was now receding, and going out fast. If a place can have a star, then Waimea's star was waning.

It was partly the fault of the Eddie, Bradshaw reflected once more as he paddled out another day – far far out – in search of some waves he could surf all alone. There was some kind of bad karma about the whole show. He had to concede that Foo had a point here: the more you wanted to hold the Eddie, the less Eddie-worthy waves there were to go around. He looked back to the pre-Eddie days, of the early eighties, when there were 20-foot days stacking up like planes over LAX. Everybody looked back to it. The age of harmony. Waimea had been consistently huge, it had been the biggest of the big-wave spots, the Holy of Holies. And now: it was flaky and, what was worse, it was crowded. Another lost paradise. Too many surfers, driven by the dream of easy Quiksilver money, had battened on to Waimea like leeches, and were sucking it dry. It was the exact opposite to rats deserting the sinking ship – *they* were sinking it.

Bradshaw couldn't help but feel that a lot of this was Foo's fault. So long as he, BRADSHAW – HAWAII, was ruling the roost, there had been order. Like a bull in a field, or a mad dog in the backyard, Bradshaw tended to keep the crowds away. He was the bouncer on the door and the club was already full to his way of thinking. Now Foo had arrived, and he had brought with him the media attention, and the circus, and the masses. Now every damn stinking kid who'd ever ridden a 2-foot wave in Florida or Atlantic City thought they should be having a crack at the Big One and flocked to the North Shore. That was the trouble with living in Mecca: too many pilgrims going past your front door. Bradshaw tried not to think too hard about when it had just been him and his gang, a handful of big-wave barons, benevolently distributing waves among one another. Waimea had had a rough democracy thrust upon it, in which every Joe had a constitutional right to be on the next big swell.

Bradshaw laughed at the crazy stunt the Willis Bros had been pulling. They already felt excluded, so they had had printed up a 'Manifesto of the Surfing Masses' – a kind of communism for beach bums – which aimed to extend the constituency, enfranchise every passing tourist and armchair wave-watcher. *Surfers of the world unite!* The Willises thought that if everybody was out there surfing the world would be a far better place. Bradshaw shook his head as he came up from under a 15-foot wall of white water. He knew better: the surf was already over-populated. There were just too many consumers for such a rare commodity, and the more demand there was the more the supply seemed to be drying up. All the media attention, the multiplying photographers on the beach, their giant lenses sticking up in the air like the quills of a porcupine, all the Foo-inspired phenomena were driving the waves away. Bradshaw knew that there was no such thing as a neutral observer, one that did not impact in some way on the thing observed. Every observer necessarily corrupted the data. And the more observers there were the more the data – in this case the waves – became corrupted.

In short, Waimea Bay was not what it used to be. Maybe it was better when it was taboo and nobody dared go out. They should have kept it a secret. Now everybody wanted a piece of the action. It wasn't right.

Which explained what Bradshaw was doing out here, beyond Waimea, and still paddling, his massive arms still churning like the blades of a paddle-steamer, powering him out into the unknown. Well, not quite unknown. It was a break which Bradshaw had pioneered. He didn't want everyone else turning up there too, so he called it 'Alligators'. An outer-reef deep-water break, a 'cloudbreak', a good mile or more out to sea. It was a big day, but only about 18 foot at Waimea. The place was packed, almost worse than Pipeline. He didn't even know half the people there. Brazilians, Japanese, Australians, even a couple of Brits – Jesus, the place had become a tourist trap, the Waikiki of the North Shore.

Bradshaw paddled out there, but, like some kind of asteroid that just bounces off the atmosphere and swerves away, he kept on rolling, not stopping to pass the time of day with any of the crowd, kept his head down and stayed on course. He just prayed that nobody followed him. He hated crowds. They could have Waimea, for all he cared.

Foo saw him go. He'd seen him go by a few times like this, ignoring Waimea, and assumed Bradshaw was doing his usual fanatical training. Paddle a few miles out, then paddle in again, and walk along the bottom lugging a great boulder. But it wasn't like him to miss a quality sub-Eddie day like today. Foo suspected he must be up to something. Had he found a spot? A set was shaping up nicely on the horizon. About a dozen guys, and most of them younger than Foo, started cautiously edging into position. He would have to outpaddle them to have a decent chance at the next wave. As all that liquid energy vaulted up and solidified into another lumbering, seething form, Foo looked up at it and paddled towards it and made it over the top and kept on going, out to sea, in the rough direction of Japan, and wondering all the time where Bradshaw was going.

The conflict between the two men was the stuff of legend. It was more than legend, it was history. A couple of years before, in 1987, Foo's old buddy (and editor of *Surfer*) Matt Warshaw had come over from San Francisco, where he was based, and interviewed both men and written a finely balanced piece ('Divided Rulers of Waimea Bay') for *Outside* magazine. They had posed together for pictures, glaring at one another some of the time, at other times grinning for the camera. Bradshaw had been his usual condescending self. Tweaked a stray hair on Foo's chest and cracked something about 'Hey, Foo-Foo, you *are* becoming a man!' Said that he thought of Foo as his 'little brother'. 'He's like I used to be.' He still thought of himself as King of Waimea Bay and Foo as some kind of pretender. Still objected to everything he did, the way he looked, his thirst for glory, that oversized ego.

They had always been like chalk and cheese. The hedgehog and the fox. The hulking hairy Texan, the corn-fed cowboy, and the smooth-skinned skinny Asian with a black belt in surfing. King Kong and Kung Foo. Big blue eyes and almond brown eyes. And yet the strange thing was that now they didn't look that different any more. There had been a gradual rapprochement between the two men over the years. Bradshaw had shaved his beard off and had his hair cut. Now that he was well into his thirties, approaching forties, he didn't have to make himself look imposing and scary any more. He was no longer one of the Old Men with Beards. He looked younger without the beard, a little bit more like Foo in fact.

Foo hadn't grown a beard but he had definitely filled out, grown a few more muscles where there had been none before. It was partly down to North Shore Neck & Back and all that iron he had been pumping, but partly to getting out here as often as he could, contending with the heavies, and mixing it with Bradshaw. Foo, in other words, was starting to look a lot more like Bradshaw than ever before. Maybe he really could pass for his younger brother, at least from the neck down.

And just as Foo, secretly, in conversation with Dennis Pang, had admitted to putting more emphasis on strength and sheer power and – although he would shy away from the word, the idea was there – conquest, overcoming the ocean (in an article about an expedition to Peru, Foo would describe himself and a couple of comrades as 'conquistadors'), so Bradshaw had picked up some style lessons from Foo. You didn't see him eating nails for breakfast any more. When it came to interviews, he was always keen to stress that he had never seen big-wave surfing as just a matter of duking it out, having the cojones to stand up and take off and make it down the face, no matter how intimidating, and just straighten out or start looking for the shoulder. No, carving out the biggest waves just gave you a bigger opportunity to make a style statement on the face; you had to be able to perform on the wave, play some complex melodies, not just open the lid and hammer away. Any idiot could do that, and there were plenty of idiots out there now; the point was to be creative and trace new lines in the water. *Finesse* was the word: you had to surf with finesse. Bradshaw spoke as if he'd always felt that way, even if everyone else remembered the jock, the football player manqué.

Foo couldn't believe his eyes. Bradshaw screaming down the face of a solid 25-foot wave. Eighteen at Waimea and twenty-five out here. A long right-hander, maybe the longest wall he'd ever seen on the whole of the North Shore. It was a hell of a long paddle-out, his arms were virtually dropping off, but now he thought it had been worth it. Foo sat up to watch. He hadn't really watched Bradshaw in a long while; he was too intent on what he was doing to worry about Bradshaw. But he had to admit that Mad Dog was not bad. He didn't remember him surfing like this before. Bradshaw arced into a bottom turn, pulled up towards the lip in a low crouch, stalled, and vanished behind the curtain. A 25-foot tube. Foo's jaw dropped.

Bradshaw was still punching the air after that last wave, in solitary splendour, just him, the wave, a few dolphins, a fleet of flying fish, and a turtle – wasn't this what surfing was all about, nothing to do with being better than the other guy, just chiming with the whales and everything? – when Foo entered his perceptual field. Foo-Foo. He knew damn well that someone was ultimately going to follow him out and spoil everything, but did it have to be the Kid? Would he never get any peace? He had a good mind to go over there and . . . But no, he'd enjoy that, wouldn't he, write an article about it, blow it up out of all proportion, it was just more attention, that was why he was out here, Foo wanted him to take notice of him. Well, he wouldn't. He'd just flat out ignore the guy, as if he didn't exist. Bradshaw congratulated himself on a new and brilliant strategy for outmanoeuvring Foo – pretend he wasn't there and, who knows, maybe it would come true and he would give up and quietly go away.

But Foo didn't go away. He wouldn't have had the strength to paddle back in even if he wanted to. But he liked it out here. It was quiet, apart from the explosion of the occasional immense passing roller. No crowds. Of course there was Bradshaw, but then he tended to pop up everywhere, he was almost part of the scenery, he didn't have to pay him any mind at all. He was tired after all that paddling and he had intended to pause and regroup. But then something huge and wet picked him up and flicked him out into space and he really didn't have a lot of choice in the matter. It had to be destiny.

Bradshaw had to admit that Foo had style, and plenty of it. Maybe, examining his conscience scrupulously, he would have to admit that *that* had never been his strongest suit, much as he had striven for it. It didn't come to him naturally somehow, nobody had ever drilled style into him as a kid: it was just neatness and brutality, that was all that mattered, nothing fancy (how fancy were you going to get with a bunch of pipes laid end to end and 6 feet under the ground?), just stick to the rules and you couldn't go wrong. But what possible rules could apply out here, where everything was water, nothing was solid and precise? You had to make it all up from scratch and reinvent yourself endlessly. It was pointless trying to be rigid and relentless in this environment; you had to be fluid, adaptable, yielding. He watched Foo floating down the wave with a kind of envy. There was something weightless about the Kid, effortless, he barely left a trace through the water, as if he was gliding, almost hovering, over the surface. Whereas he, Bradshaw, tunnelled down into the core of the wave like a fugitive from Cell Block 13 digging his way to freedom, always fighting, labouring to come back up for air, Foo looked like a radiant band of light vectoring through space, not a thing of mass and matter, immune to the laws of gravity and time.

Bradshaw watched Foo being covered up, folding himself into the wave like a butterfly wrapped up in the embrace of a flower. The wave closed up again, with a thunderous sigh, and Foo was still in there.

No big deal. A heavy wave, but Foo was light, he would bounce back. He always did. Something popped up out of the froth: it was Foo's board. An ageing 9 foot 6 inches (Bradshaw took it in at a glance), purple and green: a little small for this magnitude of wave. It looked kind of familiar though. And there it was, just as he was expecting, when he flipped it over and examined the bottom – the shadow of a line where Foo had had it filled and reglassed, after somebody had taken a bite out of it. And, yes, those fins, they'd been replaced too.

– Come back for another bite? Foo had finally come up another hundred yards away and swum back to collect his board.

– Who fixed it for you? Bradshaw said. Good job.

− Michael Willis.

Bradshaw grunted his assent.

− Said I ought to bin it and start fresh. I didn't want to waste it though. I always liked that board and then . . .

− Yeah, said Bradshaw, nodding, sensing, perhaps for the first time, how Foo must have felt. I understand. I would have been the same. A stubborn son of a bitch.

Bradshaw pushed the board gently back to Foo and Foo swung himself back on. They paddled back out together, discussing line-ups and currents and zones. Foo said something like: 'You know, this is it. It doesn't get any better than this.' Bradshaw didn't say anything; he was dumbfounded because he realised that Foo was saying what he, Bradshaw, was thinking too.

I don't honestly know what happened, in any detail, the rest of that bright, sunny February afternoon in the early nineties. I heard that they both caught a lot of good clean waves and were actually cheering each other on by the end of the session. *Go, Mark! Go, Kenny!* And possibly even *Your wave*. After so much strife between them, it's hard to credit. Maybe after so many years there was the beginning of a grudging acceptance that each of them deserved to exist, that the ocean was big enough to accommodate them both, and that, for all their differences, they were similar in so many ways.

In a sense, Bradshaw was right − they were like brothers, they wanted the same thing, they faced the same difficulties. And, at certain points, they both had to back away from the biggest waves out at Alligators, waves in excess of 30 feet. They just weren't humanly makeable. They both knew that. You just couldn't get up enough speed to get down the face. You either slid off the back or you got too far forward and the whole great mass of it unloaded on your head and that was the end of you.

I do know that when they paddled back in, with evening drawing on, there was an argument between them, a classic Foo–Bradshaw dispute. Foo was tired. He had paddled far more than he had ever intended. And there was still a mile to go. He loved it way out here at the outer reef breaks, far from the madding crowd, and yet just getting there and back drained so much energy out of you.

– You've got to have a boat, he puffed, with Bradshaw carving through the water ahead of him relentlessly, looking as if he could paddle all the way to the mainland.

– What do you want a boat for?

– Or a chopper maybe. To drop you off at the break and pick you up again. It's too far.

– Why don't you go with Ace next time? Bradshaw kept going forward, cuffing the water even harder.

A man on a board on a wave, that's all there was to surfing, nothing more. Bradshaw was a traditionalist, a DIY classicist among surfers who didn't want any newfangled modern technology coming between him and all that raw unmediated primitive experience. He was like a naturist who insisted on going naked into the woods, regardless of bears, and here was Foo suggesting he might like to slip on an overcoat, a hat and scarf, to protect himself from the elements. It was heresy. Typical Foo. Bradshaw lay down again and steamed away: the last noble savage. *Wasn't anything sacred any more?*

Foo took his time, easing his way back to shore, trying to free-ride any passing rollers, his whole body aching. He really couldn't fathom Bradshaw. What was wrong with a few accessories, if they made life easier? He used the phone, didn't he? Didn't he take the plane when he wanted to go back to the mainland? So what was the big deal about hitching a ride out to the waves? He pulled his special webbed gloves (guaranteed to shift more water) tighter around his hands and kept on paddling.

It was a good six, seven or eight months before Foo and Bradshaw met again in the water. Sometime in the fall. Still short of the full-on heavy winter swell, but there had been a few harbingers of greater things to come. This was one of those days, medium power, a good training day, clear skies and a warm offshore breeze cleaning up the faces.

Bradshaw was heading out to Alligators again. It was good at Sunset and perhaps 12–15 at Waimea, but he couldn't face the throng. They were all getting into training for the Eddie, they wanted to be ready, but he had been ready for the best part of a decade and it still hadn't really happened for him. To hell with them: they could do what they wanted to do, but he was going to keep coming out here, doing his thing, the way he always had done. Then he heard the sound of an engine coming his way, boat of some sort he guessed, two-stroke only, you could easily tell, and he knew even before it went by that he was going to have the stink of gasoline up his nose. Funny place to come fishing out here though. He hoped they knew what they were doing. He didn't want to have to go fishing himself, rescuing any idiots, he had better things to be doing, getting himself in shape for a big winter to come. Maybe the biggest.

– Yay, Kenny!

Bradshaw barely heard it above the roar of the engine. Foo carved around and gouged up a great spout of water that sprayed down on him. Ace was driving, standing up in a Zodiac boat (an inflatable) like he was doing rodeo, and yelling, and he was towing Foo behind him, who was balancing on a surfboard as if he was water-skiing. Bradshaw couldn't take it all in at once. What the hell was he doing water-skiing with Ace right out here? And what was it with that board anyhow? He could see that Foo had stuck a couple of straps into it to enable him to keep his footing. What kind of stunt was he pulling? It was a bad joke. A bad dream.

Ace circled around.

– Hey, Old Man, grab a rope and we'll tow you out there, you're going too slow! He laughed hysterically and gunned the engine and he and Foo skimmed away into the distance.

Clowns! Buffoons! Bradshaw kept on paddling, chopping down arm after vindictive arm. *An abomination in the eyes of the Lord*, as the preacher back in the Spring Branch Pentecostal Church used to say. Bradshaw waxed wrathful and called on God to smite them down and cast them into a deep pit with vipers.

When he finally came in sight of Alligators he realised two things. One, on the positive side: these were probably the best waves to be had anywhere in the whole of Hawaii today, standing up clean and stiff and tall, combing up great quiffs of white water. Two, more negatively: they were already polluted by Ace and Foo. Ace Cool and Mark Fool. They made a perfect pair. They were careering up and down the waves, treating them with no respect at all, as if they were some kind of racetrack. Alligators had become a circus, too. Cool and Fool might as well be wearing red noses, oversize shoes and stupid braces. This place was sacred water and they were pissing in it. With a mixture of indignation and incredulity, Bradshaw saw Foo take off on one of the bigger waves, approaching 20 feet, way ahead of the curl, given extra impetus by the Zodiac and then letting go of the towrope, with a kind of whiplash effect, while Ace scooted off in the direction of the channel. Flashy – but where was the *paddling*? Bradshaw asked himself. This was tantamount to cheating. You had to *earn* the wave with the sheer hard labour required to match its speed. There had to be a balance between reward and punishment. And now here was Foo just having fun, making light of serious, heavy waves. It wasn't right. In fact, it was *cheating*.

Bradshaw felt sick at heart. He fumed and raged and prayed to God to make the crooked way straight again. And yet, at the same time, in a small, secret part of his mind, he couldn't help but take notice and, almost unconsciously, despite himself, make calculations. So, if this is what could be done on a 20-foot wave, what could be done on 30 feet? Or – pushing back the limits still further, into what Foo had called the 'unridden realm' – even forty.

Nobody knew how it had all started, any more than anyone knew how surfing itself had begun. The original inspiration must have been water-skiing. Matt Warshaw once showed me a video of Pottz out at second-reef Pipeline in the eighties, skiing into a 12-foot wall. There were other isolated experiments, but it was the lifeguards (like Darrick Doerner and Melvyn Pu'u, Brian Keaulana and Terry Ahue) who adapted it for big-wave excursions. There was a limit to what lifeguards could do in certain extreme situations. It was generally surfers they were rescuing, who had got in the way of some heavy water. They had to go in and pluck them out of harm's way. But they wouldn't be doing anyone any favours if they got themselves into trouble, too. They had to get in and get out again, with the victim if possible, in the fastest possible time. They were limited by how fast they could paddle the rescue board. Boats, even Zodiacs, were often worse than useless in these cases. They just got in the way, and then you had a ton of technology bearing down on you as well as the wave. The invention of the jet ski (or 'wave-runner') in the 1980s gave them a valuable new tool. Suddenly they could outrun the waves. Even the fastest waves were going no more than 25 or 30 knots; the jet ski could reach that speed and beyond. The lifeguard could dash in, pick up their man and dash out again, before the next mountain avalanched down upon them. Sometimes they would tow surfers out of the way of waves while they were still on their boards. It didn't take a genius to realise that if you could tow people out of the way of waves, you could tow them into waves too, give them a head start, the kind of edge that even the best of the big-wave maestros could hardly scorn. Soon non-lifeguards, like Laird Hamilton, started noticing. Of course, there were dissenters: this was not *real* surfing. It was a perversion of the truth. Whatever happened to just grabbing your board and running down the beach? But, in the early nineties, the tow-in phenomenon was already spreading irresistibly, like an irides-cent oil slick.

And there was a knock-on effect: even though nobody was quite sure what the new style was going to be called – 'power surfing'? 'post-modern'? 'new millennium'? – everybody knew that old-style surfing, classical surfing, *surfing*, was henceforth to be known as 'paddle-in' – only one possibility among others, and a rather lowly, old-fangled one at that.

It was the day of what came to be known as 'the Half-Eddie'. In the morning it was only 12 feet at Waimea, fifteen at most. There had been rumours of the swell building, but nobody could seriously believe the Eddie could be held that day. Bradshaw and Doerner, the Willis Brothers and Ace Cool: they were all out at Outdoor Log Cabins, north-east of Waimea, down the coast towards Sunset, and a mile or more out. The great José Angel himself was supposed to have studied the mystic break for years, but cautiously, from afar. Bradshaw had been the first to paddle into the wave here in 1986. Now they were all towing into waves twice the size of anything Waimea had on offer. Nobody was saying how big exactly. Milton Willis: 'It went totally off the scale.' Darrick Doerner: 'After 35 feet it's all the same – scary.'

Bradshaw was a convert. And, like all converts, he had an evangelical passion for his born-again faith. The jet ski opened up a new level of performance and hitherto unexplored terrains. This was like flying to the moon and floating up and down in low gravity. Paddle-in was still good in anything under twenty. But above that, and especially when it came to 30 foot and beyond, the jet ski and the tow-in team came into their own. And the sheer wave count went up too, the quantity as well as the quality. Now you could take almost every single wave that was out there: take off, fly down the face, bottom-turn, off the lip, and then your partner would be there, if you were astute enough, to tow you back into position for the next one to come along. You could take them all. Stiff and unbending though he was, even he had had to come around in the end.

Then one of the Quiksilver water-patrol guys from the contest turned up, also on a jet ski.

– Hey, guys, he yelled, over all the whooping and the din of two-stroke engines. You'd better get your asses over to the Bay. The Eddie's about to start.

They were all down to compete in the Eddie. If the Eddie was on, they had to be there. A siren call: the call of duty, a categorical imperative. It was Bradshaw who started the mutiny.

– I'm not going, he said.

– What'd he say? said water-patrol.

Bradshaw steeled himself.

– Give Quiksilver a message from me. Tell 'em I said: *Fuck the Eddie!*

Everybody turned to stare at Bradshaw. It was like hearing Moses bad-mouthing the Ten Commandments.

– I'm having too much fun out here. Why would I want to go back to Waimea?

One or two guys meekly followed water-patrol back to the Bay. But a few remained behind. Bradshaw was right. What was the point? They didn't need another contest. The Eddie was a circus, a carnival, a zoo. The real contest was out here.

As if to confirm their analysis, the Eddie started but stopped again halfway (with Brock Little in the lead). The swell dropped alarmingly in the afternoon and the contest was never completed. John Callahan, who had been stationed on the beach for the Eddie, studied the pictures of what had been taking place on the outer reefs. He whistled and said to himself, 'Waimea is a joke.' The place had been the sacrosanct inner sanctum of the North Shore, the *locus maximus*. The idea that Waimea, *Real* Waimea, could ever be a joke was unthinkable. But the unthinkable was now being thought. The golden age of Waimea Bay was over.

15

Maverick's

'You're going with *who*?!'

SharLyn's reaction to the news was understandable in the circumstances. The circumstances, in this case, being that her little brother Mark and Ken Bradshaw had been at war, on and off, for around a decade. For years Foo had been telling her again and again about what a monster, what a pathological maniac, wave-hog and tyrant the guy was. And now he was going surfing with him. Of his own volition. Without, so far as she could see, getting paid for it. Like it was some kind of romance.

'He's mellowed,' said Foo. 'I think maybe I misunderstood him. You have to be a head case to go out in 30-foot waves.'

'So what does that make you?'

'A head case.' Foo grinned. His sister had always supported him, without question, since he was a kid, defending him against his parents. Then she defended him against Bradshaw (she had once thought of going over to Bradshaw's house with some heavy blunt instrument). And now she was having to adapt to the new mood of *glasnost*. A kind of peace had broken out between them. You could call it 'mutual respect' so long as you prefixed it with the word 'grudging'. Foo was finding it hard to adapt himself. But it made good commercial sense in the new environment they were having to work in.

Foo and Bradshaw still went out when it looked good at Waimea, but it was as if it was for old time's sake. Brock Little, ten years younger than Foo, had captured the public imagination: he had moved in and now fully occupied the role of New Kid on the Block. And Darrick Doerner, as far as most commentators were concerned, was probably more accomplished, technically, than either of them. There was a moment, absurd though it was, which seemed to define the shift in the balance of power.

Kathryn Bigelow, a big-shot Hollywood director, had been shooting *Point Break*, with Patrick Swayze, on the North Shore. The final scene was supposed to be in Bells Beach in Australia. Swayze, playing a character known as Bodhi, was on the run from the American police, having carried out a string of bank robberies, and therefore would hardly take refuge in the land of *Hawaii Five-0*. But he was supposed to be mystically waiting for the kind of swell that only comes around once every fifty years. And, in truth, Bells, although long and well formed, never gets much above 10 feet. So Bigelow and Swayze came to Waimea and stuck up a sign reading 'Bells Beach'. It wouldn't fool any serious connoisseurs of fine waves, but it would have to do. And they couldn't wait fifty years either. So they took an average 18-foot kind of day at the Bay and shot it big. As a rule, Swayze liked to do his own stunts, but he was scripted to wipeout and die on the biggest wave for fifty years, and he wisely backed out. The question was: who was going to be his stand-in? It had to be one of the top guys – Bodhi was supposed to be an outstanding surfer. But who? From a distance any one of a handful could have done the job. The part of the pseudo-Swayze, the surf double, went to Darrick Doerner. He did a few suicidal take-offs and got paid a thousand dollars per wipeout.

It was no big deal but it rankled with Foo and Bradshaw. And 6-foot 3-inch, 220-pound, highly photogenic Laird Hamilton (from Maui) had not only been included in *People* magazine's list of the '50 Most Beautiful People in the World' but had gone to Hollywood, where he would eventually double for Pierce Brosnan in the James Bond film *Die Another Day*. Foo's inventive mind naturally turned to thoughts of celluloid. Which is how he came up with the XXL project (alternative titles *The Endless Winter* or *Destination Extreme*). The idea was that he and assorted partners would make up their own grand tour and come up with the biggest waves on the planet. Waimea wasn't exactly out, but it wasn't entirely in either. Once it had been a singularity, the lone star in the big-wave firmament. But now there were other places, undiscovered countries, coming up all the time. Foo, to borrow the title of an article he wrote in 1990, was 'OUT THERE'. As a boy he'd watched a television show with his father (who was keen on fishing) called 'The Flying Fisherman'; Foo's new dream, or revised 'Plan' ('Plan A+' he was calling it) was to become *the Flying Surfer*, chasing all the swells around the Pacific. He trawled the coast of Peru, for example, and lingered at Pico Alto (fitting in an excursion to Machu Picchu); he toured Tahiti and checked out Indo.

Bradshaw, on the other hand, fantasised about going up to Iceland. He'd heard there were some mighty waves in Iceland. 'What are the women like?' he once asked me (as if I had an encyclopaedic knowledge of more northerly climes). Every now and then Foo and Bradshaw would coincide. On 23 December 1994 they coincided at Maverick's.

Bradshaw had been the first North Shore inmate to do a reconnaissance. There had been unbelievable rumours about a big-wave spot in Northern California circulating for a few years, but nobody took it too seriously. How could it be bigger than Hawaii? And then, in 1992 (see, for example, 'Cold Sweat', *Surfer*, June), the story broke: a solitary soul (Jeff Clark) had been surfing a 20-foot-plus wave, maybe thirty, Waimea-level and beyond, in a spot only a short drive south of San Francisco on the road to Santa Cruz. Half Moon Bay, and the break known as 'Maverick's' (after the dog that had first sniffed it out), had been one of the best-kept secrets of surfing history. Daniel Duane (author of *Caught Inside: A Surfer's Year on the Californian Coast*) wrote: 'to understand the discovery, in the early 1990s, that the world's greatest big-wave break lay just outside San Francisco, imagine, next week, a climber stumbling upon a mountain both bigger than Everest and harder to climb, right outside Denver'. There was an element of writerly overstatement here: it was only the West Coast crew (of whom Duane, hailing from Santa Cruz, was one) that was pushing Maverick's as the biggest ever anywhere. But if Waimea was Everest, then Maverick's probably had a claim to being K2. Whatever, Bradshaw naturally had to go and see it for himself.

The locals, the handful of guys who (following Clark) regularly surfed it, were ambivalent: on the one hand, they were gratified that their own spot had managed to attract the attention of a Hawaiian living legend; on the other hand, they wanted to keep it all to themselves, they didn't really want anyone else muscling in on the act. But they were wise enough to acknowledge one thing: it was no longer possible to keep the lid on this one. This wave was bigger than all of them and belonged to the world.

Bradshaw was struck by how different it was from Waimea. No wafting palm trees here, only tall, stark, spiky pines. It was grey and cold and murky at Mav's. Sinister, hooded waves sprang up at you like muggers from underwater alleyways. A thick wet suit was *de rigueur*. There was a small harbour around the point (Pillar Point) and an off-limits USAF tracking station up on the cliffs sprouting a crop of radar dishes like giant mushrooms. When I went to Half Moon Bay, one day in spring, there were a few scattered signs of life: a black-headed gull, a lone man in an overcoat walking his dog, a driftwood shack with smoke spiralling up from the chimney. But it had a cut-off, isolated feel about it as if it were located somewhere near the end of the world, one of those spots where if you went too far out you might fall off the edge and down into the void. 'Voodoo wave' is what *Surfer* called it, 'inherently evil': 'The reef is surrounded by deep water, and lies naked to every nasty thing above and below the Pacific: Aleutian swells, northwest winds, southeast storms, frigid currents, aggro elephant seals and wilder things that snack on aggro elephant seals.' Bradshaw went there two or three times and reported back to Hawaii. Soon there was a lot of two-way traffic between Honolulu and San Francisco. When a big swell spun up out of the Pacific, people were scrutinising weather charts fanatically to check if it was heading towards Hawaii or more east, towards the mainland, and Maverick's. Depending on the winds and the currents and the look of the weather charts, big-wave searchers had to make an agonising call on whether to stick where they were or hop on a plane.

It was all Bradshaw's idea. He was the one who invited Foo along in the first place. They had caught a sunlit 18-foot wave together at Outside Alligators (Waimea wasn't big enough), crisscrossing and weaving in and out of one another's tracks on the long green wall, matching move for move, carving out intersecting lines like a pair of skaters. As they paddled back out, Bradshaw reached over to Foo and held his board, almost tenderly, in his big hairy arm. 'I love you like a brother, man,' he said. 'Do you want to come to Maverick's with me?' Foo had been wanting to check the place out and build it into his scenario for the XXL project. They made a vague agreement. And then, on 22 December, Bradshaw called him. He'd already been over there the previous week and flown back again, and now he was getting phone calls from the West Coast and the thought of missing out was tormenting him.

– Mark, it's due back up tomorrow. The buoys are looking good. If we want to be there we've got to take the night flight.

– I'm in, Foo said.

– What about Christmas? Lisa said, when he put the phone down.

– Don't worry, I'll be back for Christmas, he said. We're flying back on the 24th. Nothing has changed.

– You're going to be exhausted.

– I'll be fine. I'll grab some sleep on the plane.

Lisa Nakano was Foo's live-in girlfriend. His 'fiancée'. Aged twenty-eight, she was an ex-model, winner of the Cherry Blossom Queen pageant of 1988, who worked in the Levi Strauss marketing department in Honolulu. Lisa had made him give up Brazilians, and a Japanese girl, and he didn't really miss them, not much. Maybe she was the one, he didn't know, but they were officially engaged. Foo wasn't too sure about this idea of settling down. At thirty-six, he still felt too young. But he was talking about buying her a ring. He was talking about children. Perhaps they would spend the rest of their lives together. They would certainly have Christmas together at least.

Bradshaw picked him up around nine o'clock that evening. 'Take good care of him,' Lisa cried out into the night, waving, as the pair of them drove away. 'Make sure he gets back OK.'

Foo tried to sleep on the midnight 'red-eye' to the coast, but he was too excited, amped, whipped up to a fever pitch of expectation by Bradshaw's descriptions of Maverick's. It was on this United Airlines flight that Bradshaw made his offer, wedged right in next to Foo, their elbows bumping up against each other, in coach class.

– You know all those waves we let go? he said.

– We shouldn't have, said Foo, half-dreaming.

– Well, now we don't have to, said Bradshaw. Not any-more. With a jet ski there is no limit. One of these days we're going to look back and realise that thirty feet is nothing.

– You're talking about *the unridden realm*.

– Take thirty and double it. Or triple it.

– Wow! You think Maverick's could be that big? said Foo, sitting up, wide-eyed.

– Who knows? said Bradshaw, who didn't want Foo to get Maverick's out of all proportion. But he was convinced that there would be times and places that made Waimea look like a kindergarten sandpit.

– You mean like those waves in 1985 where we had to let 'em slide by?

– They were nothing, said Bradshaw.

– How big? said Foo.

– A hundred, said Bradshaw. A hundred foot is possible. If you're there. With a jet ski you can be there.

– I've got to get one, said Foo.

– *We* have to get one, said Bradshaw.

– You mean, go in together?'

– I've been thinking: we could share the initial investment, divide up all the costs, 50/50. And . . .

– Foo and Bradshaw?

– Bradshaw and Foo.

– I'm not going to drive all the time, Foo said.

It was a done deal. They actually shook on it. The old enemies were now partners. They were a team.

They had got their timing all askew. By the time they landed in San Francisco at 5.20 a.m. local time (2.20 Hawaiian time), Foo was ready for bed. But they weren't going to bed. He kept dozing off (having extracted his massive two-board bag from 'odd-size' luggage, he promptly flopped down on it and shut his eyes) and Bradshaw kept waking him up again. 'You drive,' Foo said, rubbing his eyes, when they picked up their Alamo rental car.

They fixed the boards to the roof rack. Bradshaw drove and Foo snoozed on the back seat. They stopped at Mark Renneker's house at Ocean Beach for breakfast. They agreed that Foo and Bradshaw would crash at Warshaw's that night, before catching the plane home again, in time for Christmas. After toast and orange juice, it was back on the road. By the time they pulled into the car park at the bottom of the cliffs at Half Moon Bay, dawn was breaking.

If there was any natural equivalence between the weather and the fate of human beings, it should by rights have been dark and stormy. But it wasn't. It was the beginning of what would be a bright, clear day, almost sultry by Northern California standards, with gentle offshore breezes. It shouldn't have been too much of a shock for the visiting Hawaiians as they got out of the car, snaked into their wet suits, pulled on their hoods and walked down the trail that led to the sea, their boards cradled under their arms, past the signs saying 'No Swimming' and 'Contaminated Water' and 'DANGER – extremely hazardous waves even on calm days'. Whatever its state of purity, the water was 25 degrees colder than what they were used to at Waimea. One and the same ocean, the Pacific, but breaking on a different shore, and looking more like the North Sea or the Baltic: now familiar to Bradshaw but entirely novel to Foo. It was a massive wake-up call when they hit the water, around 9 a.m.

– Where's the channel? said Foo. All he could see, in the bleak half-light, was a chaos of leaden grey breakers, an opaque maelstrom.

– Just follow me, said Bradshaw. There is no channel here. Just don't paddle into the rocks, that's all.

– Doesn't look like a twenty-foot day to me. Foo took a last sceptical glance at the break. Guess we won't be needing that jet ski today.

As it turned out, a jet ski, particularly with its rescue capability, would have come in very handy on this day. For Foo it was an away game, a foreign terrain to which he would never have the opportunity to acclimatise. One of the strange things about Maverick's: you approach it sideways on. Whereas, at the Bay, the waves marched directly towards you, breaking right (mostly) or left (occasionally) but nonetheless broadly oriented towards the beach, at Maverick's they (as a general rule) appear indifferent to the last spit of land surfers step off and go thundering on elsewhere, seeming to take no notice, steering themselves gradually in the direction of the harbour to the south. The way in is to paddle out north and swing around behind them. You don't face up to the breakers at Maverick's, you sneak up on them, hoping to take them by surprise. Bradshaw and Foo plunged into the icy water together and paddled in the rough direction of Hawaii, a few thousand miles away.

As they were going out, Matt Warshaw was going in. He had already been surfing for more than an hour, and didn't like the look of it. Warshaw and Foo had been travelling on separate, semi-parallel tracks since their days together on the circuit. While Foo had become an occasional diarist and documentary film-maker but was, above all, a big-wave hunter with one of the highest profiles in the realm, Warshaw was now a professional journalist and writer even though he had not relinquished his personal stake in the surf. Warshaw had graduated from Berkeley and he was the closest thing in surfing to a professor of wave history. He generally wore glasses (switching to contacts to go surfing). At one time he was editor of *Surfer* magazine and he would ultimately go on to write *The Encyclopedia of Surfing* (often referred to as the surfer's Bible) and the definitive *Maverick's*. His house was stacked with old magazines and books and videos about surfing, it was like a museum, an archaeological archive exclusively dedicated to waves and wave-riders. He was probably the most knowledgeable man in the water that day – any day – and could answer all and any questions about who did what to whom and when and possibly even why. He had written the key article on the feud between Foo and Bradshaw, he respected both men, and he was as bemused as Foo's sister SharLyn by this recent outbreak of *perestroika*.

Warshaw had once published a story about a Californian surfer on a world tour of all the greatest breaks and who had accidentally stopped off in Berlin. For want of anything better to do he had wandered around the Wall. When he saw the heavily armed guards in their watchtowers, keeping the frontier between East and West under machine-gun surveillance, he stopped and yelled up at one of them. 'Man!' he cried out, 'You are bummed – because you will never know what true surfing really is!' The story kept echoing in Warshaw's brain now – he thought of the evolution of the relationship between Foo and Bradshaw as somewhat akin to the fall of the Berlin Wall. It looked as if the Cold War was finally over. And he felt a little as John le Carré must have done with the end of the Soviet Union: slightly nostalgic for a conflict he understood and recognised, and wondering what the hell he would find to write about next.

Warshaw knew practically everything that was worth knowing, but unlike Foo and Bradshaw he was not a great aficionado of outsize waves. He admired them, he respected them, but from afar, with a degree of academic detachment, and had no desire to tangle with them at close quarters for any length of time. Warshaw did not have the same sense of a mission that had preoccupied both Foo and Bradshaw for more than a decade. He felt comfortable in anything up to around 10–12 feet. Anything more than that and he was tentative and a little apprehensive. He could handle just about anything, but that didn't mean he went out of his way to pursue it, religiously, fanatically, uncompromisingly. He wasn't religious, he was anything but a fanatic and he preferred to compromise. 'I love the little ones,' he once bravely announced sounding an oddly Christ-like note.

In his introduction to Warshaw's book about Maverick's Dan Duane had written of 'the kind of surf that destroys bridges, sinks ships, and rearranges coastlines'. That December day wasn't one of those days: it wasn't Mav's at its most violent, its most severe. And yet it wasn't exactly a cakewalk either. Warshaw has a couple of phrases for what he was doing that morning. 'I was just doing my duty,' he says. 'I was paying my respects to Mav's.' By eleven o'clock he felt he had done enough to satisfy his ego. Caught the obligatory handful of waves. Didn't really like the feel of it, stayed out on the shoulder by and large. He wanted to stay in control and he didn't enjoy the prospect – he'd seen it happen a few times – of getting 'washed through', hammered by the waves and dumped on the massive, punishing rocks that loomed up out of the water and guarded the harbour mouth like extremely bald and broad-shouldered bouncers outside a nightclub.

The day before, Warshaw had seen Jay Moriarity 'crucified' (as he would put it) at Maverick's. Moriarity was a polite, disciplined young man, just sixteen, who trained hard like a black belt among surfers. He thought of surfing as a form of martial art and would eventually teach my own son to surf in Devon. A few days prior to 23 December he had taken off on a granite-coloured slab the size of an apartment block and was flipped over – probably by the wind – and ended up upside-down, briefly pinned to the face of the wave, his arms out to his sides, as if on the cross. Moriarity had survived (he would die at the age of twenty-three in the Maldives, sitting on the bottom of the Indian Ocean, practising breath control), but it was the harshest wipeout Warshaw could ever remember seeing anywhere. And he was loath to go through the same near-death experience himself.

Mike 'Snips' Parsons had evolved into Southern California's answer to Bradshaw and Foo. He was tall and stringy and amiable with a boy-next-door smile and excellent manners. Like Foo and Bradshaw, he had graduated from the pro circuit, with a respectable CV (he made fourteenth in the world), to the dedicated pursuit of extremely large waves, cutting his teeth on Todos Santos, in Baja California. Like Foo and Bradshaw, he was responding to the siren call of a giant swell at Maverick's. He had driven up through the night the several hundred miles from San Clemente. Like Foo, Parsons was making his debut at Maverick's, but he was nearly a decade younger. He looked up to Foo and Bradshaw as his elders, his precursors, if not necessarily his betters. He had just as much of a shot at the biggest waves as they had. It was an open door; you just had to be able to walk through it. There was no one out there stopping you. No qualifications required, although experience, bravery and an incalculable degree of insanity would definitely help. The predicted giant swell was, in truth, a slight disappointment. It was 15–18 feet at best. Sub-Eddie. Not 'real' Mav's.

But it must have seemed real enough when Parsons and Brock Little took off together on a promising, well-formed wave at the top end of the spectrum and ran into a bumpy face that folded on them sooner than either of them had anticipated. Brock had flown in from Los Angeles. He had heard about Foo and Bradshaw going and didn't want to miss any opportunity to spoil their party, 'blow their bubble'. Ever since he'd topped them at the Eddie, he'd taken it upon himself to laugh at their claims to dominance. It was his first time at Maverick's, too. The place was unusually populated by debutants. It seemed like a good day, bright, airy, not too punishing, for a first encounter with the place. But both Parsons and Brock got thrown, held down, tumbled along and dumped somewhere in the vicinity of the rocks, the area known as 'the Boneyard'. Sometimes it was hard to choose which was worse: water or the hard stuff. Water could be hard, too. Nevertheless, Brock called it 'a user-friendly day'.

Even when it wasn't a contest, Foo and Bradshaw were always competing. Neither wanted the other to steal a march, get an edge, or (as in the arms race) acquire more firepower. 'It's good,' Foo said to Bradshaw during a lull. 'I'm stoked. Glad we came.' And added: 'Wish it had a little more size, though.' They were out there doing their own thing and, at the same time, they were keeping a close eye on their old adversary – cheering him on maybe, exchanging a few words from time to time, but forever trying to match what the other guy was doing. And so it was that they were both paddling hard, jockeying for position, when the set that Brock and Parsons took off on began to take shape. Bradshaw got outmanoeuvred and came in third. Parsons and Brock took the second wave. Foo streaked ahead of everybody and took off on the first wave of the set.

He was tired, he was cold, he hadn't had enough sleep, and yet he was still surfing with all the old panache. And he was muscular too, really hustling for every wave. After all, he had a reputation to preserve. *Foo turning up at Maverick's*. In the realm of hard-core surfing, it was like hearing that Elvis Presley had blown into town. 'Surfing's pre-eminent big-wave rider', and 'consummate living legend' – *here at Mav's*! The news caused a ripple, a minor sensation among the regulars. They were too cool to make a big deal of it, but they knew he was there all right, and he knew that they knew he was. In this respect, Foo was a little like Harry Houdini. The show always had to go on, no matter what. He was always performing for the grandstand, for posterity in a way. He didn't like to disappoint his audience: over a hundred spectators – Maverick's' biggest ever crowd – had gathered in the sun up on the cliffs. And then, of course, he had made sure he had a cameraman in place to shoot film for the XXL project. He wanted to make it look good for the viewers too.

Eric Nelson, surfing videographer, kept the camera on Foo

whenever he could. There was something about the guy which was irresistibly photogenic. The lens loved Foo. When Nelson saw the ocean ruck up promisingly, around 11.20 a.m., and watched Foo paddling into the lead wave of a set, he automatically checked the light reading and the battery status and pressed record. He was set. He sure didn't want to miss this one.

Foo was on it. Everyone else backed off. Only he and Bradshaw could have made it, and Bradshaw was probably too deep, too close to the peak. *Let him have it!* thought Bradshaw, what the hell, there's always another train coming along behind. He was growing more philosophical as he got older. Or at least *he* thought he was. Maybe this was the new team mentality? Solidarity among surfers. Togetherness. Tolerance. These were concepts new to Bradshaw. Or was it just a night without sleep that made him think like this?

Foo made his move and went over the edge. He got to his feet and swivelled his 9-foot-6-inch purple and yellow Rusty board down the face. Below him, the Pacific, above him, sky; to his left, America, and somewhere far away to his right, Hawaii and Waimea Bay.

The painter James Whistler was once asked how he could justify the exorbitant price for a painting he had just completed. How long had it taken him? And how much did that work out per hour? He dismissed the questions with a wave of the hand. 'You're not paying me for a couple of days' work,' he said. 'You're paying for a lifetime of genius.' Maybe Foo would have said something similar as he took off and flew down that wave at Maverick's. His whole life went into that ride.

Nelson followed Foo's trajectory down the face. He was glued to it as closely as Foo to his board and the board to the wave. In fact, more closely. His mesmerising footage shows Foo falling in slow motion. He is slightly askew on the board, he doesn't have the right angle to hold it, he tries to correct and adjust and flatten out, but it's too late, he can feel himself going, and he decides to let it go and surrender to the forces. He bails, pitching forward. He goes down. Such is the effect of gravity. The incredible and paradoxical fact is that, in the next instant, he is being dragged back up the wave all over again, almost as if someone has pressed the rewind button. It is the ascension of Mark Foo. Perhaps to minimise the impact he has his arms pressed together, his hands folded neatly one on top of the other, almost as if he is praying. He is in a loop, rolled around in the barrel, but behind the curtain. It is still visibly Foo, but more remote, as if seen through a greenish glass darkly, a face caught frozen in the ice, or preserved inside a museum display case. And then the glass shatters: he is flung down all over again and stomped on by the cascading water and he vanishes beneath the surface and the camera turns away and looks elsewhere. There is no more to be seen.

Warshaw, by now up in a photographer's helicopter over the break, saw Foo go down. 'If anyone should have seen what happened to him, it was me,' he says. 'From the air, Foo's wipeout didn't look like much.'

Bradshaw saw Foo go down, he saw him come up again, for the last time, and he saw him finally shoved down into the pit and given a hammering for good measure. He couldn't resist a small grin of wry satisfaction. Foo was fallible, he was never going to make that late take-off. Tut-tut. Then he saw Parsons and Brock go down after him. What a crew! Maybe Mav's was a tricky sidewinder of a wave. But somebody had to be able to deal with it. He took off on the last and biggest wave of the set. He was careful to line himself up nice and square and get in early and stand up and really dominate the damn wave and crush it and force it to let him ride down it. He didn't glide down the wave, he burrowed into it, used the board like a shovel, furiously excavating great chunks out of the granite water like stepping stones. It was bumpy, but Bradshaw flat out refused to get thrown off. He was not giving in to any forces. No surrender. Bradshaw was on top of it. He looked down as he sailed by, knowing that, somewhere down there, beneath the great turmoil, Foo and Parsons and Brock were eating it. He was riding right over the top of them. *Schadenfreude*: pleasure in someone else's misfortune: Bradshaw was not averse to it. It would look good on the video, he reflected with satisfaction, if they left it in the final cut: Foo, Parsons, Little all felled by the grizzly beast while the great Bradshaw comes out on top, unscathed, immortal, godlike. The idea that any one of them might not come up again never really crossed his mind.

Brock Little and Mike Parsons were being spun around underwater, laundered like old socks in a particularly cranky washing machine. Then squeezed through the mangle of the harbour-mouth rocks. Then finally disposed of. Brock was laughing his head off as he got pounded. Parsons remembers bumping into something or someone while he was down there, his senses reeling, being turned upside down and inside out, reduced to a barely functioning residue of instinctive self-preservation. He knows now that it must have been Foo down there, underneath him, deeper down, still struggling to get up, even though he was on the wave in front. So this had to be his second wave hold-down.

It was a long, leisurely wave, longer than Waimea (maybe thirty seconds as opposed to fifteen), and Bradshaw rode it to the point of extinction, flipped off only when he was sure it was really dead. As he paddled back out again, hungry for another wave like the last one, he cruised past the photographers' boat, *The Deeper Blue*. In fact he paused to check that everyone had captured that last wave of his for posterity. As he pulled his head over the gunwales, he spotted a couple of fragments of Foo's board lying in the bottom.

– Anyone seen Mark? he said.

– I think he's gone in to get a board, somebody said.

– He sure needs a new board after that! chuckled Bradshaw. He looked back towards the cliffs and the beach, but he couldn't make out Foo. Must be already in the car park getting his spare board. Bradshaw slipped away and headed back to the break. Can't wait for Foo, he said to himself, gotta cram in a few more before he gets back and starts cluttering the place up again.

Foo was not, in fact, on the beach or in the car park or swimming back or paddling back out again. While Bradshaw and the photographers exchanged words on the surface, he was several feet below them. Perhaps he could even see them in the world up above.

The wave, having tantalisingly raised Foo up towards heaven, had now thrust him down towards hell. At this moment Foo was doing the opposite of hanging by a thread: he was attached by his leash to the bottom. His leash, the famous leash that he introduced into big-wave surfing, the leash that traditionalists like Bradshaw scorned (and then finally adopted by and large), had snagged on a rock and twisted solidly around it. Foo was temporarily stunned by the force of the wave. When he came to enough to realise he shouldn't be sticking around much longer, he naturally made for the surface, the light and the air. Only he didn't make it. The leash tightened like a noose around his ankle and he was stopped short, several crucial feet short, of the surface. He yanked at the leash but it was held tight. Wearing those gloves didn't help. Then another wave barrelled through and smashed him down again and squeezed whatever breath was left in his system right out of him, like toothpaste from a tube.

'You have to fight to hold on to consciousness,' Foo had said in 1986 after a close call at Waimea. 'That's a fallacy, you know – when people say to relax and go with it. That's a crock of shit. First you relax, but after a while you have to fight. You gotta have your eyes open. You have to find out which way's up, where it's bright and green, not black. You actually look at death in these situations, if you just relax and go with it, the wave's going to hold you down for ever.' Drowning at Maverick's came in two phases: the phase of resistance, and the phase of surrender. Foo exhausted his last ounces of energy and strength in trying to wriggle free of the web he was caught in, succeeding only in digging himself in deeper, tighter. It was the entrepreneur, the operator, in him: there had to be a deal he could strike, he could duck and dive and weave and come up with some plan or scheme that would get him off the hook. But there had to come a point where he recognised that further struggle was useless and in any case impossible. His body was already drifting with the currents, flapping like a sheet in the wind. As his lungs started to suck in water rather than air, equalising the pressure inside and out, he knew he was finished.

He couldn't have been that surprised. This was a moment he had been planning for, anticipating, living, for years. And he had written the script. 'If you want the ultimate thrill, you've got to be willing to pay the ultimate price.' 'You can't breathe water.' So this was destiny. The truth of the Tao flooded into him: 'Nothing in the world can be compared to water for its weak and yielding nature; yet in attacking the hard and the strong, nothing proves better than it. For there is no other alternative to it.' *No alternative*. For Foo everything was water. He and water were one. Perhaps, before he died, or as he died, Foo may have tasted the sense of *satori*, the moment of enlightenment. In the cold, hard, clinical discourse of the coroner's report, he had suffered 'conscious drowning'.

Bradshaw, meanwhile, just kept right on surfing. This was what he did. This was all he did. Ever. 'If you ask me to choose, I'll choose – to surf.'

Time is not something people keep a close eye on in surfing. Even so it is surprising that nearly two hours passed before someone noticed something in the water. Foo's body, with all the life laundered out of it, had finally been released from its anchorage and floated limply now, still strapped to a fragment of his broken board, the tail section, only a matter of yards from *The Deeper Blue*. They pulled him out of the water, tried to revive him, pumped him, thumped him, gave him the kiss of life, realised he was long gone.

When Matt Warshaw heard the news radioed through – 'They've found Mark: he didn't make it' – up in the helicopter, he couldn't believe it. It had to be some kind of terrible mistake or a prank. Foo? On a 15–18-foot day? It didn't make sense. Foo had survived wipeouts on waves twice that size at Waimea and come up smiling. He landed, ran down to the harbour. But it was Foo all right, still lying in the bottom of *The Deeper Blue*. The strange thing was that he appeared completely unmarked, still as handsome as ever, smooth and immaculate, his face serene, as if nothing had happened to him. And 'nothing', Warshaw reflected, was just what had happened to him, it was the something – the realm of transient events and experiences – that had stopped for Mark Foo. He was still wearing the coral necklace, a talisman given to him by his mother, that he had shown to Warshaw that morning, inscribed with Chinese ideograms that translated as 'life', 'luck' and 'death'.

Much later, some wise guy would make the crack that this was Foo's 'smartest ever career move'. Going out on stage, on film. Now he was dead Foo attracted even more attention than when he was alive. He would have loved the article in the *New York Times*, the elegy in *Rolling Stone*, the pictures in *Paris-Match*, the heroic quotations from Jack London and Ernest Hemingway. Had he not said in an interview broadcast on the BBC that dying in big waves would be 'a glamorous way to go – a great way to go'? A tide, a torrent, of tributes, memorials, obituaries, poems, valedictions, eulogies, TV programmes followed. Some people argued that he had engineered it that way, had it all worked out from the beginning. He didn't really want to get old anyway: live fast, die young and be a good-looking corpse.

But as he looked down at Foo Warshaw had to think that this, in some twisted, absurd way, must be what surfing secretly aimed for. Not necessarily dying, although a lot of surfers were half in love with easeful death it was true, but that sense of the great nothing, the void, the thing that Foo had, that was part of surfing, maybe it was the essence, if it had an essence. The point of surfing was to understand that everything else in life was meaningless: all the jobs (or lack of them), the money (or lack of it), family, friends, lovers, pets, bills, the shopping list, telephone numbers, gods, demons, pizza, perfection and imperfection, what clothes you wore, what car you drove, the name of your favourite shaper (well, no, maybe that really was significant) – none of that really mattered, and the idea of surfing was to transcend all of that stuff and concentrate all of your attention on something that was obviously devoid of all meaning and therefore deeply, unfathomably important.

The thing that Warshaw regretted above all was that now his old friend was going to be turned into a tombstone, a dead hero, a martyr to surfing. A character in an epic tale. The apotheosis of Foo. He knew that now all the talk would be of Valhalla and fallen warriors and (Foo's favourite word) *destiny* – not of a random confluence of atoms. He saw in advance that Maverick's would earn immense kudos from being the wave that killed Foo (Maverick's merchandising, T-shirts, cafés, movies soon flourished). And he foresaw too that surfers everywhere would swell up with pride, feel perversely more gung-ho than ever, elevated by his operatic fate, obscurely more glorious than they ever had been or deserved to be. Maverick's was doomed to become a myth. Surfing was fundamentally stupid, he had to admit, but he didn't want it to be stupider than it had to be. It was nothing and it was everything. Spectacularly futile. What was it Dan Duane had called it? 'An inexplicable and useless urge.' It wasn't going anywhere and it wasn't achieving anything and it didn't bring you any closer to God either.

Ten years on, sitting outside a café in San Francisco, Warshaw says that surfing is devalued by all the inflated talk of gods and heroes: it is nothing but a 'rhythm', a 'pulse', 'an alternating tension and relaxation – and that is grand enough, I don't need all the religion too'.

In a museum on the North Shore you can see, pinned to the wall like a butterfly, the pair of shorts that Foo gave away to a friend of his the day before he died.

A few months later, in the spring of 1995, Bradshaw was out at big Sunset. Darrick Doerner was out there too. Doerner saw him, paddled over to him. 'You could have saved him, man!' he spat in Bradshaw's face. 'You could have saved him.' And with that he paddled away again. Bradshaw didn't have to ask who he was talking about. Bradshaw and Foo at Maverick's: the Old Man and the Karate Kid. It wasn't exactly like Woody and Dickie at Waimea all those decades ago, the older guy getting the younger guy into trouble, but it wasn't entirely unlike that either.

Peter Cole, the wise man of Waimea (now aged seventy-three), said: 'The leash killed him. He should never have been using a leash.'

The Willis Brothers said: 'He was riding a Rusty [board] – only because he was sponsored. He should have been riding a [Willis Brothers] Phazer. That board killed him.'

Recently I was speaking to SharLyn. Her house up in the hills between Sunset and Waimea, looking down over the Pacific is, in part, a shrine to Mark. There is a Buddhist altar dedicated to members of her family now dead: small photographs of her mother (ravishing) and father (dashing), her elder brother and her kid brother Mark. There is a giant picture, larger than life-size, a headshot of Foo, smiling down on the spacious living room, still radiant, still perfect, forever thirty. And on a deeply polished half-moon table stands a small metal urn containing some of his ashes.

'I blame Bradshaw,' she says. 'I'll never forgive him. Never.'

16

Code Black

On Wednesday 28 January 1998 ('Biggest Wednesday' as it quickly became known), three things coincided on the North Shore for the first – and probably last – time: the biggest swell in Hawaii for thirty years, Ken Bradshaw, and me watching him tow into it.

I woke, at Turtle Bay, to the sound of distant booming. I had my wife and two young sons with me this time around. Spud and Jack thought that surf of this magnitude was normal. One woman went out to go to Foodland and when she got home she found that a passing wave had dumped a palm tree in her front room and sucked out all her furniture. It was that kind of day. The waves were hitting the far side of the Kam Highway.

George Downing called the Eddie on. It was like a dream come true for me. At last I was going to *see* the Eddie – the real thing, and not just the ghosts of Eddies past or yet to come. The judges' tower was set up on the beach next to the old lifeguard tower and there were Quiksilver banners and pictures of Eddie all over the place and stickers announcing

'EDDIE WOULD GO'. I called up the *Independent* in London (I had left *The Times* by then) from the phone by the changing rooms at Waimea and raved incoherently down the line about 'incredible waves' and 'the Eddie!!!' and 'the BIGGEST sports event on the face of the planet'. Half an hour later I had to call them back again. It was all off. Eddie Would Not Go. Again. Downing had backed off. I was furious with him. The Willis Bros, even more so.

There had been a lot of dropouts that day after people turned up at the Bay and took a look at the surf. The Willises stepped in to fill the gaps. They were willing to go. They were in. Their names were down on the list. At last they were going to get their shot. Brock Little didn't drop out, he liked it like this, he didn't care one way or the other.

'You can't get in,' said Bradshaw, decisively, eyeballing the surf. 'There is just no way. Look at that.' He gestured dismissively at a thirty-plus wave that was shutting down like a steel trap in the middle of the Bay.

'You can get in,' said Michael Willis.

'Come on,' echoed his brother Milton more contemptuously. 'I've surfed it bigger than this and it was a piece of cake. What are you worrying about, you pussy!'

Bradshaw glared at him then walked away. He wasn't going out at the Bay and that was that. The Willis Bros blamed Bradshaw for pulling the plug on the whole thing. If he had been willing to go, maybe Downing's hand would have been forced and he'd have had to run it.

As it was, the Hawaiian police drove up and declared the whole of Waimea Bay off limits. It was illegal to venture on to the beach. 'Code Black' was their name for it. They taped up the entrance to the beach, put up ropes and barriers and warning signs and guards around all the key points. It meant you could be arrested for going surfing. You couldn't even park your car in the car park. They'd been looking for a good excuse to arrest a few surfers and this was it. One North Shore dissident, Jason Majors, who had once provided Brock Little with a role model, and who may or may not have been high at the time, couldn't resist the challenge. To the cheers of the crowd, he managed to elude the police patrols and get in off the rocks (an unorthodox and risky point of entry), dreamed his way out there, got hammered and was eventually dragged back in by lifeguards, dazed and confused, babbling deliriously about seeing 'tunnels of light', and then handcuffed on the beach and driven away in a squad car. They got him for reckless surfing and a whole bunch of unpaid parking tickets.

Probably the biggest loser of the day was Brock Little. He and a group of other guys headed west and drove down to the harbour in Haleiwa. That was the way out. They had two or three jet skis between them and they were planning to conquer and colonise one of the outer reef breaks like Avalanche. But the police got there first. Code Black again. Nobody could go out at Haleiwa harbour either. Brock wanted to go anyway and risk arrest and imprisonment; he just didn't care. But a couple of the other guys were lifeguards, and their jobs were on the line. Brock was left high and dry.

There was, however, a secret and illegal take-off point to the east beyond Sunset. The Willis Bros drove me up there and I saw them sail off through the tiny cracks and crevices between some of the biggest waves I had ever seen and ever hope to see. Milton was driving the jet ski and Michael was clinging to the back with a board under his arm and they were grinning as they gunned the engine and steered between Himalayan-size peaks of water on one side and the abyss on the other. Ultimately, they would argue that, although they had blazed the trail, Bradshaw 'elbowed' them off the break.

I could see Bradshaw (Dan Moore had taken Foo's place as his partner) through my binoculars from Robbie Paige's backyard at Outdoor Log Cabins, north west of Waimea. At this distance – it must have been almost a mile out – the waves seemed to rise and fall with majestic languor. They made all other waves look puny and pushy, as if they were trying too hard. These waves didn't have to try: they simply *were*. For a few hours this was the most powerful natural phenomenon on the planet. It was like watching volcanoes erupt. The closest I've ever felt to Krakatoa. Even the beachbreak, which made the earth tremble, was a good 20 feet, Waimea-sized. But out there the usual statistics ceased to apply. These were waves that seemed to have lurched into being from somewhere outside time and space. Then people were calling it 'above 40, maybe 50'. This was the maximum imaginable size.

Years later, when the measuring system evolved, and people started focusing on 'face-height' (more like the hypotenuse than the vertical), this was revised upwards, into the sixties. When, in 2001, Bradshaw saw the picture of Mike Parsons' '66-foot' wave at Cortes Banks, a hundred miles off San Diego, he said, 'If you're calling *that* 66, I'm calling my wave 70 or maybe 80.' He had a point. You could have called it a hundred and you still wouldn't have been wrong. All I know is that when Bradshaw and his bright orange board hit the bottom of the wave and it reared up in all its magnificence and splendour over his head, he looked about as big as a shrimp slipping down the throat of a whale.

Whatever size it was, Bradshaw – by general consensus – had surfed the biggest wave on the biggest day. He had the photograph (shot by Hank, the *Surfing* photographer) to prove it. Was he not the high point, quite literally, of a video, *The Moment*? There were other claimants – 'He's calling his 50? I'm calling mine 60,' said Milton Willis. 'Easy,' said Michael. 'Bradshaw was out on the shoulder,' said Milton. They had ended up at Outside Sunset, where there was nobody out and 'the waves were twice as big'. But Bradshaw, Foo-style, almost *à la* Ace, had cornered the market, flooding it with photographs of 'the Biggest Day' starring Ken Bradshaw at Outer Log Cabins.

The funny thing is, Bradshaw remains slightly disappointed about the whole thing, because *that* was NOT, in fact, the Biggest Wave: he reckons he rode one some 10 to 20 feet in excess of the one in the picture, and all that remains of the *real* big one is a strip of grainy video footage, shot from land, with not enough pixels to sustain any propositions one way or the other. And there is one more rub, the tragedy of actually attaining his dream: 'How can I ever get that high again?' he groaned. His girlfriend of the time noted, with some exasperation, 'He basically waited twenty-five years for that day. And afterward – he just wasn't doing very well.'

Perhaps dispirited by the lack of acclaim for their achievements (they didn't make it, for example, into Warshaw's *Encyclopedia*, and complained mightily about the omission), perhaps (it was speculated) on the run from the local mafia, the Willis Brothers betook themselves finally to San Diego, where they set up shop as surf gurus. They published a series of self-help manuals (with titles like *Go Hard!*, *You Can Make It Happen* and, most recently, *How to Discover the Greatness Inside of You*) and could boast a regular column in the *La Jolla Light* newspaper, applying the wisdom of surfing to everyday, landlocked life. Michael, sick of working with toxic materials, dreamed of coming up with a mass-produced fully biode-gradable organic surfboard. 'If we don't take responsibility for disseminating our knowledge,' Milton says to me when I see them at a party in the hills, 'then mankind could be set back or stalled.'

Ted Deerhurst, the 'lord on a board', missed out on the Biggest Day. This is how. He once telephoned me in England in the middle of the night (and he transferred the charges) to tell me of his plans to acquire a jet ski and a good partner. And to marry Camille, the exotic dancer from the Paradise Club in Honolulu. He had made the strategic error of falling in love with her and remained convinced, despite the lack of any hard evidence, that she was in love with him. 'It's the real thing,' he told me one time as he dropped me off at the airport. It must have been shortly after that telephone call that the two men in suits knocked on the door of his condo at Turtle Bay.

You didn't see too many people in suits in Hawaii so they stood out. One of them didn't say a thing, just stood there sizing Ted up. And the other was polite. But there was something about the politeness (which was almost unknown in Hawaii) that scared the living daylights out of Ted. Fat Eric thought that Ted ought to concentrate on his surfing and forget all about Camille: that was the message. Anything else might *interfere* with his ability to surf. Fat Eric owned Paradise. And it was rumoured he was Camille's boyfriend, not just her employer. People who came up against Eric had a habit of being found down alleyways with holes in them, great gaping holes with the light coming in and the life pouring out. Nobody messed with Fat Eric, neither lord nor commoner. Ted had rejected the theory of sublimation in the past, but now it had all the force of a shotgun behind it.

'Sad,' Ted said, telling me about it one day at the Coffee

Gallery in Haleiwa, 'that a guy like Fat Eric can't stand the heat.'

'What do you mean?' I said, genuinely perplexed.

'It's obvious, isn't it?' Ted shook his head at the frailty of human nature. 'Camille told Eric she was leaving him for me and he couldn't take it. So he sends in the heavies. It's jealousy, pure and simple.'

'What are you going to do?'

Ted looked up at the purple mountain that lay between the North Shore and Honolulu. 'It would never have worked out between us anyway. I was starting to have second thoughts about the wedding. I have law exams coming up soon. I really should be concentrating on that. It was great while it lasted though. Do you want to know who I feel sorry for?'

'Who?'

'Camille. She really did love me. This has probably broken her heart.'

Bereft of a good woman, he sank to something like 231st in the world rankings, and went out and half-killed himself snowboarding. He was sick of surfing. His last words to me were: 'Hey, at least you can't drown up a mountain.' You could see him walking around (although 'walk' is an exaggeration) in some kind of wire cage contraption that held him together. He died at Turtle Bay in October 1997, aged forty, more than a year before the Biggest Day.

Sometime in the nineties Roger Erickson got a job as a lifeguard and married on the beach in front of Bradshaw's house. They had two daughters and then his wife, disenchanted with Hawaii, took them back to the mainland. Roger followed but couldn't stick it back east and working in a stables in Virginia. The last time I saw him he had 'gone underground': he was recovering from a dislocated collar-bone, torn neck muscles and marital meltdown. 'I'm an open wound,' he said and waxed lyrical about how great things used to be.

Towards the end of the millennium Brock Little, now thirty, had a crisis. He started to think about things. And he realised, one day while he was lying on the seabed, semi-conscious, and it was 50/50 as to whether he was ever going to come up again, that he didn't really want to die, not just yet anyway, and so he fought his way to the surface. He was never the same after that. He found that he couldn't look at a big wave with the same degree of unambiguous pleasure. Pain no longer made him laugh hysterically. 'You have to believe it's mind over matter,' he said. 'But sometimes there's just too much matter.' So he took up a safer career as a movie stuntman instead. He did all the hard work in *Baywatch*, *In God's Hands* and *Pearl Harbor*. The last time I saw him, in the summer at Waimea, where he was out training with the lifeguards, running up and down the beach in the sun, then swimming several laps of the Bay, he had just returned from shooting *The Da Vinci Code* in France. He took over from Tom Hanks whenever he had to jump off tall buildings or get hit by a truck.

Ace never gave up his pursuit of the biggest wave, fame and fortune, women, power, love, respect, whatever. He never lost heart. And he never stopped talking either. He adopted tow-in as if he had invented it. In fact he claimed he *had* invented it, sometime in the eighties, a claim I don't alto-gether dispute either. One winter in the new millennium, a new car sticker started to appear around the North Shore and spread quickly to all points of the globe. The old slogan 'Eddie Would Go' was dead. The new message was: 'Eddie Would

Tow'. If Eddie had lived, he would surely have been out there hanging off the back of a ski, riding waves double anything Waimea could tee up. That was all Ace's bright idea. He had stolen Foo's original line, which had been appropriated by Quiksilver, and adapted it to his own purpose: to advertise a tow-in contest that would take place every winter, conditions permitting, at Avalanche, or anywhere between Haleiwa and Kaena Point that was big enough.

'Hah! They're just B-team guys,' said Randy Rarick when we were talking about the contest. 'They're good, but they're not that good. Some of these guys can tow in to 30-, 40-foot waves, but they couldn't even paddle out at Waimea.' Surfing big waves had always been about the ultimate truth. There was a view that the whole tow-in phenomenon had introduced falsehood. With all that technology, now anyone could do anything. It wasn't 'real' any more.

'It's a lower frequency,' Milton Willis said in San Diego. 'With paddle-in, you're more in tune with the earth, you achieve harmonic convergence' (at a frequency he specified as 7.83 megahertz).

It was not a view that Bradshaw shared. The sheer size of the waves trumped everything else. Quantity was indistinguishable from quality. The old approach was history. He was so keen to get his views over that he became a professor. Really. Now he gives classes on 'Ocean Safety' at Hawaii State University (Kaneohe campus, on the east side), telling anyone who will listen (and there is no shortage of serious, respectful students) how hard it is. You can't rely on your buddy to come and pluck you out of harm's way. You have got to be able to rely on yourself and duck under 50–60-foot walls of water, and come up laughing. He'd had a two-wave hold-down and was starting to think it was 'interesting' while he was down there, unable to get up. And he was glad, on the whole, that he hadn't had to endure a third. But his training had saved him: 'You can prepare yourself for ANYTHING by training,' he tells his flock. 'Your body can do anything. Your mind gives up long before the body does.'

Bradshaw had been Foo's buddy at Maverick's. But he did absolutely nothing to save him. He knew it was Foo's first time at Mav's; he didn't know his way around, Bradshaw should have been keeping an eye out for him. When he went down, his first thought should have been to make sure he came up again, and not 'hey, this is a good wave, I'm on it'. You could say it was a cavalier disregard for Foo. But there was an extreme school of thought to the effect that Bradshaw deliberately took Foo out there, lured him into harm's way like some soft-shoed Pied Piper.

'Did I kill Foo?' Bradshaw says, giving it careful considera-tion. 'Did I actually want him dead? It's a fair question. I thought about that for a while. But my conscience is clear.' He went back, for the first time, in the winter of 1998, and introduced tow-in to 25-foot Maverick's, setting out from the harbour where everything had ended the last time. But he says now that he wishes that he had 'never even heard of Maverick's'.

'What happened to the buddy system?' Lisa Nakano, Foo's fiancée, asked tearfully. As far as Bradshaw is concerned, there is no buddy system in surfing and there never was. That is all an illusion. It is every man for himself: we are all, ultimately, alone, in the water as in life. You live and die on your own. There are no guardian angels (although he does recommend a PFD, or personal flotation device). That is his credo and that is what he teaches at the university. Foo wasn't the only one to go: there was Todd Chesser at Alligators and Donnie Solomon at Waimea and others. Bradshaw says he wants 'to reduce the number of dead bodies in the water'. It could be seen as a kind of atonement for what had happened at Maverick's. In fact, he wants to reduce the number of bodies in the water in general, dead or alive: he hates crowds. The last 60-foot day at Jaws (where his old buddy Dan Moore, who towed him into the Biggest Day, caught a wave calibrated at 68 feet that took the Billabong XXL prize for 2005) saw fifty to sixty craft in the water. What with all the noise and the diesel fumes, it was getting to be like a traffic jam on the Kam Highway out there.

Over the last decade Bradshaw has been haunted by the spectre of Foo. He can't quite manage to get all the history out of his head. Probably not a day goes by that he doesn't miss Foo, the old rivalry, in the way that McEnroe misses Jimmy Connors or Bjorn Borg. And, at the same time, he still resents him since he is forever being seen in relation to him. In fact, the rivalry is as intense as ever, maybe more so, if inevitably a little more one-sided. Bradshaw was given an insultingly brief mention in the 2004 Stacy Peralta documentary *Riding Giants*. The main men were Da Bull and Laird Hamilton (who, to Bradshaw's way of thinking, paid to have history rewritten with his name in lights as the grand synthesis, the last man, the happy ending, by way of investing heavily in the movie). Bradshaw appeared alongside Foo and Eddie Aikau. 'Me and two dead guys,' as he put it. 'And it was stills.' Bradshaw was 'burned'. 'History,' he concludes, 'is written by the guy with the most money. I'd like that ten acres above Jaws [the big-wave spot on Maui, also known as "Peahi", where Hamilton lives], but it's not going to happen.'

He has done his utmost to exorcise the ghost. The Biggest Day helped. He starred at Jaws in 60-foot surf and took ninth place in the inaugural Tow-in World Cup. In 2001 he joined the Billabong Odyssey, the quest for a 100-foot wave, but felt underappreciated and marginalised by mainly West Coast guys usually associated with Maverick's. Cape Disappointment (100 miles south of Seattle), where they were doing their initial training, littered with the wrecks of great vessels that had ventured too close to shore, couldn't have been more aptly named. The fix had already gone in, according to Bradshaw: was all being set up for Mike Parsons.

He met Layne Beachley, a decent performer on the women's pro tour, and set about training her up and coaching her, took her out at big Sunset, Waimea, the outer reefs, instructing her even when she was in the water (via a radio attachment in her ear – I remember it caused a faint ripple of scandal when it came out he'd been passing her tips like this at a Rip Curl contest in Jeffrey's Bay). She took six world titles and became the greatest female big-wave surfer of her generation, maybe ever. You could say he fell in love with her, but that phrase doesn't seem to suit Bradshaw somehow. Some people said they were married. They looked and behaved like a married couple, it was true. Cintra Wilson, writing for Salon.com about a pro contest in France, described them as 'the Tom and Nicole of the watersports set' (and she didn't mean it kindly). They split a year or so ago. Bradshaw 'can't accept unconditional love', Beachley said when I bumped into her at a funeral ceremony at Pipeline, by which time she was dating a guitarist with the rockband INXS. The last time I saw Bradshaw another young Australian contender, Mandy, had moved into his house, and he was training her up and making her smoothies and taking her out at big Sunset.

* * *

We are driving back from one of his seminars in his 4 × 4. He is wearing glasses, tennis shoes, and cut-offs with white socks.

He is in philosophical and melancholy mood. 'You know, I've screwed up all the way down the line, I can see that now. Foo was right – I should have been a publicity hound like him. He was right and I was wrong. Laird was right. He went off to be a model in Hollywood, we didn't see him for six years, he got himself a lot of influence and contacts in the right quarters. I never did any of that. He limited the contact with waves, so as to increase the mystique. Smart business! Doesn't surf unless there's a camera. Would never compete, not the Eddie, not Jaws, not if he can't control it, can't write his own script. All I ever did was surf. That's all I ever wanted to do. I'd like to call it "integrity". Maybe you can call it "arrogance". But guys with less integrity will do better. Look at Enron: the more conniving, unscrupulous, secretive you are, the better you do. In the *real* world – the one on MTV – Laird is right.'

Bradshaw's geometry is linear and unwavering. He still believes in the One Big Thing. He still sounds like Sheriff Bradshaw: 'There are rules and there are laws – and this [tow-in] is covered by both.' He can legitimately say, along with Popeye: *I am what I am and that's all that I am.* He has, in effect, remained eternally faithful to surfing, never betraying his one true love. Foo had betrayed him by dying. And, it seems to him, managed to carve out an edge for himself. Even in the midst of his endless winter, he is still outmanoeuvring Bradshaw. He'd had the big Eddie-type funeral service, not just one but two, at Waimea Bay *and* Mav's, with all the flowers and the eulogies times two. He had the memorial plaque cemented into the sand. He was idolised, he was a martyr, he was a saint of surfing, he could do no wrong, especially now he was dead. 'I'm the one who's having a hard time,' says Bradshaw. All he can do is repeat himself or deteriorate. No wonder he bought himself a house in Mammoth, up in the mountains in California, and goes snowboarding. He never did come up with the tape that would, allegedly, tell me everything I ever wanted to know about Bradshaw: perhaps he wanted to keep me guessing; perhaps he thought I knew enough.

Some say that Bradshaw has 'mellowed'. The last time I was on the North Shore I heard two stories about him. A reliable source told me he'd been terrorising some fifteen-year-old girl out at Sunset, on a 3-foot day, yelling at her because she had got in his way and taken his wave. It was classic Bradshaw. And then there was the story of the Japanese guy.

Bradshaw had been in the saddle of a full 10-foot wave and was galloping down the face. This was quite recently, at Sunset. The Japanese guy was going in the other direction, trying to get out of the way of this huge great thing coming right at him. He went to duck under but the force of the wave was too great and his board squeezed up through his legs and went flying. The board went straight at Bradshaw like a javelin. Bradshaw bailed but it got him anyway. Blood everywhere and Bradshaw fearing some massive life-threatening or at least surf-threatening injury. More to the point, furiously convinced that the guy shouldn't even have been out there if he couldn't handle it. 'Somebody's gotta do something,' says Bradshaw. Despite everything, he summoned up the energy to paddle over to the Japanese guy, grab him by the throat, threaten him, then let him go and took hold of his board instead.

He flipped the board over, ripped the fins off, methodically, one by one, then sank his mighty teeth into the rail and took a good bite out of it. A few hours later (Bradshaw had kept on surfing regardless), the Japanese guy was waiting for him on the beach. Bradshaw didn't know what to expect. Was he some kind of kung fu expert? The Japanese guy bowed and apologised. He was sorry if he had injured Bradshaw-san in any way. 'He wanted to thank me,' Bradshaw says, 'for teaching him a valuable lesson.'

Foo, permanently thirty-six, cannot change. Neither, now past fifty, can Bradshaw.

There is one thing that grates with Bradshaw. He has to grit his teeth when the Eddie is on. He refuses to go along to the opening ceremony. The fact is – and it's a manifest injustice – he is no longer on the list of invitees. He is not considered a contender at Waimea any more. But what probably hurts more than this is that Foo *is* still on the list. He is down as 'honorary invitee'.

17

Twilight of the Idols

Perhaps, as some have argued, the wave is the fundamental form of the universe and everything is waves, wave after mighty wave, rising and falling for ever and ever. But, in another way, the wave is nothing, a ghost, an empty, eva-nescent architecture. The wave leaves no trace behind it: for all its size and delinquent energy, it dies and disappears. But it lives on in the memory and the mind of those who were there to see it pass and bear witness. Just as a tree falling in a forest, with no one there to see it fall, makes no noise, so too a wave seems to require someone on it in order to exist as a wave, and acquire shape and meaning, without which it is only a transient misshapen mound of water.

When I heard the news of Foo's death, on Christmas Day 1994, back in England, I was like Warshaw: at first I couldn't believe it either. 'Foo?' I gasped down the telephone, 'I thought he was immortal.'

'Andy, he is immortal,' Michael Willis said, with mystical calm and reverence. 'He blows Elvis and James Dean clean away.' Michael told me that there was a good swell on the

North Shore and he was going out there to celebrate and to give thanks to Foo and he was going to 'surf harder than ever' and nail waves that were 'bigger, meaner, badder than ever'.

In surfing, everyone knows where they were and what they were doing the day Foo died. There are still occasional sightings of Foo. Some say that he has taken the form of a turtle.

No one has yet surfed a 100-foot wave, although Ace Cool claims that there is a nanotechnologist somewhere in Arizona who is planning to build one for him. And I, for my part, never did manage to surf that 20-foot wave – nowhere near. I take consolation from something Buzzy Trent used to say: 'A wave is not measured in feet and inches, but in increments of fear.' It could have been Foo dying that spooked me. Everything spooked me. The last time I was on the North Shore I was writing two stories. One was about a Tahitian boy who died at Pipeline; the second was about a surfer girl from Kauai who had had an arm torn off by a shark. He went by the wonderful name of Malik Joyeux but now he was dead; and she was about as brave as anyone can be, but she was still missing an arm. I keep coming back to something the comedian Jerry Seinfeld once said about the insanity of surfing: 'The ocean doesn't really want you in it at all; the wave is like a bouncer in a nightclub: it is the ocean's way of trying to kick you out of there.'

I still admire and respect Bradshaw and Foo, but I don't want to be them any more. I've probably had it with heroes. If I had to have a hero, I would probably choose Canute, King of the English at the end of the first millennium. When, after his brutal conquering youth, he planted his throne on the sand and waited for the tide to roll in, he wasn't really crazy enough to think he could exert any authority over the waves. Rather, he wanted everyone else to see that, even though he was king, there was still nothing he could do to hold back and control the force of the sea. He was only a king. There was something out there that was simply beyond the power of any human being to command. Canute was the first Zen ruler and understood that nothing in the world can be compared to water for its weak and yielding nature; yet, in attacking the hard and the strong, nothing is more powerful.

But Ken Bradshaw does not subscribe to this opinion and he never will. And he'll never stop surfing either, not unless surfing finally stops him. Until that happens, he will just go on rolling his stone up the next great hill and rapturously rolling on down again.

BIBLIOGRAPHY

I am particularly indebted to the following:

Books

Coleman, Stuart Holmes, *Eddie Would Go: The Story of Eddie Aikau, Hawaiian Hero* (New York: St Martin's Press, 2001)

Cook, James, *A Voyage to the Pacific Ocean* (London: Nicol and Cadell, 1784), 3 vols. (vol. III by James King)

Duane, Daniel, *Caught Inside: A Surfer's Year on the California Coast* (New York: North Point Press, 1996)

Grigg, Ricky, *Big Surf, Deep Dives, and the Islands: My Life in the Ocean* (Honolulu: Editions Limited, 1998)

Jenkins, Bruce, *North Shore Chronicles: Big-Wave Surfing in Hawaii* (Berkeley, California: North Atlantic Books, 1990)

Le Roy Ladurie, Emmanuel, *Montaillou, village occitan de 1294 à 1324* (Paris: Gallimard, 1975)

Lao-Tzu, *Tao te Ching*, translated by Ch'u Ta-Kao (London: Allen and Unwin, 1970)

Long, John, editor, and Sponholz, Hai-Van K, *The Big Drop* (Guildford, Connecticut: Globe Pequot, 1999)

Mailer, Norman, *The Fight* (Boston: Little, Brown, 1975)

Noll, Greg, and Gabbard, Andrea, *Da Bull: Life Over the Edge* (Berkeley, California: North Atlantic Books, 1989)

Obeyesekere, Gananath, *The Apotheosis of Captain Cook: European Mythmaking in the Pacific* (Princeton: Princeton University Press, 1992)

Warshaw, Matt, *The Encyclopedia of Surfing* (New York: Harcourt, 2003)

—— *Maverick's: The Story of Big-Wave Surfing* (San Francisco: Chronicle Books, 2000)

—— *Surfriders: In Search of the Perfect Wave* (New York: HarperCollins, 1997)

Articles

Brady, Leonard, 'Whatever Happened to Big-Wave Riding?', *Surfer*, May 1983

Foo, Mark, 'Occurrence at Waimea Bay', *Surfing*, June 1985

Jenkins, Bruce, 'The Nation of Ken', *The Surfer's Journal*, Spring 2001

Krakauer, Jon, 'The Life and Death of a Legend', *Outside*, May 1995

Marcus, Ben, 'Cold Sweat', *Surfer*, June 1992

Warshaw, Matt, 'The Divided Rulers of Waimea Bay', *Outside*, May 1988

A NOTE ON THE AUTHOR

Andy Martin was born in London and lives in Cambridge and New York. He learned to surf on the west coast of Australia. He is the author of *Walking on Water* and has written about God, Napoleon and Brigitte Bardot, and reported on surfing for the *Independent* and *The Times*.

A NOTE ON THE TYPE

The text of this book is set in Bembo. This type was first used in 1495 by the Venetian printer Aldus Manutius for Cardinal Bembo's *De Aetna*, and was cut for Manutius by Francesco Griffo. It was one of the types used by Claude Garamond (1480–1561) as a model for his Romain de L'Université, and so it was the forerunner of what became standard European type for the following two centuries. Its modern form follows the original types and was designed for Monotype in 1929.